SPEARHEAD

SPEARHEAD

AN AMERICAN TANK GUNNER, HIS ENEMY, AND A COLLISION OF LIVES IN WORLD WAR II

ADAPTED FOR YOUNG ADULTS

ADAM MAKOS

DELACORTE PRESS

To those brave American tankers—the "power and might" of the
New World—who went to the rescue of the Old

CONTENTS

INTRODUCTION

Prepare to meet the youth of 1944.

You're about to witness World War II from *all sides*. Our side. Their side. And the people caught in the middle. And ultimately, you'll see what happens when their lives collide. Why do these stories still matter so much today? Because I believe we can learn from anyone who lives through tough times. We can find courage to face *our* fears by watching them face theirs. We can draw strength to get through anything when we see the hardships they survived. Now they're going to tell us how they did it.

People like Clarence Smoyer. A gentle giant assigned to the gunner's seat of his Sherman tank, Clarence comes to realize that the only way to keep his friends alive in battle is to shoot straight and never miss. You'll meet Gustav Schaefer, a German teenager who's been taken from his farm and made to fight for the Nazis. Sealed inside his Panzer IV tank, Gustav struggles to decide what's more important: serving his country or answering his conscience. And your heart will go out to Kathi Esser, a German civilian caught between the lines. In a small car, she'll attempt a daring escape from war-torn Cologne.

These real-life characters all share a common bond: none of them wanted to be in World War II. Clarence wanted to be back home, roller-skating with his friends. Gustav loved watching the trains go past his farm and dreamed of someday becoming a conductor. And Kathi had just earned her diploma in home economics and was eager to start her first teaching job. Each of these young people had dreams for the future. But who would live to see them come true?

Prepare to climb aboard. In a few short pages you'll be behind enemy lines with Clarence and his buddies in the 3rd Armored Division. Are you ready to meet the youth of 1944? There's one way to find out.

Close the hatches.

Tighten your helmet.

It's time to roll out.

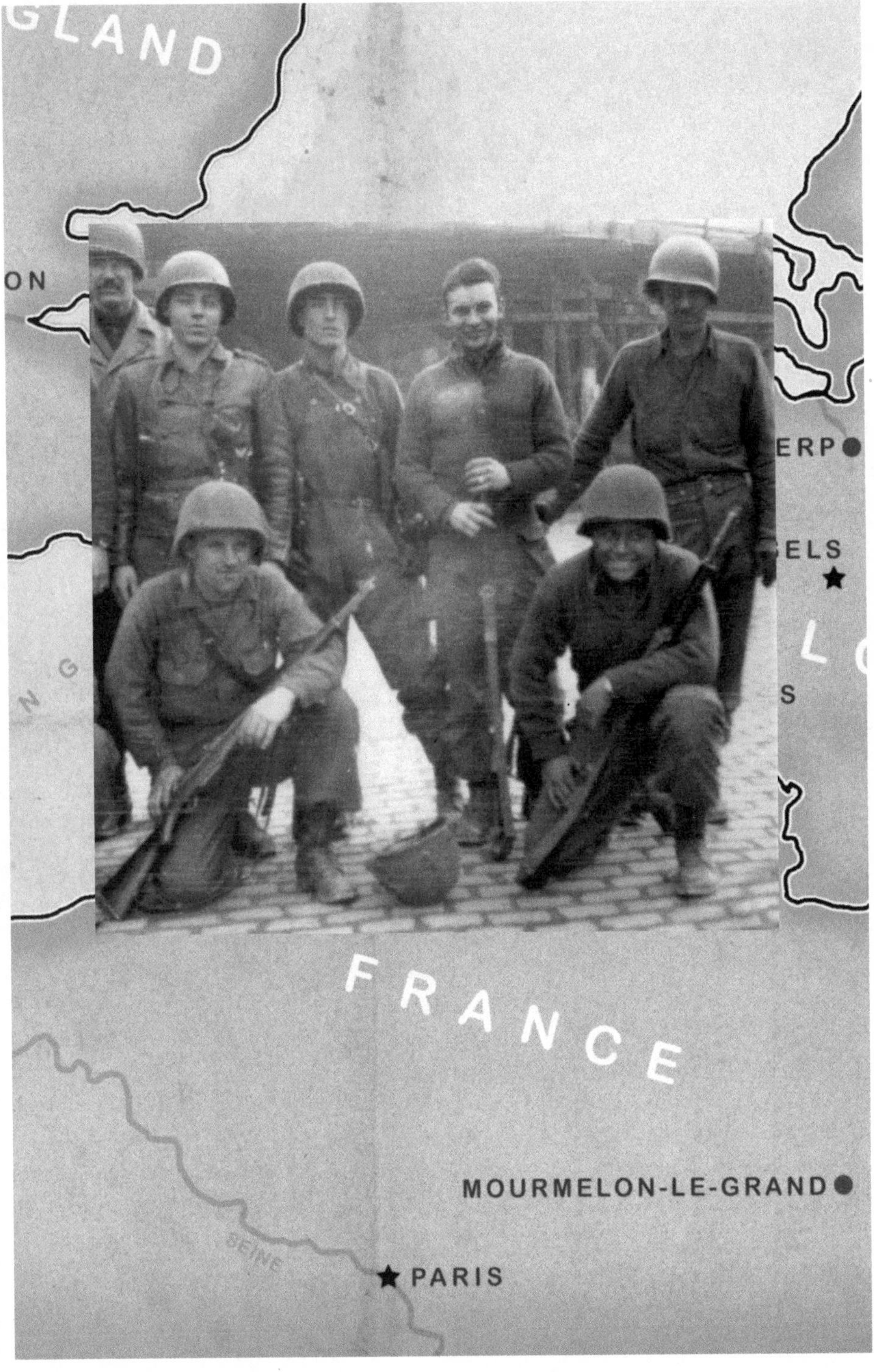
FRANCE
MOURMELON-LE-GRAND
SEINE
PARIS

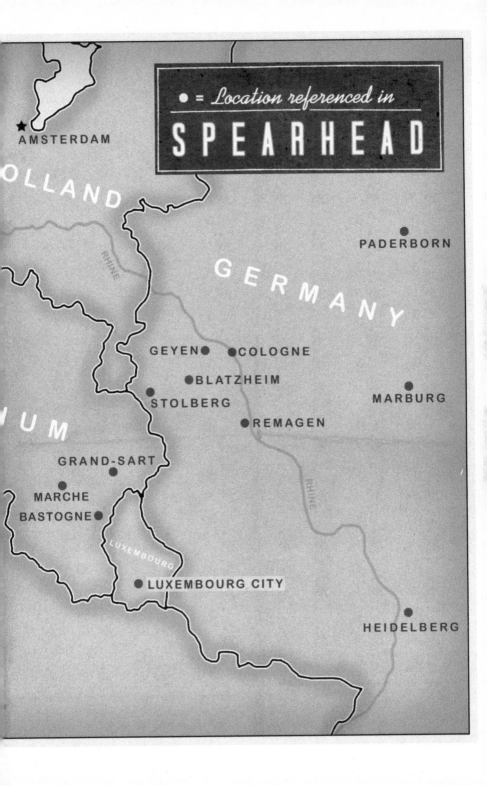

CHAPTER 1

THE GENTLE GIANT

September 2, 1944

OCCUPIED BELGIUM, DURING WORLD WAR II

Twilight fell on a country crossroads. It was quiet except for the sound of insects buzzing in the surrounding fields. But there was something else, too. Metallic. The sound of hot engines ticking and pinging, cooling down after a long drive.

Silently and efficiently, American tank crewmen worked to rearm and refuel their Sherman tanks. They were trying to finish before the last streaks of color fled the sky.

Crouched behind his tank's turret, Corporal Clarence Smoyer carefully passed 75mm shells to the loader inside. Even the slightest clang of these explosive projectiles could give them away to the enemy.

Clarence was twenty-one, tall and lean with a Roman nose and a sea of curly blond hair under a knit cap. His blue eyes were gentle but guarded. Despite his height, he was not a fighter. He'd never been in a fistfight. Back home in Pennsylvania he had hunted only once—for rabbit—and even that he did halfheartedly. Three weeks earlier he'd been promoted to gunner, second-in-command on the tank. It wasn't a promotion he had wanted.

Beside Clarence's tank, there were four more olive-drab tanks fanned out, "coiled," in a half-moon formation. The *platoon*—a unit of 20 to 50 soldiers—was in place. Farther north, the city of Mons was just out of sight. To their left lay darkening fields of a forested ridge.

The Germans were out there. But how many were there? And when would they arrive? No one knew. It had been nearly three months since D-Day. Now Clarence and the men of the 3rd Armored Division were behind enemy lines.

The division was made up of 390 tanks at full strength. They had dispersed across the area, from the place where the enemy was situated all the way up to Mons.

Survival that night would come down to teamwork. The commanders at company headquarters had given Clarence's platoon, 2nd Platoon, a simple but important mission: block the road, and guard it. Let nothing pass.

Clarence lowered himself through the commander's hatch and into the turret. It was a tight fit for a six-foot man. He slipped into the gunner's seat, leaning into his periscopic gunsight. This five-inch-wide relay of glass prisms and a 3x telescopic gunsight would be his windows to the world.

There would be no stepping out that night. It was too risky even to urinate outside. That was what they saved empty shell casings for.

Beneath Clarence's feet was the main body of the tank, known as the hull, with its white enamel walls and three lights.

In the bow at the front, the driver and bow gunner/assistant driver slid their seats backward. They'd sleep in the same seats where they'd ridden all day. The gun loader, meanwhile, stretched a sleeping bag on the turret floor. The tank smelled of oil, gunpowder, and a locker room, but the scent was familiar, even comforting. Ever since they'd come ashore, this M4A1 Sherman had been their home in "Easy Company" of the 32nd Armor Regiment, a unit of the 3rd Armored Division.

For eighteen days, the 3rd Armored had been leading the First Army. They had also led two other divisions in the breakout across northern France. Paris had been liberated, and the Germans were retreating. The 3rd Armored was earning its nickname: the Spearhead Division.

Then came new orders.

German armies had been spotted moving north, hightailing it out of France and heading for Belgium. On the way, they'd pass through Mons's many crossroads. So the 3rd Armored turned on a dime and raced to catch them—107 miles in two days. They'd arrived just in time to lay an ambush.

Tonight, though, sleep would come quickly. The men were exhausted. The tank commander, Staff Sergeant Paul Faircloth, dropped down into the turret. He lowered the split hatch covers, leaving just a crack for air. He slumped into a seat behind Clarence. Paul Faircloth was also twenty-one, quiet and easygoing, with a sturdy build, black hair, and olive skin. Some assumed he was French or Italian, but he was half Cherokee and had grown up in Florida.

For two days Paul had been on his feet in the commander's

position. He was always the first person out of the tank to offer help or support.

"I'm taking your watch tonight," Clarence said, figuring he'd give the guy a break. "I'll do a double."

The offer was generous, but Paul resisted—he could handle it.

Clarence persisted until Paul threw up his hands and finally swapped places with him to nab some shut-eye in the gunner's seat.

Clarence snatched a Thompson submachine gun from the wall and took the commander's position. For the next four hours, he kept watch for enemy foot soldiers. Everyone knew that German tankers didn't like to fight at night.

Partway through Clarence's watch, the darkness came alive with a mechanical rumbling. The moon was smothered by clouds. He couldn't see a thing, but he could hear vehicles moving beyond the tree-lined ridge.

Start and stop. Start and stop.

The radio speaker hummed with static. No flares illuminated the sky. The 3rd Armored would later estimate that there were 30,000 enemy troops out there, mostly men of the German Army. Yet no order came to attack them.

That was because the enemy armies were losing precious fuel as they searched for a way around the maze of roadblocks the Americans had set up. Spearhead was content to let them wander. The enemy was desperately trying to reach the safety of the West Wall, also known as the Siegfried Line. This wall was a German defensive line stretched along the western border of the country.

If these 30,000 German troops could get there, they could bar the Allied troops' way into Germany and prolong the war. And so, they had to be stopped, here, at Mons. Spearhead had a plan for that—but it could wait until daylight.

Around two a.m. a distant rumble arose. Clarence tracked the distinctive sounds of tank tracks. Vehicles were coming down the road in front of him. He knew his order: let nothing pass. But doubt was setting in. What if these tanks were American patrols? Whoever they were, he wasn't about to pull the trigger on friendly forces.

One after the other, three tanks clanked past the Shermans. They kept going. Clarence exhaled slowly.

Then one of the tanks let off the gas. It began turning and squeaking, as if its tracks were in desperate need of oil. The sound was unmistakable. Only full-metal tracks sounded like that, while an American Sherman's were padded with rubber.

The tanks were German.

Clarence didn't move. The tank was behind him, then beside him. Clarence braced for a flash and the flames that would swallow him. He'd never even hear the Germans' gun bark. He would just cease to exist.

The flash never came. Instead, a whisper shook Clarence from his paralysis. It was Paul. Without a word, Clarence slipped back into the gunner's seat and Paul took over.

Clarence strapped on his tanker's helmet. It had goggles

attached and headphones sewn into leather earflaps. He clipped a throat microphone around his neck and plugged into the intercom.

On the other side of the turret, the loader sat up, wiping the sleep from his eyes.

Clarence mouthed the words *German tank*. The loader snapped wide-awake.

From his hatch, Paul tapped Clarence on the right shoulder, the signal to turn the turret to the right.

Clarence hesitated. The turret wasn't exactly silent. What if the Germans heard it?

Paul tapped again.

Clarence obeyed, turning a handle. The turret whined. Gears cranked, and the gun swept the dark. When the gun was aligned, Paul stopped Clarence. Clarence pressed his eyes to his periscope. Everything below the skyline looked inky black.

Clarence told Paul that he couldn't see a thing. What if they call in armored infantrymen—soldiers who fought on foot—to kill the tank with a bazooka? he suggested.

Paul couldn't chance some jittery soldier blasting the wrong tank. "We'll take care of him," he said.

We'll take care of him? Clarence was horrified. He had hardly used the gun in daylight. Now Paul wanted him to fire in pitch-darkness? At what? A sound? An enemy he couldn't see?

He wished he could return to being a loader. On a tank crew, the loader was pretty much just along for the ride. That was the good life. A gentle giant, Clarence simply wanted to slip through the war without killing anyone. Or getting killed himself.

No time for that. By now, the German tank crew had probably realized they were surrounded.

"Gunner, ready?"

Panicked, Clarence tugged on Paul's pant leg. Paul sank into the turret, exasperated. Clarence rattled off his doubts. What if he missed? What if he hit their own guys?

Paul's voice calmed him: "Somebody has to take the shot."

As if the Germans had been listening, they suddenly cut their power. The hot engine hissed, then went silent.

Clarence felt a wave of relief, which quickly faded. His indecision had cost them whatever advantage they'd had. And against a German tank, they'd need every advantage they could get. Especially if they were facing a Panther, the tank of nightmares. Rumor had it that a Panther could shoot through one Sherman and into a second.

That July, the U.S. Army had placed several captured Panthers in a field in Normandy. Men blasted away at them with the same kind of 75mm gun that was in Clarence's Sherman. They'd busted up the German tank's flanks and rear, but not a single shot managed to penetrate the Panther's frontal armor.

Clarence checked his luminescent watch, knowing the Germans were probably doing the same. The countdown had begun.

Three a.m. became four a.m.

Clarence and Paul passed a canteen of cold coffee back and forth. They had always joked that they were a family locked in a sardine can. And like a family, they didn't always see eye to eye. Unlike Paul, who was always running off to help someone outside the tank, all Clarence cared about was his own family on the inside—him and his crew.

This had been his way since childhood.

Growing up in industrial Lehighton, Pennsylvania, Clarence lived in a row house by the river, with walls so flimsy he could hear the neighbors. His parents were usually out working to keep the family afloat. His father did manual labor for the Civilian Conservation Corps public works program, and his mother was a housekeeper.

With the family's survival at stake, Clarence had been determined to contribute. When other kids played sports or did homework, twelve-year-old Clarence stacked a ballpark vendor's box with candy bars and went selling door-to-door throughout Lehighton. Just a boy, he had vowed: *I've got to take care of my family because no one is going to take care of us.*

Now, there he was in the Sherman, trying to take care of his own. Clarence checked his periscope. He kept his eyes glued to the glass until a blocky shape appeared about fifty yards away.

"I see it," he whispered.

Hurry, Paul urged. If they could see the enemy, the enemy could see them.

Clarence settled the crosshairs on his periscope, known as the *reticle,* on the dark shape that looked like a tank. He was ready. The trigger was a button on the footrest. His boot hovered over it.

"Fire," Paul said.

Clarence's foot stamped down.

Outside, a massive flash leaped from the Sherman's barrel.

For a moment, it illuminated the olive-drab American tank and the sandy-yellow German one.

Inside the turret, smoke hung thick in the air. Clarence's ears throbbed and his eyes stung. Again, he hovered his foot over the trigger.

"Nothing's moving," Paul said from above.

The intercom came alive with voices of relief. Clarence moved his foot away from the trigger.

Paul radioed the platoon; the job was done.

Through his periscope, Clarence watched the dark clouds fade, revealing the boxy armor and the 11-foot, 8-inch-long gun of a Panzer IV tank.

Known by the Americans as the Mark IV, the design was older, and it had been the Germans' most prevalent tank until the Panther began taking over. But though it was no Panther, the Mark IV was still lethal. Its 75mm gun packed 25 percent more punch than Clarence's. Clarence had nearly placed his shot right on it.

Clarence envisioned a tank full of moaning, bleeding men and hoped the crew had slipped out in the night. He had no love for the Germans, but he hated the idea of killing any human being. He wasn't about to look inside his first tank kill.

"I'll go." Paul unplugged his helmet.

Clarence tried to dissuade him. It wasn't worth looking inside and getting his head blown off by a German.

Paul brushed away the concerns and radioed the platoon to hold their fire.

Through his periscope, Clarence watched Paul climb the

Mark IV's hull and creep toward the turret with his Thompson at the ready. Carefully, Paul opened the commander's hatch and aimed the Thompson inside.

Nothing happened.

He leaned forward and took a long look, then shouldered his gun.

Paul sealed the hatch shut.

CHAPTER 2

BAPTISM

That same morning, September 3, 1944
MONS, BELGIUM

After the tense standoff of the previous night, the American tanks were on the move.

With the rising sun at their backs, Shermans flooded across the Mons countryside. The goal was to spread the division out so they could cover as much ground as possible, squeezing the enemy out. Every country lane and every farmer's path had to be roadblocked.

With his goggles lowered, Paul rode above his open hatch. His jacket flapped in the wind. The machine around him seemed alive. Everything vibrated: helmets hanging from the turret, a machine gun on a mount, spare wheels tied down wherever they would fit. The tank seemed to clear its throat with each gear change. It was run by an engine that had to be cranked awake by hand.

This Sherman was a "75," owing to its 75mm gun, but to Clarence's crew it had a name. Eagle. Someone had even painted an eagle head on each side of the hull. Every tank's name in Easy Company began with the letter *E*.

Paul raised his field glasses to his eyes and studied the terrain ahead. The tank was bound for the tree-lined ridge where the commotion had been that previous night.

One by one, the neighboring Shermans vanished from sight. They plunged into patches of woods or slipped around the edges of fields and set their guns toward the enemy. Every tree, every shadow now seemed laced with danger.

Paul's orders were to set a roadblock right where the German tank had been the day before. He had assured Clarence that the German crew had escaped the Mark IV alive. Paul knew Clarence didn't want to harm anyone. Clarence had a suspicion that his friend was just trying to protect him. Paul had done it before.

One night, way back in September 1943, when Easy Company was stationed in England, Clarence was punished for returning to base late, past curfew. His sentence? He was ordered to cut the grass around Easy Company's Quonset huts every night—with just the butter knife from his mess kit. He'd take a fistful of grass, saw away, and then move to the next clump, from about seven to eleven each night.

Paul would sit against a hut and keep Clarence company while he worked. Over the course of three months, they talked. Clarence learned that Paul's mother was Cherokee, and that his father had been a train engineer who died when Paul was in sixth grade. Paul had quit school and become a clerk at a general store to support his mother and sisters. Surprised by Paul's keen mind for numbers, the store owner soon had him doing the bookkeeping.

While Clarence toiled away at his punishment, a few tankers

from the company would tease him. They took to urinating on grass that he was about to cut. Paul had called them together. "It's the latrine that separates us from animals," he had said.

That had put an end to it.

At the top of the ridge, Clarence peered through his periscope. There was nothing to see but sky. For now. As the tank settled forward, a sudden spit of sparks left him reeling. *We're hit!* A gonglike sound echoed through the walls.

Paul dropped into the turret and screamed at the driver to reverse downhill. Instantly the tank headed backward, onto a sunken road lined by trees. Once they were safely out of the line of fire, Paul and Clarence climbed out to inspect the damage. Atop the turret they froze at the sound of thunder in a perfectly blue sky.

A battle was raging beyond the nearby hills. Smoke rose into the sky. American fighter planes—P-47 fighter-bombers—powered overhead. Meanwhile, it was reported that German vehicles were stuck in a "delicious traffic jam."

Clarence eyed the gun barrel with concern. A shell had struck its side before deflecting over the turret. A few more inches to the right and the shell would have come straight through his gunsight, killing him instantly.

Clarence gave Paul the bad news. The gun barrel was collapsed on the inside. If he fired, the shell could get jammed. Worse yet, its backblast could come into the turret, wiping out the crew.

That settled it. It was simply too risky to fire.

Back in the safety of the turret, Paul radioed Easy Company's headquarters for permission to retreat. On the other end, a shaky voice reported that the Germans were still on the attack. The situation was dire.

The orders to Paul were firm: "Hold your position." Paul asked for reinforcements, anyone they could spare. It was clear that the situation was desperate.

Clarence asked the loader to get extra ammo for the coaxial, a .30-caliber machine gun that was set on the loader's side. Paul reviewed everyone's roles in the tank. He and Clarence would cover the tree-lined ridge, they agreed. Meanwhile, the bow gunner would guard the front with his coaxial gun. The driver would keep the engine running.

Paul rose from his hatch and swiveled the machine gun mounted on the roof.

Then he took aim.

Silhouettes appeared, about two hundred yards away on top of the ridge.

Soldiers waded cautiously down the slope, clambering down the field in groups. There were about a hundred of them, some wearing German gray, others in green smocks. Sunlight beat down on their faces.

The enemy had come far enough.

Paul clenched his trigger, sending fire leaping from the muzzle. Clarence's coaxial added its earsplitting roar, its smoke rising in front of Paul.

The Germans fell in droves—many killed or badly wounded. Others pawed for cover in shallow gullies. A few fired back.

Clarence's foot came down, the coaxial thumped; then he turned a handle, an electric motor whined, and the turret swung his reticle to the next target. It was kill or be killed—them or his family.

Almost as quickly as they had appeared, the enemy stopped coming over the hill.

"Cease fire!" Paul shouted.

Clarence caught his breath. More than a dozen German bodies dotted the slope, and survivors limped away. It was over. Or so Clarence hoped.

Within thirty minutes, engines revved behind the Sherman.

An American M3 half-track armored personnel carrier pulled up, followed by an M8 Greyhound, a scout car with a 37mm gun. A squad of infantrymen leaped down from the half-track and took up firing positions. These soldiers were known as "doughs"—in homage to the "doughboys," or foot soldiers, of World War I. They were the division's infantry arm and often rode tanks or half-tracks into battle. They had arrived as reinforcement.

Paul was about to brief the doughs when popping noises came from the ridge. It sounded as if the Germans were opening champagne bottles.

The doughs took cover. Paul slammed the hatch cover down. Shells whooshed overhead. Explosions and shrapnel thumped the tank's steel hide. The Sherman was blocking the Germans' route homeward; this was their revenge.

Above the chaos of the barrage came bone-chilling screams. The horrifying sounds leaked through the cracks into the turret. Clarence twisted in his seat, wanting to plug his ears and bury his head. Something terrible was happening outside.

A hand shook Clarence by his shoulder. "Clarence, you're in charge!"

Clarence turned and found Paul swapping his tanker's headgear for a steel helmet. He was going out there.

Paul grabbed his Thompson and opened his hatch.

Clarence sprang from his seat and gripped Paul's leg, desperately trying to hold him back. No stranger's life was worth throwing away his own.

Paul kicked free. "We gotta help those guys!" he shouted.

Clarence watched Paul running through dark smoke, toward the cries.

The Greyhound had taken a direct hit into the turret. The men inside were suffering.

An orange burst leaped from the road. Then another. They blew the leaves off the surrounding trees. Clarence rose back to eye level. He could see that Paul had almost reached the Greyhound. That was when a mortar shell landed right next to Paul. The explosion flung him askew through the smoke. Clarence's legs weakened.

When the barrage lifted, he frantically searched for his friend.

Paul had landed almost upside down on a bank. The blast had shattered his arm. His right leg had been blown completely off below the knee.

Clarence stared, horror-struck.

This can't be happening.

He fumbled for the radio and called company headquarters, stuttering, and begging for any medics to come quickly.

Before Clarence could run to Paul's aid, the sound of rifles crackled like a string of firecrackers. The timing couldn't have been worse. The Germans were back in full force.

On the intercom, Clarence heard his crew panicking. Without Paul, he was the highest-ranking crewman; they wanted to know what to do.

Clarence felt an emotion welling, one he barely recognized. He glanced at Paul. His friend still hadn't stirred.

Dropping back into the gunner's seat, Clarence told the crew, "We aren't going anywhere."

He swung the turret into action.

The Germans were moving tactically. They would fire at the dirt in front of the Sherman every few yards, then come closer and repeat. Clarence's foot smashed down on the coaxial trigger. He could feel himself venting his rage.

The gun devoured one belt of ammunition after another. The loader kept them coming. Soon the coaxial overheated, requiring a barrel change. There was no time to stop.

Clarence emerged from the commander's hatch and swung a roof-mounted machine gun into play. He kept on firing, this time in bursts.

Germans fell. His bullets danced across the dirt and through them. It was impossible to tell who had been hit and who was taking cover.

Soon, bullets began pinging off his own tank. The Germans were hitting them directly, forcing Clarence lower in the hatch.

Clarence returned to the gunner's seat and pressed his eyes to the periscope. The enemy was closer than ever . . .

The field in front of the tank was a graveyard.

Morning had become afternoon. The roaring sounds of battle had faded.

The bodies of German soldiers littered the slope to the ridgetop. Those left alive were struggling to step over fallen comrades on their way down to surrender.

"You Americans don't want to fight," said one prisoner, "you just want to slaughter us."

Countless scenes like this played out across Mons.

The 1st Infantry Division would come in to finish what the 3rd Armored had begun, and out of the 30,000 Germans who came to Mons, 27,000 would leave as prisoners of war.

"Probably never before in the history of warfare has there been so swift a destruction of such a large force," concluded the 3rd Armored Division history.

The American victory was resounding. And yet Clarence could only focus on Paul's lifeless body, lying at the medics' feet. Clarence silently pleaded for his friend to cough or flinch or show any sign of life.

That time had passed.

The medics packed up their bags to move on. "Can we take him back with us?" Clarence asked with a trembling voice from his perch in the turret.

The medics were sympathetic. "Graves Registration will be along soon."

At the words, Clarence buried his face in his sleeve. He sank down into the turret and shut the covers.

Paul's body. The field of dead Germans. All this death. And they hadn't even reached Germany yet.

CHAPTER 3

"BUBI"

Five days later, September 8, 1944
EIGHTY-FIVE MILES SOUTHEAST—LUXEMBOURG

The thunder of heavy artillery echoed over the village of Merl, on the western outskirts of Luxembourg City.

Beneath leafy trees on a country lane, Private Gustav Schaefer, a young German tank crewman, performed a balancing act as he carried five mess kits brimming with food.

Gustav watched the explosions in awe. Barely five feet tall, he was seventeen, blond, and square-jawed, with a quiet disposition. His dark eyes did the talking for him. On this, his first day in combat, they spoke volumes. Despite the explosions detonating nearby, Gustav was having fun.

As the crew's radioman, who doubled as the bow gunner, he also was expected to fetch food and fuel the tank. Gustav accepted the tasks without complaining.

Up the road, his crewmates were running back to their tank, which was parked in the shade. Branches camouflaged the Panther, masking its sharp lines. The men shouted for Gustav to hurry before disappearing inside.

Another thunderclap rippled. He had only about forty yards to go and he'd be safe, a returning hero with the crew's food rations. Just then, the field to his left exploded.

A blinding flash. A deafening crack. An invisible hand seemed to pick him up and sweep him across the road into a ditch.

Gustav opened his eyes to a rain of dirt. His eardrums throbbed with pain and he felt a burning sensation on his chest.
I'm hit!

He bolted upright before he could end up a casualty along with the now-spilled food.

With an athletic leap he grabbed the gun barrel and swung himself onto the frontal armor. Scampering higher, he entered his hatch.

Safe in the tight, oil-scented confines, he collapsed against his machine gun. The others couldn't see him. The men in his crew were all veterans with plenty of experience. They teasingly called him *Bubi,* or little boy. It was too soon to show them his fear.

After their units had been devastated on the Russian Front, they had been placed in the 2nd Company of the Panzer Brigade 106 and sent to Luxembourg City. With a strength of forty-seven vehicles—thirty-six Panthers and eleven Jagdpanzer IV self-propelled guns—the brigade's orders were straightforward: delay the American advance at any cost.

It was a tall order.

Gustav would have given anything to be back on his family's farm in Arrenkamp, in the windswept fields far in northern

Germany. Home was a humble ranch house lit by candles. There was a stable with swallows fluttering around inside. Abiding by folkloric tradition, his father always cut a hole in the roof so the birds could build their nests within the walls and bring the family luck.

Gustav's parents had one bedroom, while Gustav and his younger brother shared the other with their grandparents. His best friend was his grandmother Luise. A short, sturdy woman who wore her blond hair in a bun, she would read fairy tales to the boys, including Gustav's favorite, "Snow-White and Rose-Red." It was a simple life, but far better than in any tank.

No one spoke after the shelling stopped.

Gustav stayed hidden. The tank wasn't big enough for him to stay like that forever. Sooner or later his crewmates would notice that he was crouching—and that their dinner was spilled all over his uniform from the fall.

Should he blame the kitchen crew? he wondered. No. His feeling of embarrassment couldn't overcome his upbringing. "Always be modest," his grandmother had taught him, "and always be honest."

Facing an entirely different kind of fear, Gustav showed himself and finally broke the silence. "I lost it . . . I lost all our precious food!"

The men were furious, as Gustav knew they'd be. This was their only chance at eating that night, after all.

As the crew grumbled, the commander reassured them: "He'll be punished."

• • •

Once the shadows had shifted with the afternoon sun, the camouflage branches were cleared.

The tank idled on the dirt road. It was a Panther G model. It was sandy yellow-colored, with green and brown swirls of camouflage. A forward-leaning turret sat atop a sleek hull that had a long gun, stretching more than half the tank's length. Everything flowed from a slanted two-ton slab of frontal armor. It was about 5.7 inches thick—easily dwarfing the 3.5-inch front plate on an American M4A1 75mm-armed Sherman.

Normally after a road journey it was the driver's job to tighten or replace the pins that held the tank's tracks together. Today it had been Gustav's punishment. His hands were greasy and his knuckles were bloody as he wiped the tools down with a cloth.

The commander approached Gustav. Staff Sergeant Rolf Millitzer was tall and lanky. Beneath a black cap, his long face was lined with the stress of command. The war had aged him far beyond his twenty-six years. In the early hours that morning, three sister companies had crossed the border into France before running into American lines. They hadn't radioed back since. The silence could only mean one thing: the Americans were approaching Luxembourg and coming here next. Clearly, Rolf thought there were larger concerns than Gustav spilling food.

He squatted to Gustav's level, his dark eyes friendly. "You need to be more careful," Rolf said, referring to the night before. "There's no need to push too hard any longer. The main thing now is to stay alive."

Rolf departed, leaving Gustav puzzled.

They were German soldiers on the eve of battle, on the verge of losing the war, and Rolf was urging thoughts of survival already?

Gustav held no illusions himself—victory was impossible. The Sixth Army had been wiped out at Stalingrad in southern Russia. The Afrika Korps had surrendered in Tunisia. Germany was at war with the entire world. There was no way to win.

But what about their "duty"?

As Gustav carried his tools back to the tank, Rolf's advice wouldn't leave him.

The main thing now is to stay alive.

CHAPTER 4

THE FIELDS

The next morning, September 9, 1944
MERL

The farm courtyard was cool and quiet around seven a.m., as Gustav prepared to shave. Sure, he barely had any stubble. But today was his eighteenth birthday and this was his gift to himself.

He wasn't about to tell the crew about the occasion; no one was in the mood anyway, after what the Americans had done to other German tanks. Last night, he'd heard stories from survivors who had limped back from the massacre.

What happened was this: under the confusion of darkness, their sister companies had mistakenly wandered into American lines in a forest. They were quickly surrounded and lost twenty-one tanks and self-propelled guns—nearly half the unit. In the first day.

Still, Gustav didn't feel right about fighting Americans. As a boy, he had enjoyed reading books about cowboys and Native Americans, and even Mickey Mouse. And back home, nearly every farmer had relatives who had emigrated to the New World or sent their children there when there were too many mouths to feed. Gustav had pondered the idea too.

Gustav had barely swiped the razor when a message arrived for Rolf: it was time to fight.

Sizzling with power, the line of twelve Panthers rolled into the fields of Merl. The throaty growl of their engines coursed through the air as puffs of smoke rose from their exhaust stacks.

Fearsome as the Panther was, it had its defects. All that armor made the tank heavy in front. Plus, the tank's interlacing wheels were easily clogged and jammed. A year earlier, 200 Panthers had debuted at the Battle of Kursk. After five days of action and wear and tear, only 10 were still operating.

Gustav and the driver rode with their hatches open. The Panthers were driving toward an area in the distant forest, where they expected the Americans to arrive. Gustav wore a throat microphone around his neck and a headset over his cap. As radioman, he listened simultaneously to the intercom and the company frequency.

Behind them, smoke rose in Luxembourg City. Their fellow soldiers were destroying the city's phone grid and water lines as they fled. In the process, they were also leaving Gustav's brigade to operate without these necessities.

Across the continent, Allied units were jockeying to reach Germany. They were pushing against the Germans' defensive in Italy. Soviets were already in Poland. And now the Americans' 5th Armored Division found itself in position to reach Germany first, after Spearhead's unexpected detour to Mons. All that remained for the 5th Armored was to charge into Luxembourg City and then race to the border.

With just twelve Panthers, the German Army's 2nd Company would try to spoil that feat.

They had barely gone a mile when a voice erupted in Gustav's ears—"Fighter-bombers!" High overhead, twelve silver planes with red noses were curving through the sky. They were American P-47s, Thunderbolts of the 50th Fighter Group.

Gustav stared in awe as the planes leveled their wings and dove toward him.

From his commander position, Rolf disappeared from above the turret; the driver sank from sight and sealed his hatch. Gustav dropped into his compartment and slammed the hatch cover just before a torrent of bullets sprinted across the tank. It made a high-pitched ringing noise that reverberated through the hull.

The radio squawked. The company commander's order rang out loud and clear: the tankers had to disperse. It was every crew for itself.

The tanks, which had been clustered, now fanned out across the field, trying to put more space between them. This would make it more difficult for the planes to hit them.

Rolf's Panther pulled up to the formation. Its interlacing wheels rose and fell with the terrain, absorbing the bumps. The cannon stayed level, ready to shoot if necessary.

But the American planes were hot on their trail. The P-47s made pass after pass, mercilessly targeting the Panther's engine. But the Americans couldn't quite land a deadly blow. The planes abandoned the hunt and departed, off into the horizon.

Gustav could breathe again, but he couldn't relax for too

long. The Panther had to take cover in a thick grove of trees. Gustav opened his hatch and stood to help the driver steer. Even in the midst of combat, his job was to stick his head out and watch out for threats.

In the shadows of the spruce trees at the edge of the forest, the Panther halted with a sigh. Everyone inside rose, hungry for fresh air.

Gustav was surprised to find they had traveled the farthest of anyone in their company. Everyone else was on the other side of the field. None of them moved as they waited in ambush.

Gustav surveyed his once-pristine tank. The planes had scarred it badly. Bullets had raked the turret numbers and blasted away the tow cable.

Rolf lowered himself to the hull beside Gustav. "I need your mirror, Bubi," he said. "Mine caught bullets."

Rolf was mysterious to Gustav. He received letters from Dresden but never spoke of his family. He wore the silver Panzer badge for surviving twenty-five tank engagements, but he never told stories.

Gustav removed the mirror from his periscope and gave it to Rolf. It was more important that the commander could see outside than that he could.

In the surrounding woods, farmers worked, pushing wheelbarrows and digging for potatoes. Life went on. Gustav envied the men and women with their boots caked in soil. He had always loved farmwork. The vision before him brought back fond memories of harvesting rye in fields similar to these. His family sometimes did it by the light of the moon.

Gustav was a reluctant fighter. Membership in Hitler Youth, the youth organization of the Nazi Party in Germany, had been mandatory since 1939; he hadn't had much choice but to join. Although he enjoyed the camping, marching, and sports, he'd never wanted to be a soldier. In fact, Gustav's dream was to be a train conductor.

Every Sunday, after church, he'd pedal his bicycle far from home to watch the trains chug past on the Hamburg–Bremen line. After the war began, he'd even applied to work in a factory that built locomotives. He hoped it would be a first step toward becoming a conductor.

But when his father was drafted into the army, the family found itself shorthanded and Gustav's grandmother asked him to remain on the farm. To Gustav, this duty to his family and farm came first. It was simple. His dreams would have to wait.

When Gustav's own army orders arrived in autumn 1943, he went to an army doctor for his physical. The doctor took one look at his compact frame, a perfect fit for small, tight spaces, and sent him straight to the armored forces.

Gustav's headset crackled. The sound was scratchy but alarming. The voices coming through were American. Gustav alerted Rolf—if he was picking up the enemy's transmissions, they *had* to be close. Possibly close enough to shoot.

The crew withdrew inside and buttoned their hatches. The local farmers fled from the fields once they noticed the army men scrambling. As if on cue, the Shermans appeared two miles away in a gap in the forest.

Following the road, the column of the U.S. 34th Tank Battalion flowed into the fields without hesitation. Obviously, they were intent on liberating Luxembourg City that day.

A motorized whine sounded behind Gustav. The gunner was tracking the column of American tanks with a gun that was nearly 17 feet long. It was a 75mm gun like the older Mark IV's but could hold a nearly 3-foot-long shell that fired with earsplitting "super velocity."

"Wait for my call," Rolf, who was perched at the turret, told the gunner.

Sweat trickled down Gustav's face. The whites of his knuckles showed as he gripped his machine gun. It was useless against tanks, but it was comforting to hold.

The Shermans motored farther from the safety of the forest toward where Rolf and the Panther lay in wait. They were now only a mile away. But Rolf wanted them closer. He'd learned on the Eastern Front to wait until the target was within a half mile—and then to shoot the last tank in the column, followed by the first. This created a deadly jam. After that, the hunting was easy.

Suddenly, green tracer ammunition zipped up and over and slammed into the lead Sherman.

Gustav couldn't believe it. *Someone had fired too soon!* The Sherman's hatch covers flung open and the crew came tumbling out.

Rolf cursed. The golden opportunity to capture the American tanks had been squandered.

The Shermans began firing, trying to drive a Panther into retreat.

Rolf had to act. He directed the gunner's attention to the second Sherman in line—then gave the order as if frustrated to have to do so. "Fire."

With an earsplitting bark, flames leaped from the tank's extra-long muzzle. A 16-pound warhead blasted downrange. The green tracer covered the mile in barely two seconds. The American Sherman tank shuddered as it absorbed the punch.

"Hit," Rolf said.

Gustav watched the crew come pouring out of the Sherman as it burned in the field. He was pleased to see them escape. Even if they were the enemy, they were fellow tankers who endured the same miseries that he did.

The remaining Shermans turned back the way they'd come.

Gustav glanced over at the driver—*That's it?*

He'd barely finished the thought when a shell smacked the Panther's front armor with a low-pitched resonance. The battle was just beginning.

The intercom came alive with cursing as Gustav reeled from the attack. Smoke wafted inside the tank, stinging his eyes and nostrils. He tasted acid on his tongue. "What is this?" he asked, wiping his watering eyes. The others couldn't stop coughing. No one answered because none had seen white phosphorus before.

It was an incendiary weapon used mostly by the Western Allies—a chemical substance so volatile that it was stored underwater for safety. When packed into exploding shells, it ignited on contact with the air, burning at 5,000 degrees for almost a minute. A single waxy flake could burn a man to the bone. And this was just the smoke from it.

Gustav was still pawing his eyes when another, heavier, shell slammed the Panther.

Rolf called for the driver to reverse—"Get us out of here!"

Ears ringing, Gustav crept back to his post. The tank shifted gears and lurched backward into the shady woods. A dark shape seemed to be waiting for them there. It was an American M7 self-propelled artillery vehicle, housing a massive 105mm gun. Nicknamed the "Priest" by the British, an M7 normally fired skyward, but now its gun was leveled at the Panther.

Gustav jumped back before the shell slammed the armor directly in front of his face. Lights flickered and the ringing in his ears returned. More shells slammed the slant armor, striking just inches from his face. In the corner of the hull, he could see fissures forming up and down the welds.

Despite the pounding fire, the driver swung the tank into the cut in the forest, striving to get behind the wall of trees. For a brief moment, the turn to safety presented the Priest with a clear view of the Panther's side. The enemy took advantage. Another shell hit, then another. The brutal impact flung the driver sideways against the shells and Gustav against the steel wall.

Gustav clutched his shoulder. The driver regained the controls in the midst of the chaos. He reported to Rolf that he could feel the damage—a shell had probably severed the left track.

Gustav and the others gripped their hatches, awaiting Rolf's command. They were eager to flee but didn't dare. To abandon a tank without orders was considered a crime that the German Army wouldn't hesitate to punish—mercilessly. By the end of 1944, they would execute 10,000 of their own soldiers.

"Keep going!" Rolf urged as they regained control from the chaos and the tank moved deeper into the cut of the forest, just before its wheels rolled off the last track link and sank into the earth.

In the sun-swept fields, one Panther sat abandoned by the road. Another burned on the hilltop. The remaining Panthers had no choice but to retreat, leaving the others behind.

And now, two thousand feet above the battlefield, an American L-4 spotter plane was circling above the earth. Known as a "Grasshopper," the L-4 was used to direct artillery fire.

There was no time to lose. American shells would be on the way soon. Rolf gave the command, "Everybody out!"

The turret was empty in seconds. But in the hull, Gustav had a problem. His hatch cover was jammed and wouldn't open all the way. He was trapped.

The tank's driver lingered guiltily. "Don't wait for me!" Gustav called to him. The driver was gone in a flash, running madly through the fields as artillery shells burst in his wake.

Gustav frantically unbuckled the thirty-pound shells and began sliding them, one at a time, back into the turret until he created a pathway out through the driver's side. He crawled for freedom.

Outside, Gustav rolled over the side of the Panther, scrambled to the tree line, and dove into a pile of fallen leaves. Every fiber in him wanted to stay glued to the forest floor. Even Rolf

himself had warned him: "The main thing now is to stay alive."
The Americans would be coming soon.

Out in the fields, a shell burst changed everything.

Other men dispersed and ran. The driver hobbled, then fell
and rolled onto his back, clutching his left knee. The shelling
didn't let up.

A gear clicked in Gustav. He had a duty to help a comrade,
even a comrade who had not hesitated to leave him behind.
Gustav leaped to his feet and sprinted toward the fallen man.
He shielded his face from flaming tree bursts and smoking craters. Another crew member was coming to help too, from the
opposite direction, pushing a wheelbarrow. It was Senior Lance
Corporal Werner Wehner, a stocky veteran with a round, ruddy
face and little patience.

The driver was screaming. His knee had been split open.
Werner gripped the man in a bear hug and placed him in the
wheelbarrow. Then, Werner took one handle, Gustav took the
other, and they began pushing the wounded man toward Merl,
steering around sizzling shells and rains of dirt to safety.

CHAPTER 5

THE FORAY

That night
WEST OF MERL

Gustav followed Werner through the dead of night. The moon lay low on the horizon as the men crouched and moved silently. Every so often, Werner paused to touch the earth and check their course. They were following a set of tank tracks pressed in the soil.

Although the night was cool, Gustav found himself sweating beneath his coveralls. He knew what they had come to do: like knights stalking a sleeping dragon, Gustav and Werner were creeping back toward their abandoned Panther. Returning there, in the middle of a dark forest, was a dangerous thing to do. Leaves were rustling. Could they be in the middle of an American trap? Gustav's eyes darted in pursuit of the noises. He wore a pistol, but that brought little comfort. What could a pistol do if they were confronted by men with rifles?

Gustav's company commander had ordered him and Werner here, and with good reason. It was *their* tank. Their duty. Their mess to clean up. And besides, they were all that remained of the crew.

Army medics had taken the driver off their hands to treat him. Rolf and the loader were missing, though. Werner had last seen them dart into the forest while the shells were coming down. And now Werner was stuck with Gustav, whom he viewed as a rookie. The thirty-two-year-old veteran had been offered many chances to lead a crew of his own, but he had turned down every promotion to avoid the headache of looking after anyone other than himself. If Werner had had it his way, he'd have done this mission alone too.

Taking cover on the field side of the tank, Gustav and Werner braced for the forest to erupt with gunfire. To their surprise, nothing happened.

Gustav crept toward his compartment to grab his personal things.

Werner's grip stopped him.

"I left my bag next to my seat," Gustav said in a whisper. Inside were his diary, letters from his grandmother, and his cigar box.

"Forget it."

Gustav's spirits sank.

Werner climbed up to the engine deck and cast a glare at his partner. "Get up here!" he said.

"But my things!" Gustav protested.

Werner had bigger concerns. A half mile to the north, a Panther smoldered on a hilltop. Across the field and beyond the road sat another one with just its turret showing. It had been immobilized by the P-47s but was still partly up and running.

And therein lay a big problem. Either of those Panthers—if

they were captured by another army—could be repurposed. On the Eastern Front, the Russians had seized enough Panthers that they printed instruction manuals on how to build them. And the Seaforth Highlanders of Canada would soon capture a Panther and gift it to the British Army.

Gustav and Werner couldn't let this happen under their watch in Luxembourg. They climbed aboard their Panther and disappeared into its turret. For a moment, they were home again. Werner sat in the gunner's seat, turning the turret by handwheel. With a shell in his hands, Gustav served as his loader.

Outside the tank, the Panther's turret crept to the right so slowly that its movement was barely noticeable. Its barrel aimed at the Panther across the road. After a moment, they sent green projectiles zipping across the field. The strike accomplished Werner's goal. A blowtorch of flame blasted upward from the turret hatches, and quickly the fire from the abandoned Panther lit up the fields and forest.

Gustav leaped down from his tank and took off running. Werner followed. Anticipating the blast that they thought was sure to follow, the men dove to the ground and covered their heads.

Thirty seconds turned into a minute, which turned into two, then twenty tense minutes. But the explosion they were expecting didn't resound. Then, the silence was broken by new sounds—sounds that were coming from the opposite side of the forest. Sherman tanks had pulled up and parked. Hatches were opening. Americans were talking.

Gustav's feet felt like lead as he and Werner returned to their

Panther. He waited while Werner disappeared around the front of the tank and eyed the turret anxiously, hoping the explosives weren't smoldering inside.

Sounds of hammering and wood splitting were now traveling through the forest from the Americans' position. Whatever they were doing, they were too close for comfort.

Werner fashioned a rope and fed it into one of the Panther's gas tanks, drenching it. With a flick of a lighter, a flame raced up the rope.

Gustav and Werner fled as fast as they could into the field behind the tank. They reached safety just as a roaring volcano of flames burst from the Panther's engine deck and licked the night sky. Side by side, Gustav and Werner watched as their tank became charred.

Gustav cringed. It was like losing a friend. The tank had taken so many beatings. It had shielded him from more shells and dangers than he could count.

Earlier in the war, a German crew might have towed their Panther back for repair instead of risking their lives to destroy it. Now, there just wasn't that option. Gustav blamed Hitler, who had personally ordered that the brigade rush into Luxembourg, without aerial or artillery support, or even a recovery vehicle, to retrieve disabled tanks.

A sweet, smoky scent caught Gustav's nose. It might have been his imagination, but he swore he smelled his box of tobacco burning. He had intended it to be a gift.

His father was a supply soldier on the Eastern Front, tasked with bringing up essentials by horse-drawn cart. In a letter, he'd lamented to Gustav the lack of good tobacco. For months, Gustav had stashed away his cigarette rations and bought any cigars he could find. Now his parcel for his father was gone, along with his diary and his mail. What would happen next? Would they even find another tank for him, or would they send him to the infantry?

Gustav wanted to cry.

Werner must have recognized that the young radioman needed some encouragement. He gently elbowed Gustav and extended an open hand. In the flickering light, the two men shook to the success of their mission.

At midnight the men rode back to Merl on a Panther.

For the return journey, Gustav found himself in charge as tank commander. Werner sat on the tank's front hull as Gustav rode in the commander's position with earphones pulled on over his cap. No one could remember why the company commander had deputized Gustav, but he was loving every second of it.

For the first time in the war, and maybe his entire life, he felt important, riding in the turret's high perch. He held the reins of a 49-ton machine. Behind them, Panthers were burning like oil wells.

Beneath an overpass hidden from the moon's glow, Gustav spread a blanket on the tank's engine deck. His eyes drooped. He could barely stand. It was nearly two a.m. in Merl, and the others had gone to scrounge for food or to plan their next moves.

At first light, their brigade would retreat for the West Wall. The Americans would soon be hot on their trail. Later that morning, American Shermans would roll into Luxembourg City. And a day after that, on September 11, the war would enter a new season.

That's when a 5th Armored foot patrol would lay their boots on German soil and gaze upon the West Wall.

That's when Allied troops that had landed in Normandy and in southern France would meet up. Together, they'd form a wall of their own, of men and machines stretching from the Belgian coast to Switzerland.

Gustav curled on the deck of the Panther and pulled the blanket over him, unaware that seven Allied armies were now converging on him.

His birthday had come and gone, leaving him with just the uniform on his back. But that was good enough. He had done his duty and survived, convinced that the days ahead would be easier. How could they be worse than this?

CHAPTER 6

BEYOND THE WALL

Four days later, September 14, 1944
SEVENTY-FIVE MILES NORTH—GERMANY

A dozen Sherman tanks of Easy Company rumbled to a stop along a country road. A darkened farmhouse stood nearby. From its second-story window, a white bedsheet was flapping.

The air tingled with tension. A storm was boiling over the surrounding forests.

Sergeant Bob Earley stood like a statue in the lead tank's turret. A pipe was clenched between his teeth. Earley had replaced the late Paul Faircloth, Clarence's commander who was killed at Mons. At twenty-nine, and hailing from Fountain, Minnesota, Earley was like a hardened old man among a unit of boyish tankers. His face was flat and stoic, with eyes often locked in a squint.

The tank he rode was one of the new M4A1 Shermans known as a "76." In the 3rd Armored Division, each company received about five 76s, and they often went to the best fighters. Behind him, other tank commanders stayed low, ready at their machine guns. Before they could all jump out of the tank to stretch their legs and take a breather, someone would have to investigate and make sure the coast was clear. This was Germany, the enemy's home turf, after all.

The day before, the 3rd Armored had opened the door to Germany. That meant it was *the* first Allied unit to punch through the West Wall—and to also capture a German town. And Easy Company had the scars to prove it. Normally it was sixteen tanks strong. By now, though, the unit was missing five tanks and crews.

There was movement ahead of the tanks. The farmhouse door cracked open. A half dozen machine guns swung toward the sign of motion. Then, a hand emerged. It was waving a white cloth. A short German farmer stepped outside. He looked to be in his seventies, with bushy gray hair and a tired face bristling with gray stubble.

The farmer spoke to the tankers as they glared down menacingly from behind their guns. They couldn't hear him over the tank engines, and even if they could have heard him, they couldn't understand him.

Earley stepped down to the engine deck with a Thompson submachine gun in hand. He cradled the gun, keeping an eye on the farmer.

"Smoyer!" he called to Clarence.

Inside their new tank, christened Eagle II, Clarence grumbled. Someone had leaked that he spoke German. Now he would have to be the one to speak to the farmer. He climbed out. Despite the white flags, he kept a hand near his pistol as he approached the farmer.

Easy Company had been placed in reserve. Now it was trailing the task force, which included tanks and doughs. It was a pause for the men of Easy Company; an opportunity for them to catch their breath. But that didn't mean they were safe.

Was an ambush waiting around the next bend? If anyone knew, it would be the farmer.

Before him, Clarence saw a tired old man. Clarence greeted him in German. The farmer's face came to life.

"You're German?" he inquired hopefully.

"No," Clarence said. He explained that his parents were Pennsylvania Dutch. "When I was a kid, they spoke German when they didn't want me to know what they were saying."

The farmer laughed and Clarence cracked a smile. The mood lifted. The tankers came down to smoke or relieve themselves in the nearby grass.

"Where are the German soldiers?" Clarence asked.

The farmer pointed back the way the Americans had come.

Clarence wasn't sold. He pressed further. With each question, the farmer became more and more emphatic. "Just farmers," he said. No Nazis.

Clearly, the German farmer knew little more than they did. Clarence thanked the man and turned to leave. A bony hand reached out and grabbed Clarence's arm, stopping him in his tracks. Clarence wheeled around and broke the man's grip, clenching his fists to defend himself. His expression softened at the sight of tears welling in the old man's eyes.

The farmer told Clarence that he hated the Nazis. He had two sons on the Eastern Front and had not heard from them for a year. "Good, healthy boys," he said as the tears slipped down his cheeks. "Good, healthy boys."

He lowered his chin to his chest and began sobbing. Some of the tankers looked away.

Clarence had always thought of the Germans they killed in battle as faceless soldiers without an identity. Not as sons, with fathers or mothers who worried about their safety.

It wasn't until now that he saw an awful truth in the old man's eyes.

War touches everyone.

Clarence placed a hand on the man's shoulder and leaned in close. "I'm sorry about your boys," he said. "We lost some good people too."

A week or two later, Stolberg, Germany
This was the end of the road—for now.

In a neighborhood nestled on a hillside, the tanks of Easy Company sat parked in the evening light.

Behind the Shermans lay a valley. A castle was tucked in the middle of the Rhineland town of Stolberg, which was divided by a winding stream. It looked straight out of a fairy tale. At the moment, Stolberg was locked in stalemate, with the Allies and the Germans each avoiding making the first move. The German 12th Infantry Division held the eastern side of the hill, opposite them.

Each crew took refuge in whichever home was nearest their tank. It didn't offer much in the way of shelter, but being indoors was better than nothing. Clarence joined Earley and the rest of the crew inside a battle-damaged, abandoned house. It was in ruins from artillery fire. Wooden slabs covered the windows, and the roof leaked.

Men slumped in stuffed chairs and on a couch. No one was in the mood to talk. They were homesick, and edgy from all the waiting. The war wasn't going to end by them just sitting there. Anything could set them off, even something as simple as opening a magazine from home and seeing a pinup girl, or hearing a familiar song on Allied radio.

"Honey I don't see where candle and lamp light is so romantic," wrote one tanker. "I am about to go nuts on them. To see a room lighted again would be a pleasure."

In the kitchen, Clarence lit the crew's small Coleman stove and heated a can of food from his K ration. He took one of the remaining porcelain dishes from the cupboard and poured his supper onto the plate, then took a seat at a table in the main room and ate in silence.

The Clarence Smoyer from before the war would hardly have recognized himself now. Back in Lehighton, he had one love above all others: roller-skating. He would go to Graver's skating rink, pay the fifty cents admission, clip rollers to his shoes, and skate to organ music, past massive murals, for hours and hours on end.

Now, he could barely muster the energy to shovel his food.

The pervasive sense of fatigue—even depression—was felt across Spearhead.

• • •

The unmistakable sound of a jeep pulling up outside pierced the crew's malaise.

The engine cut out, someone banged on their tank. Then came voices.

After a pause, the door to the house flew open, and a lieutenant ducked inside.

He stood before the crew, every inch of six-five, with a slender frame, a long face, and gray eyes. Behind his back, the men called him "High Pockets." He'd attended college for a year. In these times, that was enough to make him their superior.

The crew forced themselves to their feet. High Pockets's eyes roved back and forth. He had come to inspect them, to ensure that someone was manning the gun in the tank. And to make sure no one had sneaked into Stolberg for some unauthorized R&R. Clarence pitied the guys in 1st Platoon who were stuck with High Pockets as their lieutenant.

Seemingly out of nowhere, a shrill whistle sounded. Artillery was soaring over the hilltop. The shells were coming from the German side, in the direction of the Rhine River.

The shells thundered steadily uphill—closer and closer. The house shuddered. The crew cursed—a German artillery spotter must have seen High Pockets's jeep pull up.

Earley and the others darted into the kitchen and crouched behind the brick stove. Clarence folded his arms where he sat at the table. After all that he had seen and done, he no longer even cared what happened.

With each blast, water and plaster rained down from above. It sounded like a freight train was roaring past outside.

High Pockets tried to crawl under the couch but got stuck. Trapped, he started clawing at the floorboards. When Clarence saw High Pockets's long legs flailing behind him, he couldn't help himself any longer. In spite of the chaos outside, he broke into uncontrollable laughter.

Just as abruptly as it had begun, the shelling ended.

A month later, October 29, 1944, Stolberg

Stolberg, with its tree-lined streets, was beginning to feel like "home." The houses were more modern than any they'd seen in France or Belgium, with hot running water for baths and dry floors for their sleeping bags.

It was Easy Company's week off the line. At night, jubilant whoops pierced the quiet of residential Stolberg. Clarence and the other men drank beer and joked around. Some of the other guys played goofy pranks. One had dressed up as a woman to trick the men into thinking they could meet the woman of their dreams.

For all their fun, the men were in for it the next day. Captain Mason Salisbury, the company commander, demanded that they stand in ranks in a field behind the houses. Salisbury was furious as he paced between the men and their tanks.

Salisbury was just twenty-four years old, with a square, boyish face. He wore a visorless "overseas" cap atop curly blond hair. He hailed from Long Island high society and had been attending Yale in 1942 when he gave up his studies to join the army. He was still new to this post, and eager to enforce the rules against drinking and fooling around.

Salisbury stopped in front of 2nd Platoon. Clarence and Earley stood ramrod straight as his glare drifted across them.

"I should court-martial each of you," he said.

The culprits' faces tightened with smiles. After the first sergeant dismissed them, their barely contained laughter exploded across the company. Even Clarence had to chuckle.

Early December 1944

Under the cover of darkness, Clarence slipped from his house and darted across the street. No one saw him as he followed a cobblestone road toward a hilltop neighborhood. He wore a mackintosh against the chilly drizzle and carried a package under his arm. The castle was shadowy, and Stolberg was quiet behind him.

Life had gotten better.

In November, the port of Antwerp had been opened in northern Belgium, unleashing a much-needed flood of supplies. The company mess now served such luxuries as pancakes with butter, Nescafé, and chocolate pie.

Clarence's package contained leftover food that the cooks had slipped him under the table. Tonight, he had a different, but no less dangerous, mission: a date with a local girl.

He had seen her sitting on the steps of her home. Hungry for companionship, he had approached her, in spite of the rules. Socializing with the local Germans was strictly against army code, yet almost everyone was guilty of fraternizing by then— even Captain Salisbury. There were few other distractions from the looming dread of returning to battle.

At the top of the hill stood a row of brick townhouses. On her front step, Resi Pfieffer waited beneath an umbrella. She was a full-faced eighteen-year-old with gentle green eyes who usually wore her brown hair pulled back into buns.

The coast was clear.

Resi and Clarence slipped inside her front door. The date would be confined to the home—where they would play board games and share the food Clarence had brought, all under her parents' supervision. And whenever the MPs came knocking, they'd cover for him: "No Americans here."

To Clarence, still new to dating, this was a fine first step toward something more.

A week or two later, December 18, 1944

Wintry gray clouds hung over Stolberg, threatening to burst with snow. It was a good afternoon to be indoors. The tankers had a stove roaring, trying to stay warm. Clarence checked his watch, counting down the hours until he could see Resi again. His whole crew knew about her by now.

A Christmas tree stood in the corner. They had cut it from a forest full of West Wall bunkers. Everyone in the platoon had chipped in two dollars to buy a cow for Christmas dinner. Some of the men had even taken to going to church with Germans. It was starting to feel like a time for hope.

And then Earley blew through the front door. "Get ready to mount up!" he said. "We're leaving!"

Clarence and the others leaped to their feet. "The Germans broke through somewhere," Earley said. In actuality, that "somewhere" was the Ardennes Forest in Belgium. Still, intelligence coming from the Ardennes was murky, and Earley was as much in the dark as the rest of the men.

Clarence was stunned. The Germans were supposed to be falling apart, weren't they? They were taking a pounding from the Americans in airplanes, and from the Soviets in the east.

Someone asked Earley if they could still kill the cow and bring it along to eat. Clarence asked if he could say goodbye to his sweetheart.

There was no time for either. Earley told the crew to gather any warm clothing they could find. They had been issued only rain gear, and wherever they were headed, they would be fighting in winter. Clarence had an idea. It would not hurt to have extra food, so he volunteered to approach his friends in the kitchen crew. Everyone scattered to pack and prepare to leave.

By then, Stolberg had descended into pandemonium. The streets were a crisscross of men and urgent, honking traffic.

The division's armored infantrymen were packing up too. As one dough loaded his half-track, one soldier said, "My God, it's just like a movie, you guys running off to war!"

No one knew exactly how desperate the situation was.

The fighting in the Ardennes had been raging for two days by then. In fact, the Germans were steamrolling the American forces. They had three times as much infantry and twice as many tanks. They had also cut field telephone lines, jammed American radio wavelengths, and filled the airwaves with broadcasts of bells ringing from German towns.

To slow the onslaught, GIs were fighting fiercely. But the German forces were simply too many.

The Shermans had become battlewagons. Shovels, sledge-hammers, and spare fuel cans were attached wherever there was space. Clarence had secured food rations for Eagle's departure.

Clerks brought out bags of Christmas mail and shouted names. One man came back with a package of roasted peanuts that had already turned rancid. Another received a letter notifying him that his kids were sick. No one was receiving good news.

When he heard his own name—"Clarence Smoyer!"—Clarence seized up with trepidation. He had received a box wrapped in wax paper, which he eyed without opening. He hoped it contained what he thought it did.

German citizens were congregating on the street, whispering and pointing as they watched the tanks gear up. Clarence was distraught that he had not said goodbye to Resi and her parents. They had all but adopted him and treated him as if he were their own son.

The tank commanders huddled for a final briefing before the race to the front lines. Spearhead's parent unit, the First Army, was sending veteran divisions. A relief force of 60,000 men was already in transit.

"We will be at the battle site at first light," commanders were told.

Darkness had already descended at five-thirty p.m. when Easy Company wound through Stolberg. The tanks' headlights glowed as they set out to "destination unknown." Clarence didn't need a map to tell him they were leaving Germany. The route was leading them toward Belgium.

The column turned the corner and the tankers beheld a sight they would never forget. The sidewalks brimmed with Germans of all ages, holding lanterns and candles. Clarence was not the only tanker who had been "adopted" by the enemy.

Earley relinquished his place in the turret, and Clarence stood to look for Resi as the tank held course between the crowds. As Clarence looked left and right, countless faces swept past his vision. Women dabbed their eyes. Men waved handkerchiefs. Children ran alongside the convoy shouting farewells. If the German Army returned, anyone on that street could be branded a sympathizer or collaborator, yet still they waved goodbye.

Clarence tore off his helmet in the hopes that Resi would recognize him, but the crowds slipped by too quickly. As the tanks moved forward, he kept his eyes on the panorama behind him. Those three months in Stolberg had brought Clarence back to himself, giving him and his crew a taste of freedom from fear. Now they were leaving it all behind for some far-flung winter battlefield.

CHAPTER 7

THE FOURTH TANK

Five days later, December 23, 1944
SOUTHERN BELGIUM

One after another, the Easy Company tanks followed their leader through the snowy fields of the Ardennes Forest. Jagged pines whizzed by. A fuzzy shell of snowflakes blanketed each Sherman. Their engines puffed exhaust into the cold. Frigid winds had wiped away the clouds, and the afternoon sun was beaming brightly.

The sojourn in Stolberg had been relaxed, with the men hunkering down in abandoned homes and getting to know the area as they waited for battle. Now, things were springing into action. The 2nd Platoon was "spearheading"—the crew's slang for leading. There was a rotation for spearheading. Each platoon took a turn, and then within the platoons, individual tank crews alternated the duty. The tanks proceeded in their order of combat, each thirty yards apart. The lead tank set the pace, gun aimed forward. The second tank shadowed the first, in case the leader missed anything. The third guarded the right flank, and the fourth watched the left.

Every minute took them deeper into what would soon be the largest battle ever fought by the U.S. Army. The chaos here now had a name: "The Battle of the Bulge."

Four tanks back in the column, Earley rode low in Eagle's turret, wearing goggles and many layers of clothing to stave off the bitter cold. Without a heater, the tank felt like an igloo. With a gloved finger, Clarence etched his name in the frost that wrapped the wall. Beneath his helmet, he wore a tanker's winter hood, and he had pulled a blanket over his shoulders, but it didn't stop his teeth from chattering.

Through his periscope, Clarence took in Belgium's beauty: a stream lined by brambles, a dark forest, and snowy, hidden paths. It looked like a winter wonderland.

Easy Company had been sent there to fight in the deepest part of the bulge in the Allied lines. The "bulge" referred to the wedge that the Germans drove into the Allied lines. After an eighty-six-mile ride, they had arrived the night before and joined the 84th Infantry Division, known as the "Railsplitters," in the defense of Marche. Marche was an ancient town of cobblestone streets and narrow homes built around a fourteenth-century Catholic church.

And the Battle of the Bulge might hinge upon what happened there.

Hitler's forces were racing to reach the Meuse River before the Allies could get there. That was because across the Meuse River lay the road to the Germans' ultimate objective: the port of Antwerp. Hitler was gambling that if German troops could drive a wedge behind the American and British forces and capture that port, the setback might stop his enemies.

The German battle plan wouldn't be easy to pull off, though. They'd have to work quickly to beat the Allies. The twisty Ardennes roads passed through towns that the Germans desperately needed to control in order to pull off their grand plan. They had already sacked La Roche and St. Vith and laid siege to Bastogne. All that remained was Marche, closest to the Meuse.

That meant that the stand at Marche was shaping up to be the Allies' best chance to destroy the German offensive.

About three miles south of Marche, the terrain gently rose ahead of Easy Company. The gray roofs of Hèdrée, a settlement that straddled the road, came into view about a hundred yards ahead. The lead tank radioed for a halt, then stopped with a lurch.

That morning, the commanding general of the 3rd Armored, Major General Maurice Rose, had ordered his chain of command: "Impress on every individual that we must stay right here or there will be a war to be fought all over again and we won't be here to fight it."

For Clarence, sitting fourth in line made all the difference in the world. In most of the battles he had seen, the first tank did the fighting while the others waited. Clarence removed his gloves and unwrapped the Christmas package he'd received back in Stolberg. It was a box full of chocolate fudge—a treat he'd been looking forward to ever since he smelled it.

Back home in Lehighton, Melba Whitehead, a girl from the skating rink, had made it for him as a Christmas present.

Clarence had promised himself that he wouldn't touch it until he reached the combat zone. He figured this was close enough and dug in. He wasn't sure if it was the stress or the memories of the home he hadn't seen in over a year, but it was the best fudge he'd ever tasted. He slowly savored every bite.

Meanwhile, from the first tank's turret, a slender young commander scanned the horizon through his binoculars. In tank warfare, vision was everything. Whichever side saw the other first typically *fired* first. And a British study had found that 70 percent of the time, whoever fired first survived.

The man behind the field glasses was Lieutenant Charlie Rose—no relation to Major Maurice Rose. A dark-haired twenty-two-year-old with an All-American grin, he was a rookie lieutenant who was leading the 2nd Platoon to build experience. He'd left college behind to enlist in the army. Back home, Rose had a wife, a child on the way, and plans to sell tractors after the war.

All that would have to wait. Today, he was hunting enemy tanks.

But where were they now? Someone had to go looking.

On Rose's word, the tanks resumed clanking toward Hèdrée.

Rose's tank was pulling up to the settlement when the crack of a German gun stopped the tank in its tracks. With a vicious clang, Rose's Sherman shook from the blow.

They had found the 2nd Panzer Division. But not before the 2nd Panzer Division had found them.

• • •

In the fourth Sherman in the lineup, Earley called out, "Lead's hit."

Clarence had just reluctantly closed his box of fudge. He turned his gun forward.

The second tank, commanded by the platoon sergeant, was idling. Its turret swung side to side, searching desperately. Neither the platoon sergeant nor his gunner had seen the shot.

In the lead, after recovering from the shock of the hit, Rose and his crew bailed out of their tank and came bolting back. Rose urged the men to keep going. He'd meet up with them later, he said. Everyone watched as he climbed aboard the second tank in line. At the turret, Rose pointed the platoon sergeant's attention to where he'd last seen the enemy tank. The platoon sergeant nodded and shinnied down the turret to direct his crew. Meanwhile, Rose kept watch for movement.

From ahead, a fiery green German tracer cut through the frozen air. Before anyone could catch their senses, it slammed into the front of the turret. A glowing chunk of shrapnel punched straight through Rose's gut, nearly tearing him in half. His body tumbled over the side of the tank, lifeless.

From his own Sherman, Clarence reeled back in his seat, spilling what remained of his precious fudge. Did that just happen? Was the lieutenant really gone? Sure enough, Rose's body was seeping blood into the snow, and the platoon sergeant and his crew were pouring from their damaged tank.

"Situation report!" Captain Salisbury radioed from all the way back at the rear of the column. "Situation report!"

No reply came from the front. All the tanks that had two-way radios had been abandoned.

Clarence's eyes darted back and forth. His mind swirled with panic. Nearly three months spent in Stolberg had dulled his reactions. The first two tanks that had sheltered Eagle were nothing but useless shells. Only one remained operable ahead.

Earley got back on his feet and stood tall in the turret. "Keep your gun up there," he told Clarence. "If it's a Panther, you know what to do."

With his periscope fixed forward, Clarence waited for the enemy tank to slide into view. His heart pounded in his ears.

The commander of the tank directly in front of Clarence's, Sergeant Frank "Cajun Boy" Audiffred, suddenly veered to the right and drove off the road into a shallow gully.

Clarence couldn't believe his eyes.

Cajun Boy was a twenty-three-year-old from the Louisiana bayou, and his toughness was almost legendary in Easy Company. But here he was, driving away. So Cajun Boy couldn't take any more either? Were he and his crew booking it? Was he *abandoning them*?

Clarence kept his reticle trained on the rise. A sudden realization terrified him: They had been the fourth tank in line a moment ago. Now they were the first.

Suddenly, Cajun Boy's tank reappeared, climbing uphill this time. Clarence marveled at his audacity. Cajun Boy wasn't running. He was circling around the village to try for a side shot.

Cajun Boy's 75 Sherman churned slowly in the snow. In a twist of daring, Audiffred, a former gunner, had a high-explosive (HE) shell locked and loaded in the breech. This type of shell was typically used on buildings and troops—not on tanks—but the tactic had worked for him in Normandy. He'd stunned the enemy first before switching to an armor-piercing (AP) shell and maneuvering in for the kill shot. He'd try it again here.

The radio squawked to life. A tank commander's voice sounded the alert. "They're outflanking us!"

One of the crews had spotted movement in the forest to the left—surely German infantry.

Salisbury ordered everyone to retreat to the Marche perimeter. They had no choice but to flee and turn their backs to the enemy.

In front of Clarence, Cajun Boy's tank turned and reversed course.

It was complete and utter chaos. If the German tank—which was surely still up there—simply moved to the edge, it could hit the Shermans one by one as they fled.

Earley told Clarence to lay down suppressive fire using HE. Someone had to cover Cajun Boy. The best they could do would be to scare off the Germans as they retreated.

Clarence was confused. Since the German tank hadn't shown itself, he had no idea where to aim. "What do I fire at?"

"Anything."

The engine roared as the tank barreled after the others. Clarence took aim, foot on the trigger. Riding and firing backward, he shifted his fire from side to side. Gravel and snow leaped from the road, stone walls turned into dust, and trees shattered as he sprayed.

Clarence kept thumping shells, creating a storm that no enemy tank would want to move through.

And that was Earley's plan.

It had worked. The enemy tank never moved forward to follow up its first two kills.

Surrounded by fudge wrapping and shell casings, Clarence set his foot aside the trigger, exhausted.

CHAPTER 8

HOPE

That same night, December 23, 1944
SEVERAL MILES SOUTHEAST OF MARCHE, BELGIUM

Three Shermans sat silent beneath snowy evergreens. Behind them lay the woods called the Bois de Nolaumont. Crews covered their tanks in branches and snow, trying to camouflage the machines among the trees. Even when the moon shone directly down on them, the tanks were almost impossible to see.

The temperature hovered around zero. Across a field lay a tiny Belgian village. Now and then, the glow of candlelight would appear in the windows of the village's houses, taunting the men with thoughts of cozy indoor warmth.

Three tanks. They were all that remained of 2nd Platoon. Captain Salisbury had ordered them to this sleepy road with orders to shoot anything that moved. Every road mattered in the defense of Marche.

There was nothing to do now but wait.

Clarence wrapped himself in a blanket, stepped inside his sleeping bag, shoes and all, and brought the ends of the bag around his neck. If the tank was hit, he probably wouldn't be able to get out, but he didn't even care.

The day's events weighed on him. Everything felt futile. No matter what he did, it wouldn't matter. His Sherman's armor was simply no match for the ferocity of the German guns.

The radio was turned low. Cold wind whistled through Earley's hatch, where he sat with the cover cracked, listening for the enemy. Now and then he sprinkled instant-coffee granules into his mouth to stay awake.

Back at a convent in Marche, Carmelite nuns served soup to warm the men of the Railsplitters Division, who were defending the city proper. The Reverend Mother had asked a GI if there were many Germans in the area.

He assured her that there certainly were. .

"We will pray for you," she promised.

"Thanks," said the GI. "Yes, pray a lot."

The next Sherman over from Clarence's was named Eleanor. An old 75, it bore battle scars from its time in Normandy, including a deep gouge on one side of the turret.

In the gunner's seat, lost in thought, sat Corporal Chuck Miller. A wry Midwesterner from Kansas City, Chuck was nineteen, with heavy cheeks and narrow eyes. Beneath his tanker helmet he wore a hooded sweatshirt that his mother had sent to him.

It didn't sit right with Chuck, the way they had left Lieutenant Charlie Rose out there dead in the snow.

After the company had pulled back to friendly territory, a message had arrived. Through some miracle of family connections, the War Department had sent word to Lieutenant Rose that he had become a father. His son, Charles Crane Rose, had been born about a week and a half earlier. The news cut everyone deeply, and perhaps Chuck the deepest. A father would never know his son. A son would never know his father.

Chuck recognized his own story in the tragedy. He had few memories of his own father. He had been just a child when his father abandoned his mother, leaving her to raise Chuck, his older brother, and five older sisters on a seamstress's salary. She was Chuck's hero. Somehow, she held the family together and even now still scraped money together to send him adventure novels to read between battles.

Midnight had come and gone. It was now December 24, 1944, the day before Christmas.

Chuck had a plan, and now was the time to act.

Illuminated only by the sparse light of a half-moon, a jeep set out through the silvery fields.

At the wheel, Chuck leaned from side to side to keep an eye out. A dough volunteer sat in the passenger seat clutching his rifle. They went off-road, to avoid the Shermans. Captain Salisbury could never, ever know of this secret mission. And if the Germans saw them, they would endanger the whole company.

As the terrain began to rise, Chuck parked the jeep. He and the dough got out quietly.

Celebratory German voices could be heard. They were coming from a nearby farmhouse. It sounded like the soldiers were singing and likely drinking beer in the Christmas spirit.

With rifles at the ready, Chuck and the dough crept up a

roadside ditch toward the two abandoned Shermans. There, they found Rose's body covered in snow. It was frozen to the ground. They drew their knives and carefully pried it free. With their arms looped beneath Rose's, Chuck and the dough slipped away.

Chuck climbed aboard Eleanor and knocked on the turret.

The hatch cover opened and Sergeant Bill Hey, a commander with a thin mustache, greeted him. He pulled Chuck inside, as if he were harboring a fugitive.

Chuck fell into his seat, pale and convulsing. His mission was complete. He'd brought Rose's body back to friendly lines and left the jeep outside the command tent, with Rose's remains still lashed to the hood.

Bill covered Chuck in a blanket and lit the flame of a blow-torch for him. Chuck huddled over the flame's warmth and slowly came back to life under Bill's watchful eye.

At twenty-eight, Bill was a little older than most of his counterparts and new to command. Of his commander's many attributes, there was one that Chuck appreciated the most that night: Bill Hey could keep a secret.

The night wore on. In Eagle, Clarence dozed on and off in his sleeping bag.

A faint glow and hissing sound were coming from the bow gunner's compartment. Private Homer "Smokey" Davis was down there. Twenty-year-old Smokey came from Morehead, Kentucky. The thick bags beneath his eyes suggested he'd had a hard life. He was seldom without a cigarette and wore his tanker's hood everywhere.

Clarence leaned in his sleeping bag and saw shadows dancing in the bow. Smokey was using the crew's Coleman stove to keep warm, and the heat was rising to the turret. Clarence felt bad for his friend, down in the coldest reaches of the ice cave. Still. *It'll run out of fuel, eventually,* he thought.

Earley grumbled. He was getting it too. He grabbed the pork chop—the hand microphone, so nicknamed because of its shape—and spoke. "Smokey."

Smokey's voice came back weakly. "It's so cold, I can't stand it anymore." His feet were freezing because he had nowhere to move them, so he had removed his boots and was holding his feet over the stove's flame.

Earley grumbled, "You can afford to lose a few toes."

The stove stopped hissing and once again the tank went dark.

A mechanical rumble jolted all three tank crews awake. Engines puttered noisily, gears shifted, and heavy tracks clanked. Something was out there. It was coming from the forest, and growing louder.

Dim headlights swept the field in front of the tanks.

Clarence freed himself from his sleeping bag and settled an eye to the telescopic sight, trembling.

An armored scout car led a column.

They were Germans, all right, traveling by night to avoid Allied fighter-bombers.

"Track 'em, Clarence," Earley said.

The moonlit shapes kept coming.

Then came a noise that drowned out all others. Squeaking metal tracks clawed the road as a German tank rumbled into the open. It was followed by a second, and then a third. Their Maybach V-12 engines snarled as each roared past. It seemed like the earth was shaking.

"They're gonna hear us!" Smokey whispered over the intercom. The plea went unanswered.

The tanks kept coming.

Earley had eyes on them and told Clarence to be ready to fire on his call.

Clarence's heart pounded. He almost wanted to take a shot now. These German machines just seemed so arrogant. They were most likely the rear guard of the 2nd Panzer Division, racing to catch up with the main force. Some were sharp, possibly Panthers. Some were blocky, maybe Mark IVs—or even the legendary Tiger, a 60-ton behemoth that was so heavy that it couldn't cross most bridges.

But now Clarence could kill any of them. He could avenge Lieutenant Rose.

"How's it looking?" Earley asked Clarence. The commander sounded hesitant.

Clarence felt a lump in his throat. His answer to the question might steer Earley's commands in one direction or another.

The moonlit German tanks were slipping away. Three Shermans could each knock out a tank or two. Maybe the doughs could even get some with their bazookas. But what would happen if even *one* of those German tanks turned to face them? The Shermans had a forest at their backs. There was nowhere to run. *It'd be suicide.*

"Not good, Bob. There's too many."

If it were a smaller column, they could handle it. But attacking now would be like poking a bear.

Earley agreed, but reminded Clarence that if one of the other guys fired they would have no choice but to join in. Without a radio transmitter to communicate with Cajun Boy or Bill Hey, he couldn't tell them to hold their fire.

He hated letting the Germans get away like this. His morals felt different in the dark. Those tanks suddenly weren't machines out there with men in them; they were nothing but steel monsters hunting for something to kill.

"Let 'em pass," Earley muttered beneath his breath.

Outside, the American line of tanks and doughs remained silent. *Choose your battles,* they told themselves. *Their day will come.*

Clarence had never pondered being captured like he did now.

As a youngster, Clarence had never known quite how to pray. It wasn't until a neighbor bought him a suit that he regularly attended church. By then, he simply copied what he saw the other parishioners doing. In lieu of a primer on how to pray or what to pray, Clarence began to do what came naturally: he simply spoke to God.

He sat back from his sight and drew his arms tight against his chest for warmth. Silent, Clarence had never spoken so hard in his life.

The next day, Christmas morning

The tankers huddled behind their vehicles and warmed their hands with the engines' exhaust. It was around eleven a.m. The boom of artillery rippled through the clear sky. Sun glinted from the snow.

In addition to Easy Company, two more companies each of tanks and doughs were spread over the neighboring fields. They had been ordered back to friendly territory, a few miles away from Marche.

American engineers were laying mines nearby. The goal was to rig everything—even the sidewalks—to explode if the Germans came near. And outside the city, artillerymen's shells arced southward to disrupt the enemy. New German units had arrived to take the place of the 2nd Panzer Division, which had resumed its drive toward the Meuse River.

There were no glad tidings or toasts of cheer this Christmas. Clarence had never felt more homeless and forgotten. Back home in Lehighton, he knew, families would be coming home from church. Christmas bulbs would be strung from lampposts and front porches.

As a boy, Clarence had gone downtown and stood in line with the other needy children at the Eagles Club. After a moment inside with Santa, he would leave with a gift. He'd take it to the park, where he'd enjoy his favorite part of Christmas: a box of candy and an orange.

Clarence's upbringing gave him a healthy sense of perspective. No matter how bad things seemed, someone else always had it worse. He thought of Paul's mother, and Lieutenant Rose's young widow, Helen. What kind of Christmas were they having now that their loved ones had been killed?

Around noon, a truck parked behind the tanks. Clarence pried himself from the huddle to see if the truck had brought them more ammo.

The lift gate dropped and Clarence couldn't believe his eyes. The delivery was far better than ammo. The company cooks were crouching behind steaming containers of hot food. It wasn't too late for a Christmas miracle after all.

Clarence and his crew retrieved their mess kits and joined a fast-forming feeding line. At each man's turn, the cooks wished him a merry Christmas. At the front of the tank, Clarence and the crew set their food and cups of coffee on the fenders as they ate. It was a Christmas dinner with all the fixings: drumsticks, stuffing, mashed potatoes, gravy, and even a slice of freshly baked bread.

With every bite, Clarence's mood lifted. Someone still cared about them after all.

Soon, as the men chowed down, the sky began to buzz.

Across the field, Clarence and his comrades craned their necks to see what was making the noise. American bombers were flying westward. The planes seemed to rake the sky with white vapor trails.

The Eighth Air Force was heading home.

Nearly four hundred B-24s had just bombed western Germany. They had targeted railroad marshaling yards and road junctions to amplify the previous night's raids, when more than three hundred Royal Air Force planes had struck German airfields. The raids aimed to prevent the Germans from being able to resupply—and thus strand them in the Ardennes.

The waves of bombers flew overhead for thirty minutes, reverberating through the frozen sky as Clarence and his fellow tankers relished their Christmas dinner.

Clarence smiled for the first time in days. A great military force stood behind them and was finally back to swinging.

Perhaps, he thought, there would be no losing this battle.

CHAPTER 9

SOMETHING BIGGER

Nearly two weeks later, January 7, 1945
GRAND-SART, BELGIUM

Early that January morning, the Easy Company Sherman tanks climbed uphill through a tunnel of dead trees. A blue sky beckoned through a craggy canopy of branches overhead.

Eagle was a mess. Icicles hung from its fenders, and frozen branches stuck like stubble to the hull. The driver was putting all his effort into keeping the 33-ton machine from rolling off the slick track into the nearby ravines.

The men themselves felt roughed up and grimy. "Enough dirt on us that you could plant spuds," wrote Cajun Boy to his girlfriend back home. "Sometimes I wonder how I'll ever scrub it off."

But the end of this battle was in sight.

The 2nd Panzer Division had been stopped within three miles of the Meuse. That meant Marche was safe from the Germans, and that Bastogne had held strong. The British were about to take La Roche, and St. Vith was next in line for liberation. The tide was turning. It was time to reverse the bulge—to redraw the lines on the map of what the Germans controlled.

Light beamed from the crest of a hill. They were almost at their destination.

Once they reached the hilltop, the tanks passed through the lines of A-Company, 36th Armored Infantry Regiment—a unit of doughs assigned to accompany the attack. The doughs stopped the lead tank, Eleanor, so they could give a heads-up to the commander, Bill Hey. The night before, they had been shelled by a Mark IV, they warned him. That tank might still pose a danger to anyone approaching the village.

Bill Hey steered Eleanor toward Grand-Sart before pausing and idling in the snow. Three more Shermans took their places to his side. Today, 2nd Platoon would be spearheading. Anchoring the left flank was Eagle. Clarence sat back from his sights, concerned about the prospect of firing in snowdrifts. The top layers were powder and the 76's sizeable muzzle blast was bound to kick up quite a cloud.

Eagle's driver—a nineteen-year-old Irish American from Michigan, Tech Corporal William "Woody" McVey—didn't share Clarence's burden. Dark-haired, with darting eyes, he launched into his prebattle routine. Feigning seriousness, he asked the crew if they would pray with him. By now, they knew better than to bow their heads.

"Lord, please keep the big bullet away from us." After a solemn pause he concluded—"Amen."

The tank's interior echoed with laughter. It never failed to break the tension.

• • •

Trapped inside the tight confines of Eleanor, Chuck Miller sat brooding with his hood drawn over his ears.

He didn't like this plan one bit. Two thousand yards—more than a mile. That was how far they were being asked to go, without any cover and likely under fire. The Sherman tank's 75mm gun just wouldn't provide them with enough protection. It had been a fine gun when the Sherman first entered production in early 1942. Since then, the Germans had bolstered the armor of their vehicles and the muzzle velocity of their guns. Meanwhile, the 75mm gun's muzzle velocity remained the same—comparatively low.

"This is a bad idea," Chuck said.

Bill grimly agreed but was powerless to change the orders. Some of the crew rolled their eyes at Chuck. They thought he was living up to his nickname.

The crew's driver, a heavyset corporal by the name of Fahrni, had it in for Chuck. Possibly it was because Chuck had said he was the baby of seven kids. Or maybe it came from Chuck's payday ritual. With each check he received, Chuck saved some money for candy before sending the rest to his mother. But for whatever reason, Fahrni had given Chuck a nickname that spread like wildfire throughout the company: "Baby."

The company was in place. Captain Salisbury radioed the order for the attack to begin.

From his hatch in the lead tank, Bill made the signal: a raised hand, lowered forward. Second Platoon began rolling. The four tanks plowed ahead.

A second row of tanks, from another platoon, followed at a distance. The third rank then followed the same procedure as the second. The doughs would follow later on foot.

With the flick of a switch, Chuck turned on his gun's gyro-stabilizer. The device steadied the gun's bounce, making it easier for a gunner to hit their target on the move.

The Allied counteroffensive against the Germans—made up of British and American armies—had begun that week. The 3rd Armored and the First Army were pushing from the north, while the British XXX Corps pushed from the west. Meanwhile, the notorious General George S. Patton's Third Army was pushing from the south. In the battle for this real-world jigsaw puzzle, every piece mattered.

Chuck swept the field with his telescopic sight. A couple of yards ahead and to the left there was a dark mass—a dead German soldier. Chuck could see the black bread spilled from his bread tin. But what was he doing out there?

The tanks were almost halfway across the route when machine-gun fire crackled from the village.

Bill Hey ducked lower in his hatch as bullets whizzed by.

Wehrmacht regiments. Clearly, they had stayed back to defend Grand-Sart—and to prevent the Americans from catching up to their comrades' retreat. In reality, these German forces in the Ardennes were losing faith in the Nazis. And yet many continued fighting, afraid of defying the top commanders.

The armored assault crawled forward, steadily gaining

ground. Behind the American Shermans, the roads to Germany were a chaotic traffic jam.

To Eleanor's left, an explosion erupted from the snow—right beneath another Sherman. The blast left a black cloud blossoming around the tank.

"Mines!" Bill shouted into the radio.

Up front, Fahrni hauled back on the steering-brake levers. But by that point it was too late.

A massive explosion erupted beneath the left track, lifting the tank's nose a few inches off the ground before slamming it back down. The tank swayed. Dark smoke filtered into the turret.

Chuck gripped a bloody nose, which he'd smashed against the periscope. But he wasn't about to give the men the satisfaction of admitting to an injury. He reported that he was fine.

He was no "Baby."

In the aftermath of the blast, the company paused to take stock of the situation.

They'd driven directly into a minefield, hidden beneath snowdrifts. Everyone was thinking the same question: *Do we turn back?*

Clarence turned his turret. He had friends in every tank and was worried about the other guys. Three tanks away, a halo of smoke and snow settled around Eleanor. Clarence thought of his friend Chuck and hoped he was unharmed.

•   •   •

The crews never expected to see what transpired next.

Bill Hey jumped down into the minefield.

He worked his way to the front of Eleanor, dropping to his hands and knees to inspect the damage. Somehow, the tracks were still intact. The hull floor escape hatch wasn't damaged either.

Bill climbed back up to the turret. He was facing a difficult choice. No one would blame him if he turned back. But he wasn't about to give up now. From his hatch, he raised his hand and signaled "Forward."

Eleanor's tracks started turning again. The trailing tanks followed in one long line, trying to avoid the hidden mines. Minutes felt like hours; another blast could come at any moment.

Bill stood tall in his turret, determined to spot the next threat. Grand-Sart was just a small piece of the puzzle in the Bulge, but it was *their* piece. And they weren't going to let their fellow fighting men down.

Bill raised a clenched fist, signaling for all three platoons of tanks to stop. Through his binoculars, he saw something. "Chuck, we've got an enemy tank," he said calmly.

Chuck felt a tap on his left shoulder and turned the turret in that direction.

"Steady, steady," Bill said.

When the gun was aimed where Bill wanted, he stopped Chuck. "On!"

Chuck spotted the enemy. A long whitewashed gun barrel jutted from behind a woodpile. It wasn't aiming at them. But it was aiming at someone. Probably one of Chuck's friends in another Sherman. No one else was firing, and without a two-way radio, there was no way to warn them.

Chuck followed the gun barrel back and set the reticle where he estimated the turret should be. He stomped his foot on the trigger.

The gun thundered and the shell struck. But he saw nothing. Did the shot deflect? Did it even hit? The German tank seemed to be unscathed.

"He's coming out!" Bill said.

The German tank pulled forward. It stopped with a lurch as it swung its gun toward Eleanor.

Chuck moved to adjust his aim, but it was too late. The enemy's long barrel had disappeared. It was now aiming straight *at* him.

The muzzle flashed.

Chuck watched a green tracer flying toward him, seemingly in slow motion. The shell slammed the turret, the tank hiccupped, and a red flash filled Chuck's field of vision, sending him reeling backward.

Bill did not duck in time. The ricocheting shell cut through his tanker helmet. He fell dead onto Chuck's shoulder, showering the gunner in blood. Chuck screamed and flailed. His commander fell to the turret floor. Bill Hey's tenure as a Sherman commander had lasted just eight days in combat.

The tank heaved to a stop. The intercom came alive with panicked voices from the bow.

"Get out!" Chuck shouted over the intercom. "Abandon

tank!" The enemy was known to pump shells into a tank until it burned.

Chuck stepped around his fallen commander and pushed himself out from the turret.

Get out!

But he had forgotten that he had left the turret askew. Now its rear was dangling over the snow. With nothing to catch him, Chuck fell almost nine feet, face-first into the snow.

He sat up, stunned. Snow matted his bloody nose and tanker jacket. Bullets pinged against the tank. The Germans in Grand-Sart were targeting him. He crawled behind Eleanor for cover, but his relief lasted only a moment.

Eleanor mysteriously sprang to life.

The exhaust pipes growled and spewed hot exhaust in Chuck's face. He heard the gearshift. Tracks began clanking backward.

Chuck rolled to the right, narrowly missing being crushed.

But who was operating Eleanor? The tank stopped and a hatch opened. Fahrni slid over the side, fuming mad.

When he saw Fahrni, Chuck immediately realized his mistake. Since he'd left the turret pointing leftward, the gun had blocked the driver's hatch, trapping Fahrni alone inside the vehicle. Fahrni had narrowly escaped alive—and he was outraged.

The crew took cover in a frozen creek bed. Chuck tried to ignore Fahrni's rageful cursing. Quietly, he peered over the bank just in time to catch a glimpse of the German tank retreating. Using the village as a shield, it slipped away into the nearest forest.

Sometime after the attack

A snowstorm howled through the darkness. Light fell through the windows of a rugged Belgian farmhouse, illuminating snow flurries that were flying sideways.

Private Malcolm "Buck" Marsh stepped out the back door and into the swirling snow. He tugged his helmet low and his scarf higher, framing his dark eyes and pointed chin. An affable twenty-one-year-old Southerner, he felt for the boys out there in the tanks. At least he and the other doughs had a place to warm themselves between duties.

Private First Class Bob Janicki, a taller, burlier dough, joined Buck. His collar was turned up, obscuring a face of close-set eyes and a heavy jaw. Janicki was Buck's foxhole buddy. Combat had aged him. He seemed older than his twenty-three years.

It was almost midnight: time for the two men to relieve the ten p.m. shift that was manning the squad's .30-caliber machine gun. With his M1 rifle at the ready, Buck led the way toward the dark forest. Buck was too new to the job to be fearful. He was one of nineteen replacements rushed into the Ardennes to join A-Company.

Although the village of Grand-Sart had been secured, the woods around it remained dangerous. There the enemy wandered, searching for Belgian civilians they could beg for shelter.

From beneath his helmet, Buck saw the outlines of two men shuffling toward him. Apparently the ten p.m. shift couldn't wait to get indoors. Huddled in their long coats, the men passed Buck and Janicki without a glance. It was too cold for them to stop and chat, it seemed.

When Buck and Janicki arrived at the tree line, two doughs were clustered close together at the machine gun. What was going on? Buck was puzzled. Did he get the shift schedule wrong? It was only then that he realized who the men they'd just passed were.

Buck alerted the others in dismay. Those two men weren't doughs—they were *Germans*. And they were headed toward the farmhouse where the rest of the squad was settled in for the night. The two Germans were outnumbered . . . but who knew what could happen?

Janicki unslung his rifle. "Come on," he said, gesturing that they should go back to the house to warn the other men.

Buck started to follow him. "Not so fast!" the other doughs cried out. It was *their* turn to go home. Their shift in the cold forest had just ended. And these doughs were more eager to head home and face the enemy than to face another minute freezing outside.

Buck and Janicki sighed, took their places at the gun, and hunkered down for their shift in front of the spooky black woods. They'd have to wait to find out what happened until after their shift anyway.

Hunched over the gun, Buck couldn't stop replaying their encounter with the Germans earlier in the evening. What if they were German commandos? He had heard that some English-speaking Germans—dressed in American uniforms—had infiltrated the U.S. army lines before. The only way to identify these saboteurs, aside from questioning them about American sports and pop culture, supposedly was to check their trousers for German-branded underwear.

Janicki didn't seem worried as they kept watch. His eyes were often glazed over, and the only time they seemed to spark to life was in a firefight. Back in Illinois, he had been a motorcycle mechanic. Now all he wanted was to get home to his wife, Ruth.

Buck had grown up well-to-do in a large Southern home in Alabama. Chatty and approachable, he had been voted the "Boy with the Best Personality" by his high school classmates. As foxhole buddies went, the duo were an odd couple.

When their shift finally ended, two doughs came to replace them. They told Buck and Janicki that two German deserters had knocked on the door of the home the crew was staying in, looking for a place to surrender. The dough who opened the door took them prisoner.

Buck felt an immense wave of relief. So everyone was safe—for now.

When Buck and Janicki got back to the house, coffee was simmering on the wood stove in the candlelit kitchen. Buck did a double take. There sat the two Germans in long coats and caps. Their helmets sat beside them. When soldiers tossed away their helmets, it was a sign that they were done fighting.

A dough kept an eye on the Germans from his seat at the kitchen table, making sure they didn't escape or start a fight. The rest of the squad was sleeping near a crackling fireplace in the next room.

The Germans were pale, gaunt, and scratching themselves. They had probably been stricken with lice. One was older and larger, with a black beard, while the other was slight, fair-haired, and in obvious pain. He was in bad shape. When they'd removed one of his boots, part of his frostbitten foot had come off with it.

Janicki, unimpressed by the spectacle of the German prisoners, went to sleep by the fire. Buck, meanwhile, sat with the guard at the kitchen table and laid his rifle against the wall. Between sips of coffee, he wrote his nightly diary entry. He was meticulous about it. The habit was a carryover from days as an engineering student at Tennessee Tech. Since the guard was getting drowsy and Buck was too wound up to sleep, he volunteered to watch the prisoners. The gesture wasn't unusual for Buck. Quietly, he aspired to be a veteran, and often sought to exceed others' expectations of him by going above and beyond.

The only people awake now were Buck and the larger of the two Germans.

Buck eyed the soldiers. The one with the bandaged foot dozed with his face against the stone wall. Now and then, he whimpered in pain. The larger one with the black beard had tired eyes. He looked leery of the young American. He also looked fearful for what his future would hold. That was because the Nazis' orders had made it perfectly clear: any unwounded soldier who allowed himself to be captured "loses his honor and his dependents get no support." Heinrich Himmler, Reich Leader of the SS, demanded deserters be punished horrifically: "If there is any suspicion that a soldier has absented himself from his unit with a view to deserting and thus impairing the fighting strength of this unit one member of the soldier's family (wife) will be shot."

As the night wore on, Buck fished through his K ration. At

The Pershing approaches the Cologne cathedral after its clash at the four-way intersection.

With the cathedral in sight, a second Sherman moves alongside Kellner's tank, which is obscured from this angle.

Kellner rolls from the turret after his Sherman absorbs a second hit. The urge to escape was so desperate that his gunner would dive headfirst off the turret.

The Pershing advances through "Cologne's Wall Street," bound for its duel with the Panther.

This motion-picture frame captures the moment the Pershing fired at Bartelborth's Panther. The train station is visible beyond the Pershing, at the end of the street.

This sequence
from the camera
of Jim Bates shows
Bartelborth and
crew members
emerging before the
Panther erupts in
flames.

Bartelborth's Panther burns in this photo taken from Bates's vantage in the German Labor Front building.

A bulldozer clears the street that cost the lives of Karl Kellner and two of his crew. Their knocked-out Sherman can be seen on the far right.

The Hohenzollern Bridge—part roadway, part railway—having collapsed into the Rhine, as seen from the cathedral.

After reaching the Rhine, the Pershing stands guard in the plaza alongside the cathedral.

McVey poses with the Pershing's .50-caliber machine gun during some downtime in the war's waning days.

Clarence (far left) relaxes with his fellow tankers at the war's end.

the sight of food, the bearded German perked up in his chair. Buck set a can of processed cheese aside—he hated the stuff—and searched for something else: canned pork, or biscuits, or caramels, anything would be better than the cheese. After he finished eating, the canned cheese still sat on the table.

With eyebrows raised, the bearded German motioned to the can.

Buck pondered the suggestion. Was he allowed to feed the prisoners? Did he even want to? They were the enemy, after all.

"Sure." Buck tossed him the canned cheese.

The German caught it, smiled, and muttered his thanks.

Buck ate and was tidying up his meal when a noise stopped him in midmotion.

It was the unmistakable sound of a knife sliding from a sheath. Buck's heart raced.

The German held an eight-inch knife that he had slid from his boot.

Buck eyed his M1 rifle where it stood against the wall. It was only an arm's length away.

Before he could lunge for it, the German plunged the knife blade into the can and began sawing around the lid.

Buck resumed breathing.

The German sliced the cheese in half before waking his younger companion to pass him the food and the knife. The two soldiers ate quickly. They were clearly starving.

With their supply lines cut for weeks, the only source of food these German soldiers had to rely on was rummaging through Belgian homes.

The bearded German wiped the blade on his trousers and handed it, hilt first, to Buck.

"Thank you," Buck said.

The German nodded and sat back.

Buck marveled at the instrument, a Hitler Youth knife. It featured a wide blade and a red-and-white inlay with a swastika in the center. Weighing it in his palm, Buck felt a shiver.

Another German might have shoved the blade directly into his gut. If he was to survive in the Spearhead Division, Buck knew he had a long way to go.

The "Boy with the Best Personality" award counted for nothing here.

CHAPTER 10

AMERICA'S TIGER

A month later, February 8, 1945
STOLBERG, GERMANY

Tankers and doughs were headed back to Stolberg on their way back from the Ardennes Forest. The men were in a hurry to reunite with their German girlfriends and adopted families.

Stolberg was "home" once again. For now, at least.

As soon as he could make it over, Clarence huffed up the hill toward Resi's house. He couldn't wait to see her, to talk about their future together.

When Resi opened the door, she couldn't believe she was looking at Clarence in the flesh.

"You're back!" She started kissing and hugging him in full view of the street.

Once indoors, Resi became emotional as she told Clarence the news she had heard on the radio. "Hitler said he destroyed the 3rd Armored Division."

The absurdity of the propaganda gave Clarence a laugh.

Resi was so talkative that Clarence couldn't get a word in edgewise. He had a speech prepared, but he couldn't find the opening to launch into what he wanted to say.

Resi's mother—a dark-haired, neatly dressed woman—was clearly delighted that Clarence had returned. Unlike Resi's easygoing father, a merchant in town, she intimidated Clarence.

She had to talk with him—privately. Once they reached the kitchen, Resi's mother lowered her voice to a conspiratorial whisper. "Deutschland is kaput," she said. "There is nothing good for Resi here."

Clarence sympathized. The sentiment was widespread. But Clarence sensed something more was coming.

"You marry Resi now," her mother said. "Take her to America later."

"We aren't even supposed to be talking," Clarence said. "I can't marry her—they'll throw me in jail."

The mother's face soured. She left to let them figure it out for themselves.

The young couple sat alone together. Conversation wasn't as easy as it had been moments before. Clarence looked at Resi. She was youthful, whereas he felt old and tired. She was cheerful, while he felt hopeless. And above all, she was loyal—she had waited for him even after he'd left without saying goodbye.

Resi moved to kiss Clarence. But to her surprise, he pulled back.

Clarence finally came around to what he had been waiting to say. There was a reason why they shouldn't be together: the next battle. He didn't know where the war would take him, or whether he had any chance of survival.

"I might not be coming back," he said.

Tears streamed down Resi's face. As he gripped her hands, Clarence also became emotional.

He had come back from the Ardennes resigned to his fate. But as he held Resi, he admitted his greatest fear aloud. "I may die."

Resi threw her arms around him and sobbed. Clarence held her. He was convinced that he was doing the right thing for both of them. The war had robbed Resi of more than enough already. They had no choice but to say goodbye.

Two weeks later, February 22, 1945

The Rhineland—the area of western Germany around the Rhine River—was soaked. Its pale green fields were marshy and flooded, and dead trees stood like islands above the tide. This was partly because of all the melted snow. Most of the blame, though, rested on the German military. They had opened dams in the north—intentionally flooding the area to delay any Allied advance. Until the Rhineland dried out, Spearhead wasn't going anywhere. The tanks just couldn't navigate the swampy terrain. For American armored units, the reprieve was a blessing.

Their experience in the Ardennes lingered. The Allies' victory in the Battle of the Bulge had been through sheer sacrifice and will. Tank crews had been sent on suicide missions down icy roads. Yet still the men saddled up and went forward, many to their deaths.

The 3rd Armored had lost more tanks than it had destroyed—163 losses against 108 German tanks. And the U.S. Army had to borrow 350 Shermans from the British just to replenish their losses. Clarence and the men of Spearhead were becoming frustrated with the army's tanks and tools. They just weren't sufficient to keep the men safe.

Now, they had a chance to regroup and figure out next steps. And, perhaps most importantly, to address the problems with their tanks. Something had to change for the Shermans to survive the next push.

And, in the valleys of Stolberg, the First Army's Spearhead division had a potential solution.

Clarence; Bob Earley, who had just been promoted to platoon sergeant; and the crew gathered around a tank that was sitting on the firing line. A murmur arose. This tank was no Sherman.

Its frontal armor flowed into a sleek body with widely spaced tracks. The turret was set so far forward it seemed as if the tank were looking for trouble. The gun was almost as long as the tank itself. This tank was known as a Pershing—the Super Tank, "America's answer to the Tiger," the fearsome German tank.

The Pershing had yet to be unveiled to the American public. It was a secret weapon. The first forty tanks had just rolled off the assembly line. Half of the tanks had been sent to Fort Knox for testing. The other twenty went to Europe to the ultimate trial: live combat.

And now, one of the Pershings was all theirs. The Pershing wasn't just a small step forward. It advanced tank technology by leaps and bounds. It was equipped with a monstrous 90mm cannon, not to mention an automatic transmission that could move the tank in reverse at high speed. With twice the effective armor of a 76 and twenty thousand pounds more heft, the Pershing weighed in at 46 tons—just three tons short of a Panther.

The fact that their crew had been given one of these extraordinary new Pershing tanks befuddled Clarence. *Why us?* he asked his officer.

"Everyone figured that Earley's crew was the best one to get the tank," the officer replied.

But what made them the best? Earley had his own theory: "We just never got knocked out."

Clarence and the crew climbed aboard. The Pershing had the designation *E7* painted on its front fender. The crew accordingly christened their new tank "Eagle 7."

Standing atop the engine deck, Clarence felt a wave of anxiety. All eyes were on him—rookies and experienced tankers alike. His first time firing the 90mm would serve as a demonstration for the entire 32nd Regiment. Was the Pershing a machine that could go muzzle to muzzle with anything the Germans put on the battlefield?

The paint inside the Pershing was fresh white. Clarence took his seat by the 90mm gun. It had been touted by the army as "the most potent weapon we've ever mounted in a tank." A powerful 6x telescopic sight had been set within the periscope mount.

Clarence flipped through the notepad he'd brought with him. In it, he'd written down the targets he would shoot at to test the new vehicle's gun. The notepad shook in his hand. Once again, he felt like he was flying by the seat of his pants. He had never been trained as a gunner in the first place. If anything, he had tripped into the role by accident.

It had all started in fall 1943, when the battalion was in England for long-range gunnery training. This involved blasting table-sized targets on sand dunes. After the gunners fired, each loader was given a turn too, so that he could operate the weapon just in case.

Clarence should have missed. The target was set a thousand yards away, and yet he hit it all eight times without breaking a sweat. What was his secret? Everyone wanted to know. That night, as the crew celebrated, Paul Faircloth had confided in Clarence: the first chance he got, he would make Clarence their gunner.

Behind the Pershing, Earley and the rest of the crowd parted for a group of officers.

As the commander of the 3rd Armored Division, Major General Maurice Rose wore two small silver stars on his helmet. He was a strikingly tall forty-five-year-old with black eyebrows that arched over stern eyes. The son of a Polish rabbi who had immigrated to Denver, Rose had been climbing the ranks since he was just seventeen. He'd already commanded tank units in Africa with the 1st Armored Division, and in Sicily with the 2nd Armored Division, "Hell on Wheels."

"He goes himself wherever he sends his men," wrote the *Chicago Tribune*. Rose's men loved him for it and would follow him almost anywhere.

He was the leader of the division he named Spearhead—a group of men and machines that he called "the greatest tank force in the world." Now came Germany, where General Rose and his entourage took their places to see what the Pershing was made of.

No one had seen the Pershing fire—not even the Supreme

Allied Commander, General Dwight Eisenhower, who had rushed the tanks to the front lines. Rose watched intently, eager to assess the capabilities of the gun and gunner. The Pershing was essential to the success of his plans for the 3rd Armored Division. Thirty miles away lay Cologne, the "Queen City" of Germany. With a massive twin-spired Gothic cathedral, the city was a symbolic guardian of German territory. That was where Rose would eventually take Spearhead. If the division could conquer Cologne and leap the Rhine, they could charge deep into the heart of Germany and bring the enemy to its knees.

Usually, Clarence was glad to see Rose. This time, his presence made Clarence want to groan. Clarence had only dry-fired the 90mm of the new Pershing tank. He had no "feel" for the weapon and now the general was watching? The pressure was on.

Earley gave the command. It was time for the show to begin.

A loader hefted a 3-foot-long armor-piercing shell into the breech. The 102-pound breech block slammed shut with a clang. The technicians plugged their ears.

Clarence set an eye to his 6x zoom sight and twisted the pistol grip. A 15.5-foot barrel swept the air as the turret began turning. At the tip was a football-shaped muzzle brake with holes to funnel the blast out.

The roofs of a small neighborhood floated across Clarence's sight. He stopped turning when a damaged, abandoned farmhouse filled the reticle.

Earley gave a range estimation: "One, two hundred"—tanker-speak for 1,200 yards, about two-thirds of a mile. "The chimney."

Clarence wanted to throw up his hands in defeat. They

wanted him to shoot a narrow brick chimney? This was a tank gun, not a sniper rifle.

"Fire when ready," Earley said.

Gone was the foot trigger button from the Sherman. Clarence's index finger tensed on a red trigger on the pistol grip instead. Don't miss, he told himself. The secret to his marksmanship was simple: fear of letting down his crew.

He took a deep breath and squeezed.

A blinding flash and an earsplitting crack filled his senses. Outside the tank, General Rose and his entourage were blown clear off their feet. The tracer zipped forward and the 24-pound shell flew straight into the chimney. A shower of red bricks somersaulted through the air.

The gun's sound was like an ice pick to the eardrums. When his hearing returned, Clarence heard grumbling behind him. When he turned, he found Earley nursing his face.

No one had warned the crew that the gun breech belched a flaming orb of gases up through the commander's hatch as it exited the tank. The fireball had whisked Earley's face and singed his eyebrows.

As Rose and his entourage picked themselves up from the soggy ground, the hardened crews fought to stay straight-faced.

"Target two." Earley was back to business.

Clarence swung the gun for his next test shot. The target this time was another farmhouse, about a mile from the tank. This house had two chimneys. "I'll try for the near one," Clarence said. A white stone chimney, it was the easier of the two to hit.

Clarence's finger hovered in front of the trigger. Between the savage crash of the gun and the change in air pressure that followed in the blast's wake, firing the 90mm actually scared him.

He fired again.

With another ear-piercing crack, a shell launched forward and the breech leaped back. And just like that, the target was down a chimney. A cloud of white dust hung where the bricks had been.

Cheers streamed into the turret from outside.

I like this gun! Clarence thought.

A small brick chimney stood on the back of the house. Just the top of it was showing. This would be his third target. The chimney looked as narrow as a pencil point.

Clarence winced. At about a mile's distance, it would be like trying to shoot a helmet off a soldier's head. Clarence admitted that he'd rather quit while they were ahead. It would be better than disappointing everyone.

"Oh, come on," Earley said. "Try it."

Clarence reluctantly laid an eye to his sight, calculated his aim, and squeezed the trigger. Another ear-piercing crack sent the shell downrange. The chimney burst into red dust. Clarence eyed the target in disbelief. He had not only hit it, he'd evaporated it.

Clarence followed Earley outside to thunderous applause. A grin lined his face as he gave a bashful wave.

General Rose and his entourage were muddy but proud and clapping with the rest of the troops. Rose would soon write to General Dwight Eisenhower: "There is no question in my mind . . . our gunnery is far superior to that of the Germans."

On the ground, the crews mobbed Clarence, Earley, and the others like schoolboys. There was more backslapping and bravado than there'd been in a long time. These men had resigned themselves to eventual death. Now, they had hope.

"The army needs to rush a whole bunch of these over here," Clarence said.

"Look out, Hitler, here we come!" cried another crew member.

The enthusiasm was infectious. In the distant haze, Clarence could envision the spires of Cologne and, more important, somewhere beyond the spires, the end of the war.

Stolberg was the closest he'd been to home during his time in Europe. Now, for the first time since he'd arrived, he was restless to leave.

CHAPTER 11

TWO MILES

Four days later, February 26, 1945
GOLZHEIM, GERMANY

It was a cold morning, around eight-thirty. Fog drifted across the surrounding spongy fields. Rain spiraled from the tanks' barrels.

Spearhead had set out from Stolberg in the early morning hours. They were heading east, spreading task forces across the Cologne Plain.

For Clarence's "Task Force X"—the name of this next big operation—it had been smooth sailing: sixteen miles without a shot so far. To the left of the column, the infantrymen, in wet helmets and muddy spats, as the canvas covers for their boots were known, were moving between the puddles of Golzheim, preparing to move on, having secured the village the night before.

Taking the highway was a no-go, Earley told them. Engineers had concluded that it was likely mined. As a result, the tanks would have to go cross-country, through bleak, barren fields. Easy Company funneled from the road and the tanks fell in line.

Clarence brought himself close to his periscope. The lens was streaked with water. Two miles east was the town of Blatzheim. Cologne itself was now just twelve miles away. It had been confirmed that enemy trenches were all over.

Today's would be a full task force attack. Easy Company and its two sister tank outfits were combining forces. A few Stuart tanks of B-Company would go first, scouting for a spot to cross the trenches. Then the Shermans of F-Company would cover the left flank while Easy Company went straight up the middle to the doorsteps of Blatzheim.

Clarence was optimistic. This time, at least, Easy Company wasn't leading the charge.

Idling in Easy Company's lineup was a 76 Sherman with the name "Everlasting" written on its flanks. Inside, Chuck Miller sat in the gunner's seat. Gazing through the periscope, Chuck felt himself on the verge of traumatic flashbacks. The empty field. The spongy terrain. It was Grand-Sart all over again, where Bill Hey had met his brutal end.

Chuck had transferred to this crew after hearing that the commander needed a gunner. After Grand-Sart had fallen, any tank was better than Eleanor. Plus, Fahrni had been promoted to commander. Chuck couldn't escape being bullied by him fast enough.

The division had buried Bill in his uniform and a mattress cover. After the makeshift funeral, the army sent his belongings and his prayer book, to his mother, Lauretta.

Chuck was trying to move on, to put that pain out of his mind. And now, here he was in a new crew. The three Stuarts raced toward Blatzheim in a wedge formation. They were off.

The Stuart was a far cry from the engineering marvel of the new Pershing. It had only a 37mm gun and weak, thin frontal armor. As if that weren't bad enough, its belly was so thin that if the tank hit a mine, the blast could punch through the floor— right into the legs of the crew. In no way was it enough to keep the men safe in a battle.

As they crossed the field, the Stuarts came to a screeching stop. The gun of the lead tank was turned toward some distant haystacks. The tank's commander blasted a hole through a haystack. As he prepared to shoot another, a German shell startled him back to his senses. A green shaft of tracer punched through the Stuart and flew out the other side. Black rings of smoke rose from the tank as wounded men rolled out frantically. The remaining Stuarts spun on a dime and came racing back.

The shot looked like it had come from a farm complex about a mile north.

Chuck couldn't help but feel like it was some kind of grim warning.

After the inauspicious beginning for the Stuart tanks, it was Easy Company's turn. The tanks rolled into the soggy field in their usual three rows.

At the periscope, Clarence breathed easy. Salisbury had put the Pershing in the middle rank for safekeeping. No one wanted to see the brand-new tank suffer in its first battle. The Pershing was surrounded. Everywhere Clarence looked were the whirling tracks of other tanks.

The Pershing was worth protecting. Thanks to the longer turret, it was roomier than a Sherman. And even though its gun was big, there was still more space to slip over to the loader's side or to escape down to the bow gunner's position. A well-placed step for entry and exit into the turret didn't hurt either.

The formation split to avoid the burning Stuart, its steel skin sizzling in the rain. Earley shielded his face against the heat as they passed.

This time, the crews were ready. The lead Shermans swung their guns toward the farm complex that the earlier shot had come from. As added insurance, the A-Company doughs—including Buck—were also with them, advancing on foot, alongside the highway.

Another green lance streaked toward the American tanks, narrowly missing.

Clarence felt a twinge of trepidation. This was no warning shot. Another green lance sliced through the air, followed by another.

The lead row of tanks returned fire. Their shells destroyed the farm complex—and whoever had attacked them from it.

More green bolts came flying from Blatzheim. At first, the bolts looked like they were moving in slow motion. Then, they seemed to accelerate as they rocketed through the formation. Clarence flinched in his seat while Earley ducked. The first volley narrowly missed everyone, letting out alarming sounds.

These weren't just any shells. The Germans were firing their tank-killer gun, the 88. A fearsome gun with an 88mm mouth, the 88 could throw a 20-pound shell for six and a half miles into the sky. But when used to target tanks, it was even deadlier.

Easy Company found itself caught in a net of fire from at least six guns. The radio crackled with curses.

With friendly tanks surrounding the Pershing, Clarence was powerless. All he could do was watch. A green bolt struck a 76 Sherman ahead of him with a flash of sparks. Hatches were flung open and the crew nearly tripped over one another to escape. It was every man for himself.

When topped off, a Sherman held around eighty shells and 170 gallons of gasoline. It was a lot of artillery. It was also very flammable—a recipe for disaster if the tank was struck by enemy fire.

To top it all, the airwaves were just as clogged as their route on the road. One crew reported a jammed cannon. Another came running after a mechanical failure. It was chaos.

With the clang of metal on metal, another of the lead Shermans took a heavy hit and exploded. The commander was thrown headlong into the air. Another crewman stumbled from around the front, his shirt flapping wildly where his arm had once been.

Now reduced to two fully operational Shermans in the lead rank, Salisbury called for a retreat. Earley ordered the platoon to lay down a smokescreen to cover their fellow tankers. Each Sherman had an M3 smoke mortar launcher—a British invention, like a flare gun, that the loader fired from a hole in the turret. The platoon set them off. A cascade of smoke shells arced over the tanks and sizzled, spewing a massive white wall of smoke.

Green bolts corkscrewed through the haze as the twelve American tanks carved U-turns in the slush.

It was the Ardennes all over again.

If they were supposed to retreat, no one told the doughs.

Buck Marsh paced through the shroud of smoke with his rifle at his hip. Buck was cold and wet; his teeth chattered uncontrollably. The Germans had stopped firing, but he imagined German soldiers charging at him through the mist. Buck was the first scout. That meant he'd been chosen to strike out alone, ahead of the company. He was supposed to stay a hundred feet ahead of the main body so that he could watch for irregular terrain or motion from the enemy. He had been flattered by the assignment, until Janicki straightened him out: The first scout was usually the first one to step on a mine, or become separated in a firefight. Or get outright shot.

Buck wiped his eyes from the stinging smoke. Where were they? Were they close to the German trenches? He was disoriented.

"Buck! Keep going!"

Over his shoulder, Buck saw the reassuring outline of a six-foot-two officer standing taller than his fellow doughs. Buck's platoon leader, Second Lieutenant William Boom, was waving him forward, urging him on as a teammate would. Boom was more of a coach than a platoon leader. One by one, other doughs appeared.

Always eager to please, Buck picked up the pace. The smoke thinned. The highway was to their right. Blatzheim still lay a mile ahead, and they were only halfway there. With every step, the mist slipped behind Buck. He felt naked now that he was no longer shrouded in smoke. Surely, the Germans were watching from behind their Flak 41 guns. His palms were sweating beneath his gloves.

It was a good time to pray. In the Ardennes, with mortar shells bursting all around, Buck had prayed aloud to God. After the bombardment, Janicki had turned to him and said, "Why do you think God will help you? So you can climb out of this hole and go kill Germans?"

There was no good answer to that question then, and since he still didn't have an adequate answer now, he kept his prayers to himself.

Easy Company idled back at the starting line.

The eleven remaining machines were itching to roll.

Inside a 75 Sherman, Sergeant Frank "Cajun Boy" Audiffred had traded his commander's position for the gunner's seat for now. The tough but good-natured tanker had the looks of bayou country, with thick black hair, a sharp nose, and deep-set dark eyes. Audiffred peered through his telescopic sight. What he saw outside wasn't pretty.

The doughs were blindly forging ahead. Meanwhile,

stranded tank crews were hiding out in shell holes. One tanker was even hopping back on one foot—where the other foot had been was now a stump. A mile to the left, F-Company's Shermans were assaulting the farm complex. Until that flank was clear, Easy Company was stuck here.

Audiffred sat back and fidgeted. He wasn't one for watching from the sidelines. He wasn't one for riding in the gunner's seat either, but it was only temporary.

A new lieutenant who had just transferred over after being wounded in the Ardennes was serving as gunner for the day, to get some more experience. Lieutenant Robert Bower now sat in the commander's seat behind Audiffred, still shaking from the earlier attack. Tall, with blue eyes, brown hair, and a pale complexion, he looked younger than his twenty-six years. Bower had a boyish eagerness to learn. He was also quick to acknowledge that it was Audiffred's tank—he was just borrowing it for the day. Audiffred liked him instantly.

The radio crackled. Audiffred listened in as Salisbury briefed Bower. The farm complex was clear. Their attack could resume. This time, they would lead, which meant that Lieutenant Bower would be in command.

Salisbury's order ended on an ominous note: "There will be no turning back."

Bower's eyes met Audiffred's. "He's serious?"

Audiffred nodded. It was their job to saddle up and go forward, even if it meant their deaths.

It was time to move out. The tank began rolling.

"Just keep your head down when the shooting starts, Lieutenant," Audiffred said in his slow-rolling Southern-French drawl. "You'll be just fine."

Bower appreciated the tip.

He has no idea what he's in for, Audiffred thought.

The stranded crews cheered as the 2nd Platoon tanks roared past. Six more Shermans followed close on their heels.

Nothing stood between the lead tanks and the doughs.

Audiffred's 75 Sherman anchored the left flank, while the Pershing was assigned the right, nearest the highway. In the middle was Everlasting, the 76 Sherman whose gunner's seat was occupied by Chuck Miller. Try as he might, Chuck hadn't completely escaped Eleanor. The battered old tank was holding formation in a slot to the left.

Behind Chuck in the commander's position stood his friend Sergeant Raymond "Juke" Juilfs. Juke hailed from a small speck of a town in Iowa. Twenty-two, with blond hair and flat dark eyebrows, he looked like he belonged on a baseball diamond, not captaining a tank.

But here they were.

In Blatzheim, 88s began blinking. The terrible sound of metal on metal cut the air. Someone had been hit.

"It's Eleanor!" Juke reported from above.

"How bad?" Chuck asked.

A bow strike had stopped Eleanor in her tracks. Fahrni was rolling from the turret while other survivors were pulling the driver out by his arms.

The platoon kept going, now down to four tanks strong.

A glimpse of a green bolt zipped toward Everlasting. Chuck leaned sideways in his seat, as if he meant to dodge it. The shell thudded to the ground before skipping off to hit someone else.

That could have been me.

Meanwhile, another Sherman had fallen out of the formation. The platoon had no choice but to keep going. They were now down to just three tanks. With fewer targets, the enemy narrowed their aim to the middle tank. A shell landed right in front of Everlasting. It left a smoking hole in the ground.

"Brace!" Juke shouted.

Chuck gripped the bulkhead as the Sherman dove nose-first into the crater with a crunch. Track links went flying. The engine whined before mercifully quitting.

Chuck's head was swimming beneath his helmet after slamming into the periscope. He tried to move but realized he was pinned down by an avalanche of fallen equipment. This was not the time to be unable to think straight.

"Abandon tank!" Juke called.

Tankers the world over knew the Sherman's reputation for going up in flames. The crew fled. To prevent a spark, Chuck shut off the gun's electrical switches. He dug free from the ammunition belts, shell casings, maps, and other debris. Then he climbed for daylight, emerging into a world of noise.

Chuck slid into the crater and scrambled to join the crew, who had taken shelter behind a pile of potatoes. He hit the dirt next to Juke. Juke and the others were banged up, with black eyes and bloody noses. They couldn't stay here, but could they survive a run to Golzheim?

As Chuck turned forward, a flash burst in front of the potatoes—a crack like thunder come to earth. The shock wave sucked all the oxygen from his lungs. Ringing filled his ears as he came up panting and disoriented. Dust hung in the air. The driver, Corporal Joe Caserta, was writhing in pain as he clutched his shoulder.

Chuck turned to Juke. "We need to get out of here!"

But Juke didn't stir. Chuck shook his friend and Juke's head rolled toward him, limp. Juke was dead, never to return to his young wife, Darlene, or Jimmy Ray, the baby son he had yet to meet. Chuck couldn't believe it. His dearest friend here was gone. The crew around him were wounded and stunned, and the shells continued popping. At a time like this, another person might fall to pieces.

But not Chuck Miller. "Let's go," he hollered as he lifted Corporal Caserta, wounded but alive, to his feet. Offering a steady shoulder, Chuck steered his injured friend toward Golzheim, leading the way for the others.

The platoon kept going, though their numbers had been whittled to just two tanks.

Audiffred's Sherman charged side by side with the Pershing. Audiffred glanced over his shoulder to see Bower, who was staying low in the turret.

That was when a shell struck the turret with the clang of a

bell. A blast of molten steel swallowed the loader—and Lieutenant Bower. Audiffred was thrown into the sidewall, knocked unconscious.

Seconds later, maybe minutes, Audiffred came to and opened his eyes. Dark, acrid smoke filled the turret. Crashing waves filled Audiffred's ears; both eardrums were ruptured. He was so numb he couldn't tell whether the tank was still moving.

We got hit.

The left side of his body was naked. The sleeve of his tanker jacket and a pant leg had been incinerated. Blood seeped from his body. His jaw tingled and his head itched. The steel gun breech had shielded his eyes, but that was the only part of him that had emerged unscathed.

The lieutenant.

Audiffred turned and his heart sank when he saw Bower motionless and crushed beyond recognition.

Outside the tank, Audiffred sank to his knees in the soil. He was alone and enemy shells were still popping. Instinctively, Audiffred went for his Colt 1911 pistol, which he'd switched to his left hip.

Looking down, he saw that a jagged shard of shrapnel was wedged in the pistol's slide. The gun was holding together by a thread. The pistol had shielded an artery—and possibly saved his life.

It was then that Audiffred collapsed into the dirt. The pain had caught up to him.

Later, in a field hospital, doctors would find the shape of a pistol bruised into Audiffred's thigh. But when Cajun Boy awoke several days later in a French hospital, his good fortune wasn't his first thought. Or even his second. Instead, he was possessed by a singular thought: *That poor lieutenant!*

Lieutenant Robert Bower's combat time in a Sherman had lasted two hours.

The trailing Shermans had fallen behind. The Pershing was now in the lead—all by itself.

Inside, Clarence was glued to his periscope. He had yet to fire a shot.

Across the turret, Corporal John DeRiggi gripped a shell, eager for a reason to reload. The twenty-year-old loader had grown up in an Italian American household in Scranton, Pennsylvania. DeRiggi, usually a fun-loving guy, was now deadly serious as his eyes and ears tracked the shells outside. He couldn't take any more. A battle was raging around them and Clarence wasn't fighting back.

"Do something!" he shouted across the turret. "We're being wiped out!"

Clarence's temper flared as he snapped back, "I've got no shot!"

Five doughs bolted for the highway, seeking cover. But they didn't make it. An explosion sent their bodies flying.

From what Clarence could discern, most of the flashes came from right beneath the trees.

The trees.

Clarence had an idea. He asked Earley to stop the tank to give him a stable firing platform. DeRiggi and others protested—stopping would make them sitting ducks. It would be suicide.

Clarence ignored them and turned to Earley. "Stop the tank, I need to shoot!"

Earley had never seen Clarence so inflamed. He called for the driver to stop the tank.

Clarence turned to DeRiggi. "WP!"

DeRiggi looked confused—they normally used white phosphorus shells to mark targets.

"Now, goddammit!" Clarence leaned back to his periscope.

DeRiggi swapped out the shell in the breech for another one with a gray-painted warhead.

The Germans took advantage of the Pershing's sitting still. They fired again and again. Geysers of soil leapt from the field as dirt showered them from all sides.

Clarence looked past the chaos. He blocked out the noise and settled the reticle on the trunk of a single tree.

Don't miss. It was the usual pep talk he'd give himself, but this time, the stakes were life or death. Clarence squeezed the trigger. The 90mm barked as it blasted the shell at its target.

Downrange, the tree trunk shattered into matchsticks. Where the tree had stood, a white cloud billowed, sparkling with particles of white phosphorus, each burning at 1,000 degrees and spreading over the Germans' trench.

It worked!

Clarence could have cried with joy. There was hope, but no time to celebrate. Enemy shells were landing closer and closer.

Before Clarence could fire again, Earley told the driver—

"Reverse!" The Pershing rolled backward. Clarence called for more shells, while Earley ordered more tank movements—forward, backward—to keep the enemy gunners off-balance.

Casing after casing ejected from the 90mm's breech. Earley dodged the flaming spheres. Clarence directed his fire at tree after tree.

A pale mist, like a ground fog, hovered over the trenches. The German guns had all but stopped flashing.

A safe distance from the trenches, A-Company heard the American shells streaking overhead.

Buck tugged his helmet over his ears.

When the firing finally tapered off, he lifted his head. The fog of white phosphorus was fading. A runner dashed from platoon to platoon. It was time to rush the enemy trenches.

On Lieutenant Boom's shout, all of A-Company charged forward. Buck sprang to his feet. He threw a grenade into the trench and watched it explode with a rise of dirt. His job as the scout was to find the enemy. Buck took his duty literally. He jumped into the trench and found them.

There was a gun pit twenty yards away, where a German gun crew—still stunned by the use of white phosphorus—was huddled around an 88. After one German noticed Buck, four or five others turned toward him with their weapons lowered. Buck took aim with his rifle. They froze. Buck's finger tightened on the trigger.

Everyone's eyes were bulging in fear. But before anyone

could pull the trigger, A-Company arrived at the trench. Dough after dough jumped to the muddy floor. They pointed their gun muzzles in the Germans' faces. Others pulled pistols out of the Germans' trembling hands.

Up and down the trench, Germans removed their helmets and surrendered. A-Company claimed 173 prisoners, most of whom were older men.

Buck sank to the trench's muddy floor. His mouth felt as if it were stuffed with cotton, so he took a swig from his canteen. The water didn't help. Janicki helped him up as their squad gathered around. The others were amazed that Buck had survived. To them, he was "Shorty," and they even had a saying about him: "Shorty thinks he's invisible!" Every time Buck heard it, he had to wonder if they knew the difference between "invisible" and "invincible." He wasn't about to correct them now. They were hard-nosed veterans and he was not. And after today, he felt further from joining their ranks than ever.

When Janicki and the others unslung their weapons, Buck did the same. He wished he could just stay there and collect himself, but gunfire was still popping.

The veterans led the way.

On the edge of Blatzheim, the Pershing shut down with a battle-weary sigh. The remaining six Shermans parked haphazardly around it.

Clarence steadied himself against the Pershing. The sights of the battle's aftermath nearly made him sick. Five of the company's tanks lay derelict in the field with their guns frozen, pointing at phantom targets. A few other broken tanks limped back to Golzheim.

The human bloodshed was even worse. Medical jeeps raced forward to tend to sixteen wounded tankers, not to mention the injured doughs.

And the dead? They were still riding in cold steel sarcophaguses.

Having safely delivered Corporal Caserta to the medics, Chuck Miller hobbled to the curb in Golzheim and took a seat.

A fresh pain in his ankle had seemingly arisen from nowhere.

Chuck removed his right boot, lowered the sock, and found blood seeping from a hole on the outside of his ankle. Having lost two tanks and two commanders, Chuck would be sent to Stolberg for care and reassignment to a new job with the supply sergeant. As far as the 3rd Armored Division was concerned, Chuck Miller had seen and done enough.

Shadows stretched across the field at dusk as Clarence and crew replenished the Pershing. With its sooty muzzle brake, mud-caked tracks, and countless claw marks left by shrapnel, the tank had taken on a stalwart, rugged appearance.

Earley pulled Clarence aside to praise his quick thinking with the white phosphorus. Earley had also noticed a change in Clarence. For the first time since he'd been under Earley's command, Clarence was displaying confidence and forcefulness.

Earley looked his friend in the eye.

"From now on you fire when *you* want to," Earley told Clarence. "No more waiting on me."

Clarence was flattered by the gesture and promised Earley that he wouldn't let him down.

Personally, Clarence credited the Pershing—not himself—with their survival, with its automatic transmission and 90mm gun. The tank wasn't just a tank anymore, it was a partner in the only mission that mattered to Clarence: keeping his family safe.

That night, however, someone would come to see the Pershing differently.

Captain Salisbury drifted sullenly around his company, disgusted by their losses. Five men dead. His company had lost five men taking one small German town—and they hadn't even reached their destination, the city of Cologne.

Salisbury was known to dwell on his unit's casualties, especially the men killed in action. To him, each death was a personal failure to someone's mother. Now he had to sign five letters of consolation and send the boys' belongings home. A lighter. A ring. A chess set.

For all this, Salisbury blamed one person: himself. He had chosen to spare the Pershing. He had wrapped his company around the Super Tank only to see his Shermans be destroyed.

Never again.

It was February 1945. Although it was a painful choice, Captain Salisbury had made his decision. If his company was to live to see the end of the war, he'd have to risk one crew to protect the rest.

From now on, the Pershing would lead.

CHAPTER 12

HUNTING

Four days later, March 2, 1945
NEAR OBERAUSSEM, GERMANY

Buck stepped lightly along the path through the cold, dead woods toward Oberaussem—another town on their march to Cologne. The city was now just eight miles away.

Snow floated through the canopy of trees. All of A-Company followed Buck in single file. They had not assigned him to be first scout this time. He had volunteered.

Buck was actually enjoying the role of first scout. There was nothing quite like the rush of stalking the enemy and trying to shoot them before they could shoot you. It was just like the cowboy movies he had loved to watch. He was no stranger to the woods. His father—a rugged outdoorsman—had first put a rifle in Buck's hands when he was just twelve. In no time, Buck and his younger brothers had built a cabin in the woods, where they spent their free time playing and hunting.

Now, the German woods in front of Buck opened up to a narrow footbridge. It crossed a babbling creek. On the other side, in the backyard of a stone hunting lodge, stood a large oak tree. Shovelfuls of earth ringed the base of the tree. Something was moving in the tree's shadow, something gray.

A German helmet.

Buck pumped his rifle overhead to signal "enemy in sight." Behind him, the company hit the ground. Buck took cover behind the nearest tree.

A German soldier rose into view, then sank from sight.

Moments later, a burst of flame shot upward. Bullets from a machine gun tore the air and landed by an empty patch of woods farther up from where Buck had taken shelter.

The Germans *had* to be spooked—they were firing in the wrong direction.

Another burst ripped from the gun. When it ceased, the German gunner rose to see if he'd hit anything. Buck balanced his M1 rifle on the nearest tree knob and centered his sights on the man's helmet, taking aim just above the curved earflap.

His gun barked. The helmet dropped from sight as the shot reverberated through the woods. Then, an eerie silence filled the forest air.

Lieutenant Boom crawled behind Buck and stopped within the tree line. Boom, a gangly twenty-three-year-old, had a narrow face featuring close-set eyes and jug ears. He and Buck had bonded over their love of sports. In fact, Boom ran his platoon like a sports team. Everything was a competition that came down to "us versus the enemy," and in this match there could only be one winner.

Buck pointed out the emplacement where the German seemed to be hiding. "I'm pretty sure I hit one," he said.

With infantry aboard, this Spearhead M4 probes for resistance during the fighting in France, August 1944.

A Panther G, fresh from the floor of the MAN factory in Nuremberg, September 1944.

The real *Fury*, seen here in Normandy. This M4 belonged to the 2nd Armored, the army's other heavy armored division.

A Panzer IV H races to the front lines in Normandy, June 1944.

A Spearhead Sherman crosses a floating bridge, likely during the liberation of Belgium, as evidenced by the patriotic scribblings on the hull.

A Spearhead Sherman rolls through Stolberg on September 24, 1944, at a time when only half of the town had been wrested from the Germans.

Tanks were literally parked between houses in the early days at Stolberg. Seen here is "Cajun Boy" Audiffred (far left) and some of his crew aboard their Sherman.

At the onset of the Bulge, Easy Company tankers take a meal alongside Clarence's Sherman *Eagle*. Left to right: Smokey, unidentified, Earley, McVey, and Clarence.

A view through the periscope. Jim Bates snapped this photo from the bow gunner's seat of a Stuart during the Battle of the Bulge.

"Cajun Boy" Audiffred and his M4A3 during a lull in the Bulge. "Duckbills" can be seen extending from the tracks.

Spearhead crews assess their next move in the Ardennes. To the right of the M4A1 is one of the division's sought-after M4A3E2 tanks, an up-armored assault Sherman.

Clarence (left) and McVey display a 76mm high-explosive shell. Their tank *Eagle*, seen later in the Bulge, is now missing its logs.

This Spearhead M4 struggles for grip on the icy streets of Baneux, Belgium, during the American counteroffensive in January 1945.

An M4A3 Sherman passes a vanquished Panther in the northern salient of the Bulge.

Boom looked through his field glasses. What if anyone was left? They'd better finish the emplacement off, just in case.

"Okay, let's go," Boom said.

First, though, he and other doughs carefully circled the emplacement, to see firsthand what they were up against. To their surprise, the pit was empty. No Germans, no machine gun. The only evidence that the emplacement had recently been occupied was an escape trench that led to the wall of the lodge.

Buck turned to Boom in disbelief. "I swear I got one!"

"If you live through this war you're going to deserve a medal," Boom said, amused.

Buck picked up a trail of blood in the trench. He followed red drops around a corner and over to a basement staircase.

Buck crept down the steps, leading the way. At the foot of the stairs, he gave the "hold" signal and opened the door. When no shots rang out, he stepped inside the dimly lit basement.

There he saw eight enemy soldiers, huddled around something with their backs to him. When Buck shouted, the soldiers turned with their hands raised in surrender. Their faces were creased with dismay. Then the soldiers stepped back, revealing a young German soldier lying on the floor.

Buck stepped closer.

The soldier was blond, blue-eyed, and around Buck's age, twenty-two. He was breathing, but bloody gray brain matter was oozing from holes on both sides of his head. Buck almost gagged. His hearing faded, and time seemed to stand still. He felt so light-headed that he was afraid he was going to faint. This was the victim of his gun. No other dough had fired a shot.

It was the first time Buck had seen the results of his bullets up close.

Buck turned to the other Germans and saw grief-stricken faces. Several wiped away tears, while others were on the verge of crying. They probably weren't just fellow soldiers; they were more likely friends who had known one another for years, belonging to a unit recruited from the same town.

Buck hollered for a medic.

Moments later, Boom arrived with a medic in tow.

The medic knelt over the young German. Buck couldn't look away, as if he could somehow will the young man back to health with his stare. The wounded man's eyelids fluttered; his breaths were shallow. The medic shook his head. The young German was going to die.

Buck struggled for breath as his chest tightened uncontrollably.

Boom must have recognized Buck's anguish, because he ordered him to go upstairs to search the lodge. As Buck's feet carried him away, he looked over his shoulder, yearning to see the damage undone.

Dazed and ashen, Buck drifted aimlessly through the commotion of the hunting lodge.

Janicki took him aside. Buck told him what he had just seen.

"He wouldn't have hesitated to turn his gun on us," Janicki said. "You just happened to fire first."

Buck wasn't about to accept that he had *possibly* saved other lives by taking this one. Despite Janicki's best efforts, Buck's eyes were distant and his mind was elsewhere. He couldn't stop replaying the moment when he'd pulled the trigger. His life had changed forever.

Should I have shot over his head or into that oak tree?

Would he have dropped the gun and run?

He couldn't forget the faces of those German soldiers as they watched their friend die.

In his rush to become a veteran, he'd overlooked the downside: war is an ugly business to be good at.

CHAPTER 13

THE FIRE DEPARTMENT OF THE WEST

A day or two later, early March 1945
ABOUT 130 MILES SOUTH—GERMANY

Darkness blanketed the countryside. Meanwhile, the Kriegslokomotive, or Kriegslok, a German military train, raced north along the Odenwald Mountains. Glowing embers illuminated flatcars, which were carrying German tanks. With his goggles lowered, Gustav Schaefer rode in the radio operator's seat of a Mark IV tank three cars from the front. His blond hair blew in the wind. The coal smell was comforting; it reminded him of home in winter.

Gazing at the train tracks flying by, he was right where he wanted to be. If only his grandmother had let him follow his dreams to become a railwayman, he could have been doing *this* every day.

Ever since the battle on his birthday, September 9, 1944, the fighting had been brutal. Panzer Brigade 106 had been sent to the province of Alsace, in the southwest corner of Germany. There, they had experienced devastating losses in the line of duty. The brigade—what remained of it—was dismantled and sent northward in pieces. One battered company went ahead to defend a bridgehead at the western city of Bonn. Two went to the Rhineland. And now, the last part of Panzer Brigade 106, Gustav's part, was riding the rails toward its fate.

Theirs was now a mixed fleet of tanks that consisted of about three Panthers, three Mark IVs, and a leftover Jagdpanzer IV or two. Gustav's days in a Panther were behind him. He had been assigned to a Mark IV H, a dark-green-and-brown camouflaged tank from a disbanded unit, to use in future fighting.

Gustav leaned in his seat to see around the locomotive. There were American planes overhead these days, so tunnels were a train's only sanctuary. Surely one was coming soon?

At the start of the journey, Gustav had traveled in one of the cargo wagons at the rear of the train. Thirty men rode in each car, playing cards as the train chugged along. But soon he had sneaked out to ride in his tank, which was also on board. He would reappear at each stop just in time to show his face—no one any the wiser about where he'd been.

During a layover, the train's brakeman confided in Gustav that when they passed his hometown, he planned to jump from the caboose—consequences be damned. He knew where they were headed and wanted no part in it.

The train was bound for Germany's "Fortress City"— Cologne. The Wehrmacht was preparing the city for an American onslaught.

From the caboose, the brakeman signaled the engineer. He hadn't jumped off yet. The engineer leaned from the locomotive for a glimpse behind the train. Something he saw in the dark sky sent him into a frenzy.

A whistle bellowed a bloodcurdling wail. The train accelerated rapidly. Sparks gushed from the smokestack with a deafening roar. They were running from something, but Gustav wasn't sure what. He looked over his shoulder in a panic, but the turret blocked his view.

Gustav sank lower in his seat. More than 600 tons of train were speeding down Germany's badly patched tracks. He held on tight. A howl rose in pitch behind him. It was the unmistakable sound of air whipping through engines. Now Gustav knew what they were running from—Allied fighter-bombers were hot on their tail. Gustav descended into the tank and closed the hatch cover behind him, hiding himself in the dark confines.

Machine guns clattered. Bullets clinked against metal. The sounds danced over Gustav's steel ceiling and kept going. The locomotive gave a scream—its external pipes were fractured. A second plane roared overhead and smothered the machine's cries with a racket of blazing guns.

The planes kept running, low and straight. The train chugged along swiftly, but if it was hit, it would explode with the force of a bomb.

Gustav cracked the hatch to peek outside.

The first plane came in gunning for the train's nerve center—the locomotive. The second plane came at them higher and slower, then let loose with a bomb that crashed down, tossing up a cloud of cinders directly ahead of the train.

The tracks in front of them had been severed. If they didn't stop, they would derail.

Brakes screeched. The drive wheels locked, throwing up sparks of their own as the train skidded on the rails.

The train slowed to thirty miles an hour. Then twenty.

Behind Gustav, tankers jumped off the moving cars, willing to take their chances.

The train was almost at a standstill. Gustav braced himself for impact. The locomotive barreled over the edge of the bomb crater. It careened into the hole with a sickening crunch. Car after car violently slammed together like an accordion. Gustav lurched forward. His face came to a rest against his gunsight.

He needed a moment to take it all in.

Gustav raised the hatch and surveyed the damage. Every train car except the locomotive was still sitting on the tracks. A roar of steam rose from the bomb crater.

The P-47 bomber planes were moving on. Gustav watched them shrinking into the distance. Nobody emerged from the wrecked locomotive. In crashes like this, the coal often shot forward and crushed the men against the scalding boiler.

Gustav wished he could hug his grandmother. He could have been among them.

The next afternoon, Gustav walked through Old Town Heidelberg with some of his fellow tankers. They marveled at the old Baroque buildings and Byzantine church domes. The Neckar River lay a few streets away, and across the way lay mountains and a crumbling castle.

The most remarkable thing about the city was that it was still intact. So far, Heidelberg, home to Germany's oldest university, had been almost entirely spared by the bombings. Wandering these streets, Gustav could almost convince himself that the war was nothing but a bad dream.

The men were in high spirits. It felt good to be back in a German city, especially after their close call on the rail lines. A locomotive had had to tow them back to Heidelberg.

Gustav was surprised that the others had let him tag along. He was the youngest and lowest-ranking soldier in the group. Luckily, Rolf Millitzer had vouched for him. Gustav's commander was back, walking beside him, in the flesh. In the scramble to escape the Panther in Luxembourg, Rolf had hidden in the forest, returning just before the brigade evacuated without them. Gustav and Rolf were the only remaining members of their original crew. Everyone else had been transferred from the company, because of wounds or the needs of the war.

As the men strolled through the town, passersby drifted to the other side of the street. Some looked away. Others glared. Clearly, the citizens of Heidelberg saw something they didn't like. Gustav wondered if his comrades noticed too.

During his time away at the front, Gustav had not been privy to the latest propaganda that the Nazis had been spreading. He hadn't heard the "terror stories." To instill fear and a fighting spirit, Propaganda Minister Joseph Goebbels was employing state media to paint a horrific picture for Germans of what the country's future would hold should they be defeated.

Goebbels claimed the Americans had cut a deal with the Russians to send prisoners to camps in Siberia. Any men left in Germany would be shifted from city to city to shovel rubble and break rocks. Goebbels told his people that American officers would beat German women and that civilians would be imprisoned in their homes for all but two or three hours a day.

The propaganda quickly took root among the German people. But the campaign had an unintended consequence—a vicious blame game that was crippling morale and turning German civilians against their own troops.

In countless towns and cities, German civilians in the west now called their soldiers by a new name: "Prolongers of the War."

During his short time in Heidelberg, the scorn in the locals' eyes was enough to set Gustav's mind in motion.

If his people were now against him, who was he risking his life for?

The beer brewery kept the harsh realities of war at bay—for the time being. The tankers gathered at a table, enjoying the comforting smells of the hearth and food. Radio music played.

Seated near Rolf, Gustav felt comfortable again. Frothy mugs of beer arrived. No one took the toasts seriously any longer. Most were delivered as a laugh.

"Many enemies, much honor!" was a tongue-in-cheek favorite.

On any future battlefield they would be outnumbered. There was no escaping that reality. So, German tankers joked about it. "One of our tanks is better than ten of yours," they wanted to tell the Americans—"but you always have eleven!"

Every unit had its fanatics, to whom such jokes were blasphemy, men who still believed in Hitler's *Endsieg,* or final victory. But none of them sat with Gustav that day.

Gustav took a sip. The beer was watery. As he looked around the table he saw the others puckering at the flat taste as well. Beer was another casualty of wartime ingredient shortages, along with butter, marmalade, honey, and coffee, which were all artificial now.

Their greatest fear was German civilians. They were hiding from the very people they were fighting for. The Goebbels propaganda machine had transformed anyone and everyone into a potential mole. Apart from a swastika pin on a lapel, it was impossible to tell whether someone was a loyal Nazi Party member who would tip off the Gestapo, the Nazis' secret police.

The 1938 "Subversion of the War Effort" law made it criminal to undermine the war effort in any way, shape, or form. The punishment for breaking the law was death. Did drinking in uniform while making unpatriotic toasts qualify? At this point, after all they'd been through, they didn't care.

Loosened up and laughing, the men reminisced. One soldier, an older tanker, held a piece of metal to his mouth to re-create the resonance of a radio broadcast and did impressions of news announcers. "From the Reich Ministry in Berlin," he said.

Speaking with a crooked mouth, the older tanker launched into a mocking impression of a Goebbels speech: "If our enemies think we Germans have no art, then we can prove the opposite! Every day there is a full train wagon of *art*-ificial honey being sent to the Eastern Front! And what about our *art*-ificial coffee? And . . ."

The table broke into a fit of laughter.

Gustav laughed with the rest of them but held back from contributing any jokes of his own. He looked over his shoulder. This was fun, but dangerous.

Gustav had been twelve years old on November 9, 1938, Kristallnacht, or the "Night of Broken Glass," when church bells awakened his entire family from their slumber. Flames were rising from the neighboring village of Wehdem. Gustav's father was in the local fire brigade, so he shouldered his tools and pedaled away on his bicycle to fight the blaze. Other firemen followed, steering a horse-drawn water pump.

In the village, they discovered that the fire was coming from a burning synagogue and the town's Jewish homes. The fire brigade was able to rescue one family's belongings from the flames and was moving to another home when the Nazi Brownshirts returned. A gang of these Brownshirts, local troublemakers who joined forces in a Nazi militia, had set the fires on Goebbels's suggestion as part of a wave of violence. The Brownshirts outnumbered the fire brigade. They had forced the firemen to stand aside. As if that weren't bad enough, the Brownshirts threw everything the fire brigade had managed to save right back into the fire.

When Gustav's father returned home that night, he wept.

Germany's anti-Semitic fervor made no sense to Gustav. He knew only one Jewish person—a neighboring farmer who had loaned the family a cow during tough times, without ever asking for, or expecting, anything in return. To Gustav's way of thinking, the Jews were ordinary, hardworking Germans just like his parents. Even though he was only twelve at the time, he knew that whatever was happening, it was wrong.

It had gotten late and the brewery was winding down. Bursts of war news interrupted the music on the radio. As frontline updates drifted across the beer hall, any last traces of revelry were dampened. The Red Army (the army of the Soviet Union, the U.S.S.R.) had entered East Prussia. Soon, millions of civilians from those territories would be refugees, forsaking more than seven hundred years of German history.

The news made Rolf especially melancholy. He was worried for his family back home in Dresden. He didn't even know if his home was still standing. Several weeks earlier, nearly eight hundred British bombers had flown over the city in the dead of night, raining bombs and lighting a firestorm in the city center.

News of the horrors of Dresden spread quickly. Survivors spoke of a tornado of flames that tore people from their handholds as it sucked them into the red glow. Air-raid shelters burned. Molten rivers of tar flowed as the asphalt streets boiled over from the heat.

Gustav was worried for his commander's sake. Rolf was more than a commander; he was a friend. No matter how much he enjoyed a night out with the men, Gustav couldn't forget where they were headed. With just a few tanks, they would soon fight the most technologically advanced killing force the world had ever known. Eisenhower had 73 divisions, 17,000 aircraft, and 4 million soldiers at his disposal for accomplishing one purpose—to kill Germans like Gustav.

That knowledge gave them all a crippling sense of doom.

The tracks would soon be repaired. Another train would come, and there would be no turning back. Their train to Cologne was a one-way trip, and Gustav knew it.

CHAPTER 14

GOING FIRST

A day or two later, March 5, 1945
COLOGNE, GERMANY

The gate to the city of Cologne was barred. The Pershing shuddered to a stop. The rest of Easy Company halted behind it. Rusty leaves fluttered beneath gnarled trees. Ominous clouds were forming on the horizon. A storm was brewing.

Inside the lead tank of Task Force X, Clarence pressed his eyes to his periscope to survey the scene. The road ahead led to an underpass jammed with white trolley cars and steel cables.

"Could be an ambush," Clarence said to Earley.

On the other side of the overpass were apartment buildings. But who was inside them? This could be a perfect location for Germans to spring a trap.

Earley sent a warning to the whole company.

American crews were expecting to be met with the Panzerfaust weapon, a deadly combination of a bazooka and a grenade launcher. The American tanks' turrets swept the horizon, looking for Germans. Clarence was bracing himself for the enemy to appear.

Thunder rippled from the sky.

"Hold your fire," Earley radioed the platoon, sounding relieved. The infantry would handle this. A rush of doughs moved forward and secured the overpass without firing a shot. A bulldozer tank was coming to clear the blockade that stood in their way.

Earley left the tank to confer with the other commanders. Clarence was fidgety. Sitting in the lead tank—the most exposed target in the whole crew—was harrowing. But he wasn't alone. Smokey Davis came down from the tank and paced back and forth, wearing his pistol low on his hip, like the gunslinger he fancied himself.

A sign nearby marked the city limits of Köln, the German name for Cologne. In the distance, the famous cathedral stood blackened above a cityscape still smoking from an earlier raid. The cathedral's twin spires stared back at Clarence like sinister, all-seeing eyes.

He wished his parents could see him now: one of five crewmen on the tank that would lead the 3rd Armored Division into the Queen City of Germany. He had come a long way from peddling candy back in Lehighton, Pennsylvania.

Meanwhile, farther north of Clarence, Buck sat atop an idling Sherman with Bob Janicki, Lieutenant Boom, and a few other doughs.

During this attack, they would ride the tanks of F-Company.

Heat was rising from the engine deck. And it wasn't just the heat—the smell of oil was nauseating.

There was only one way to get off the scorching tank. Buck asked Lieutenant Boom if he could investigate the holdup ahead, and he set out alone. Even if his job as first scout was dangerous, at least he held his fate in his own hands.

Turning the corner, Buck saw that GI engineers were already on the scene. The Sherman commander was talking to the engineers. They were waiting on a tank to clear the barricade so they could keep moving. Something stirred in the group's peripheral vision. Someone was walking on the bridge that ran above the underpass. Buck and the men snapped to attention. Then, one by one, they lowered their guns.

It was just a German couple out for a leisurely stroll.

But even after he lowered his rifle, Buck kept an eye on them. Something wasn't quite right about the pair. The man and woman both wore white medical aprons bearing the Red Cross. They were dawdling, taking their time studying the Americans below. Then, suddenly, the man reached under his apron and lifted a Panzerfaust beneath his arm, taking aim at the Sherman. The Americans scattered. Buck bolted for cover.

The Panzerfaust fired with a burst of black powder, propelling a football-shaped warhead that flew down like a meteor. The warhead hit in front of the tank but didn't explode. Ricocheting off the street, the missile kept traveling. It skidded beneath the tank's undercarriage and out the backside before exploding against a curb.

The shock wave lifted Buck and threw him down.

With his chest heaving from exertion and the force of the impact, Buck leaned out from his covered position and took aim. But it was too little, too late—the couple had disappeared.

Buck and the others had just met a new breed of German soldier.

A seat of Nazi power, Cologne held 125 local offices of the party, and many neighborhoods had "block leaders," who kept tabs on which households hung swastika flags. Were the German couple a pair of rogue block leaders with no one left to harass? Had they been recruited by the military to wage war in the streets? It was anyone's guess.

Buck was fuming. Being nosy had nearly gotten him killed. It had been a close call for the tank crew, too.

Suddenly, he noticed motion on the bridge. The man and woman had come back to see their handiwork. They had heard the explosion and assumed they'd destroyed the tank. Clearly, they wanted to double-check.

Buck took aim with his rifle, but before he could squeeze off a shot, the Sherman fired first. The shell sent a hail of shrapnel. When the dust settled, it revealed a crumbling hole in the side of the bridge. Where the couple had once stood, only a pair of long red streaks remained.

When Lieutenant Boom and the platoon arrived, Buck came out to greet them as if everything were normal. They couldn't know the truth of how close he'd come to becoming a red splatter himself. If they did, he'd never hear the end of it.

One dough glanced from side to side, as if he'd lost something. He was Private First Class Byron Mitchell. When he spotted Buck, he broke from the pack. Byron's bright blue eyes radiated skittishness, like those of an animal that had been abused. A former baker from Atlanta, Byron had grown up poor, so poor that some wagered he might have raised himself.

Byron wielded the squad's Browning Automatic Rifle, or BAR, their most potent handheld weapon. He had the aggressiveness to match it. "Where'd they go?" he asked furtively. He was after the German couple.

Whenever he came across a dead German, Byron would search him for souvenirs. Pistol. Watch. Jewelry. His looting wasn't solely for personal gain. Sometimes Byron came away with valuable intelligence for Lieutenant Boom, which allowed the others to look the other way.

The boulevard into Cologne was vacant, the underpass finally cleared. The Reich lay before them. But where were the German soldiers? In the Pershing, Clarence kept looking, expecting the sight to change.

Behind him, Easy Company wound back through the underpass, followed by doughs of B- and C-Companies.

It was now four p.m. and Easy Company's march into Cologne had been delayed for four hours—but they had made it.

The radio crackled with static and the acting company commander announced, "Gentlemen, I give you Cologne. Let's knock the hell out of it!"

The words brought a smile to Clarence's face.

It was about time.

The Pershing churned down the empty boulevard. Half of Task Force X trailed close behind. The other half took another road. There were three routes into the city, but only Easy Company's led to the cathedral—directly into the heart of Cologne.

Clarence felt like a vandal, breaching the walls and sneaking into an enemy's camp. Brimming with nervous energy, he searched for a target. Any target at all. But he couldn't seem to find one.

Parched soil lay where a park had once stood. Most of the trees had been felled for firewood. Vents poked from the soil, revealing underground air-raid bunkers. The terrain was littered with bomb craters.

Clarence was astonished.

This was 1945. This was the time of the *Endkampf*, the "final battle," when Germans were urged to fight blindly for Hitler, even if the possibility of victory was almost nonexistent. This was the day when the city's Nazi *gauleiter*, as the regional leader was known, had called for the "unrelenting defense of Cologne until the end."

Yet Germany's fourth-largest city appeared empty. It seemed as if everyone had already been wiped from the earth and there was no one left to put up a fight.

Just then, a glint caught Clarence's eye.

A clock tower stood about a mile ahead to his left. High in the tower, something had sparkled. It was just one flash—possibly a burst of light bouncing off the glass—but Clarence wasn't taking any chances.

Enemy observers were known to place themselves high above the fray. What if one was up there now? If so, the doughs in their open-topped half-tracks were in serious danger.

"Bob, I'd better get that clock," Clarence said. That was all he had to say.

Earley called for a halt. Everyone watched and waited in silence. Without a fuss, DeRiggi, the loader, switched to an HE shell. Clarence sent it flying toward the clock. The 23-pound shell landed smack in the middle of the clock's face. The tower ruptured with a sidelong blast as bits of clock and brick came tumbling down, generating a huge cloud of dust.

The crew roared in approval. At the start of the battle for Cologne, time stood still.

Easy Company drove onward, but the smooth sailing couldn't last forever.

Tank commanders consulted their maps of Cologne. When the city's main boulevard ended, it branched into smaller streets. Each street led toward the big cathedral. At the first two streets that Easy Company came to, a platoon of tanks peeled off, followed by a company of doughs in half-tracks. The company's remaining platoon of tanks would wait in reserve, in case the troops needed backup. Between these two streets, Easy Company and the doughs would fight side by side to clear one block at a time, all the way to the train station. Once there, they would stand before the ultimate prize: the cathedral.

At the spearhead of 2nd Platoon, Clarence kept his eyes peeled for any movement.

Stately townhouses lined the street ahead. Their once-beautiful turn-of-the-century flourishes were now destroyed. Rubble spilled from the shattered buildings over the sidewalks, blocking the Pershing's path. This cultured major city with a prewar population of 445,000 had recently dwindled to a mere 40,000 residents. The Nazis had ordered the evacuation of all but the essential war-industry workers.

Lines of doughs moved up the sidewalks past the Pershing and began going door-to-door. Clarence felt sorry for them. Each block held more than thirty homes, and each of those homes had multiple floors. Each one needed to be searched. And the doughs' search had to be thorough. No German soldier could be left behind.

The crackle of gunfire echoed through the streets as doughs broke down doors with boots, hammers, and axes. It was late afternoon, and the army's biggest house-to-house battle of the European war had officially begun.

Start and stop. Start and stop. The column of tanks inched through the streets.

Inside the Sherman behind Clarence's tank, Chuck Miller held his breath. Chuck had enjoyed several days away in the supply depot, before the company sent word that his skills were needed back on the front. Despite the ankle wound he'd suffered in earlier fighting, Chuck had stepped forward. Even after losing two commanders, it didn't feel right, the idea of his buddies fighting without him.

Now, he was back in the gunner's seat. The Pershing in front of him spewed a steady stream of exhaust. The fumes left his head swimming. The width of his periscope marked the extent of his vision, and the rattle of idling engines drowned out all other sounds.

The enemy was near. Chuck had seen doughs bringing back German prisoners, though he hadn't seen a hostile enemy soldier yet. What he *didn't* know was that the enemy was spread thin in Cologne. The city was guarded by the 9th Panzer Division farther north and the 363rd Volksgrenadier Division here and to the south. Both divisions had been terribly battered by fighting and had lost many men. But they were holding on.

Through his cloudy mind, Chuck could see that the doughs had cleared another block and were on the move. The Pershing rolled forward. Chuck's tank followed. Chuck caught a flash of gray in the lower-right corner of his periscope. Someone on the sidewalk was running along the right side of the Pershing. It was the unmistakable gray sleeve of a German uniform. Chuck couldn't believe it. The doughs had missed someone.

The German soldier ducked into a doorway ahead of the Pershing, where he fumbled with something. Chuck caught a glimpse of the yellowish warhead of a Panzerfaust.

It was a perfect storm. The Pershing was on course to drive right past this enemy soldier. The doorway was in Clarence's blind spot, and Earley was looking in the wrong direction.

Chuck wanted to shout a warning to the tank ahead of him, but there was no time. He slammed his turret control, spinning the turret directly toward the threat, and hovered his foot over the tank's triggers.

As soon as the barrel reached the German, he'd fire the machine gun. *Faster!* Chuck urged the turret onward. The German stepped out from the doorway, raised the warhead from his hip, and aimed it toward the Pershing.

Chuck stomped for the trigger.

But in the heat of the moment, his foot found the wrong firing button. Instead of a machine gun's measured response, the muzzle flash from the 76mm lit up. The HE shell blasted the German soldier straight through the house he was standing in.

A backblast of stone and wood pelted Chuck's tank. Debris crumbled from the building onto the turret. The crew coughed.

When the dust cleared, Chuck returned to his periscope to see his handiwork. Where just a minute before, the German had stood, a pink mist had settled around the edges of the door-frame.

Chuck's whoops of elation could be heard over the tank's engine.

The crew erupted in cheers and praise. Bob Earley radioed, his voice shaking from the emotion of the close call: "Thanks, Chuck." Chuck beamed with pride.

No one in Easy Company would ever call him Baby again.

Later, Chuck would feel a pang of guilt over the use of excessive force. But not now and not here, where survival was the goal by any means necessary.

Two streets over from Clarence, Buck and the other doughs moved quickly along the sidewalk as they ventured onto a new residential block. Bodies littered the streets from the latest air raid. More than three hundred casualties remained unburied. It was a bone-chilling sight.

Buck's team surrounded him as they made their way down the street. Besides Janicki, there was Private First Class Jose De La Torre from El Paso. Sharp and streetwise, he wore a tanker's coveralls in place of trousers and was particular about his appearance—even as he tramped through a war zone. There was also Tech Corporal Frank Alaniz, a quiet soldier with a gift for operating and fixing radios. And then there was Private First Class Bill Carrier, who hailed from the backwoods of Kentucky.

Together, they had cleared houses all morning.

Cologne's remaining residents had moved into their basements and knocked "mouse holes." The tunnels ran the length of whole blocks. German soldiers were now using the passageways to move between basements and elude capture.

Just then, four Germans burst from a doorway ahead, sprinting frantically to escape.

Buck shouted for them to stop. Janicki fired warning shots over their heads. Buck observed that Janicki didn't just shoot them in the back. The Germans hung a right and took cover inside the nearest house.

The squad divvied up in hot pursuit to follow them. Buck and his team ran through the front door of the house that the Germans had entered. The upstairs was empty. They cautiously eyed the steps to the basement. Where else was there to hide?

Since a grenade was not an option because of the potential for civilian casualties, Buck shouted the only German he knew: *"Raus kommen! Wir nicht schiessen."* It meant "Come out! We don't shoot."

Buck drew a German P-38 pistol from his shoulder harness and chambered a round. He had picked it up a few days earlier and had had a feeling that it was going to come in handy. He gingerly descended the stairs. The ancient floorboards creaked in protest. He held a flashlight in his left hand. The others crept behind him.

When he reached the bottom of the stairs, Buck kicked the door to make sure no one was hiding behind it. It swung all the way open, and the men burst inside. Buck scanned the four walls of the basement. There were no tunnels or other doors to provide an escape route. So where were the Germans?

Against one wall stood a large wooden bin that was used for loading potatoes. It was as tall as a person, and deep, too.

Buck cocked the pistol's hammer. He aimed and fired. A long blue flame shot from the gun's muzzle. In the close quarters of the low-ceilinged basement, the crack resounded like a cannon.

Frantic voices shouted, "Comrade, comrade!" as four Germans nearly trampled one another in their race to come out with their hands up. They all looked tired and haggard.

Janicki gave Buck a nod of approval as he helped secure the prisoners. The fire team marched them out of the basement toward daylight.

Buck sighed. He didn't hate the Germans. They were soldiers too, in the same ugly line of work. But that didn't mean Buck was going to start shooting over heads or asking forgiveness for the young German he had killed. In Buck's mind, asking for forgiveness meant he wouldn't commit the same sin again. There in the middle of Cologne, with the rest of the war still ahead of him, he wasn't sure it was a promise he could make.

On the cusp of evening, Earley and the crews of 2nd Platoon milled around their tanks. Now was about time for a breather. Tankers stretched their legs. Meanwhile, doughs ahead were forting up in houses for the night. Clarence remained inside the Pershing, stationed at the gun. He was suspicious of the city, even if Cologne hadn't yet been the bloodbath that everyone expected.

Spearhead had paved the way into Cologne. In taking the outer city, Easy Company hadn't lost a single one of their men. They *had* taken 1,027 German soldiers prisoner, though. Yet, despite their success, the day's tension lingered. The crews had been going since four a.m. and had spent nearly twelve hours inside their tanks, on constant guard for enemy soldiers who wanted to kill them.

A tall, unusually slim soldier approached the tankers, wearing a helmet and jacket with an armband bearing a white C, the label for a war correspondent, or journalist. The "soldier" was Ann Stringer of the United Press, one of the three female reporters there on the front lines who'd soon be dubbed the "Rhine Maidens." She wore her curly brown hair pulled back to reveal a shapely face with bright eyes.

"Would any of you grant me an interview?" she asked.

Almost all of the tankers were willing to talk to the pretty young woman, including Chuck. He hoped his mother would read the story back home.

The men jostled closer, enamored with the journalist. Stringer's smile entranced them. She whipped out her notepad. She asked the men about their mounts. How were their tanks holding up? The crews let out a harrumph of disgust and aired their grievances. Sure, the American army was a strong one, but their tanks were battered, scarred, and threadbare.

"We pushed into this town with our old M-4 tanks, which the Nazis have been knocking around all through France," said Chuck Miller's new commander, Sergeant Sylvester "Red" Villa, a boisterous ex-detective from the Midwest. "It made us feel pretty blue," Villa added.

Chuck chimed in and told her: "It makes us feel pretty bad to have everyone at home talking about having the best equipment when we know our tanks lack a lot of things being the best."

The men explained that Easy Company had lost almost half of their tanks—and plenty of friends—just a week earlier at Blatzheim.

Stringer was sympathetic; she had recently suffered a loss of her own. She and her husband, William, also a journalist, had reported together until that August, when he was killed in his jeep by sniper fire while approaching Paris. Eisenhower's headquarters reprimanded Stringer for journeying closer to the front than any women—even nurses—were allowed to travel. But the scolding had only spurred her to press harder.

Earley felt the need to speak for the tankers whose voices had been forever silenced by German guns. Of the twelve Shermans that Easy Company had driven into the Fortress City, seven were 75s. Each was equipped with an underpowered gun. It simply was no longer up to the task of keeping its crews safe.

And *someone* had to say it.

So, Earley gave Stringer a quote for her story: "Our tanks are not worth a drop of water on a hot stove. We want tanks to fight with, not just to drive over the countryside."

Stringer smiled. She knew she had something explosive. She rushed off so fast that Chuck and some of the others began second-guessing the interview. How would the higher-ups react to their sounding off in the papers? Would they get in trouble?

Earley shrugged away any concern. They'd only spoken the truth.

Three streets away, Buck and his platoon entered through the back door of a townhouse. They would spend the night here, less than two miles from Cologne's cathedral.

Dusk had settled over the neighborhood. Buck gazed at the horizon, his eyes landing on a cream-colored corner house across the street. Cracks of light shone from its second-story windows. That was unusual. All the civilians he'd seen that day had been living underground, in basements. After all, Cologne was now on the front lines of the war. It was dangerous for them to be in the middle of it.

As first scout, it was up to him to investigate whether someone was there. Buck was wary. The lights looked like a trap to him. As he dashed across the road, he braced himself for a sniper's bullet. When he got to the door, he raised his rifle. This would get the attention of whoever was inside.

The door flew open. He lowered the rifle to his side and stared. He was speechless. Looking back at him was a beautiful young woman. Her blond hair was swept back from her face. Her blue eyes sparkled beneath dark eyebrows. She was nineteen and wore a pretty dress.

When she saw Buck at the door, the young woman's face lit up. She was deliriously happy, laughing and crying at the same time. She threw her arms around him and kissed him. Buck was taken aback. What was happening?

Shadows moved inside the home behind her. Maybe it *was* a trap after all.

Buck started to reach for his rifle but stopped short. A man, the young woman's father, stepped into view. Tall, thin, and gray, he was a dentist and looked the part. Behind him, the young woman's two aunts emerged timidly from the shadows.

The young woman grabbed Buck by the hand and wouldn't let go. She led him into the foyer. Speaking accented English, her father told Buck that there were no German soldiers in the house. He opened the door to the first floor, revealing his dark and empty dental office.

Buck explained the situation. The area was on the front line of the war. Civilians needed to get out to safety, he urged. The man was appreciative but seemed unmoved by the prospect of leaving. Where could they go?

Someone tapped Buck's shoulder. He turned and found Janicki, Byron, and a few other members of his squad at the doorstep. They had come to see if he was safe. The father invited everyone upstairs, and the others happily obliged.

The young woman held Buck back. She spoke broken English and introduced herself as Annemarie Berghoff. Her father was Wilhelm. Buck told her his name. As she led him up the marble steps to the second floor, Annemarie exclaimed: "Buck, first American I see!"

The home was lovely. Art hung from clean white walls. The flooring was made of polished wood. They sat down on plush couches. Annemarie's aunts brought out a glass pitcher and served drinks. Buck eyed the orange-colored beverage and wondered whether it was safe to drink. These were Germans, after all. Wilhelm gave a toast to the war's end and then everyone clinked glasses. Buck took a hesitant sip. The beverage had a metallic tang. He fought off the urge to cringe but relaxed when he saw the Berghoff family drinking. Certainly they wouldn't poison themselves.

A calming mood settled over the room. The doughs sank into their comfortable seats. For a moment, it was as if the war were really over. Buck shinnied closer to Annemarie.

She was absolutely glowing and kept repeating, "Buck, first American I see!" to herself. Buck stayed quiet. He was infamous among his fellow doughs for not talking for hours on end. He also had an uncanny knack for ducking out of a squad photograph whenever a camera appeared. And his shyness especially came out around pretty girls.

Meanwhile, Annemarie's father and aunts chatted with Janicki. Annemarie's family puzzled Buck. *Why were they so happy?* All the other Germans had seemed pained and depressed. They lived with barely any water, electricity, or telephone service, no shops or pubs, and only enough food rations to fill their bellies.

There had to be something more at work.

In the course of their conversation, Buck learned that Annemarie worked as an assistant in her father's dental office, twice a week, between abbreviated sessions of school. But all Annemarie wanted to talk about was the aerial bombings. For more than four years of her life, that was all she'd known. She spoke of a classmate whose house was bombed. When she and her father had arrived to help, they'd discovered the family's corpses, burned and shrunken.

What Annemarie neglected to mention was the time she herself was injured in an air raid in the city center. Before she could reach a bomb shelter, a white phosphorus target-marker landed nearby and seared her leg. Buck meant to ask about the whereabouts of Annemarie's mother. He had seen her in a photo on the way in but erred on the side of being polite.

After about twenty minutes, one of Lieutenant Boom's men knocked on the front door to order Buck and the others back across the avenue.

Annemarie darted to her bedroom and returned with a photograph. It was a portrait of her wearing a checkered red dress. She wrote her name and address on the back before handing the photo to Buck and pointing at the address: Eichendorf Street 28.

Buck was touched. She wanted him to come back. He had dated here and there in college, but none of those relationships seemed serious. This felt different. In the heightened state of wartime, his run-in with Annemarie felt like fate.

Annemarie led Buck to the door. She wouldn't release his hand until he promised he would return. It was an easy promise to make but would be a hard one to keep.

That night from across the street, Buck gazed at the outline of Annemarie's house in the light of a half-moon. He swore he felt her eyes on him, as if she were gazing back at him from behind the darkened windows.

Beyond her house lay Cologne's inner city—the one thing that could prevent him from ever seeing her again. If the enemy was going to fight for Cologne, that was where they would make their last stand.

Tomorrow.

CHAPTER 15

VICTORY OR SIBERIA

The next day, March 6, 1945
COLOGNE, GERMANY

In the cool light of dawn, a Mark IV tank crossed the Hohenzollern Bridge toward the city of Cologne. Gustav peered worriedly over the tank's side. The Mark IV was astoundingly heavy—28 tons. The already-battered bridge could collapse beneath them at any moment. Gustav gripped the hatch so tightly that his knuckles turned white. Below ran the murky rush of the Rhine River.

Sitting high in his seat beside Gustav, a driver steered carefully. With one slip of the controls, they would plummet over the side. The driver and the tank's gunner were replacements, new to the crew. Gustav had met them during the crew assignments only that morning. Now one of these strangers held his life in his hands.

Gustav, Rolf, and their crew had been ordered to go to Cologne, where they would take up positions in the inner city. Their mission: to hold off the Americans for as long as possible. Then they would escape the way they'd come—over this rickety bridge. And once they were safely across, they would demolish the bridge with explosives.

This wouldn't be a one-way trip.

A pair of medieval castle turrets guarded the entrance to Cologne, standing tall against the clouds. Gustav stared with wonder as the tank passed through the gate and came down from the bridge. It felt like driving into another realm.

On Gustav's left, the city's iconic cathedral reached toward the sky, with its Gothic icicles and towering twin spires. By the time Gustav rode into the city, high-explosive bombs had breached the cathedral's roof and its exterior. But it was still standing.

The driver was heading toward the train station. Gustav couldn't fathom the destruction laid out before him. Only the burned ribs of the train station's arched glass ceiling remained. The area was full of rubble. All the buildings around the station's plaza had bombed-out windows like empty eye sockets. The area had been ground zero for the British bombing campaign.

This destroyed train station, it had been decided, would serve as the Germans' defense headquarters. There were two Panthers from Gustav's company and the Mark IV. They were all that was left on this side of the Rhine. And they were the German Army's last hope to delay the Americans' conquest of Cologne.

Three tanks. In the heart of Cologne, that was it.

No one else was waiting for them. No one else was coming to their aid.

Second Company's other tanks, which were in poor mechanical shape, were back on the other side of the Rhine. Their sister companies in the Rhineland were missing or wiped out; no one knew which, because radio communication had broken down. The 9th Panzer Division had at least twenty tanks in the northern outskirts of the city, but the Americans had them pinned against the Rhine.

While Gustav and his crew lacked adequate manpower, at least they had leadership. Their respected company commander, Second Lieutenant Wilhelm Bartelborth, sat in the turret of the neighboring Panther. Twenty-nine, with pale blond hair and blue eyes, Bartelborth—much like Gustav himself—was descended from humble stock in northern Germany. In his life before the war, Bartelborth had been a teacher. Gustav didn't know him personally but had heard the man was a skilled fighter.

First Lieutenant Otto Leppla, an older officer, emerged from the train station's wreckage. Rolf and the other two commanders dismounted from their tanks to hear Leppla's briefing.

Gustav knew there would be no holding off the inevitable: the city would fall. But maybe Lieutenant Leppla had a plan? Maybe they could survive long enough to hear the call to retreat?

When Rolf returned, he was tight-lipped about the meeting, telling the driver only to follow Leppla.

Gustav could read Rolf like a book. He could tell something was wrong. Gustav looked behind the tank and saw the Panthers turning in the opposite direction. They were headed back toward the train station—away from the enemy.

"Where are they going?" Gustav asked.

"They're staying back to defend the bridge," Rolf said. He sounded dejected.

It didn't make sense to Gustav. The *Panthers* should have led the way toward the enemy, not them. Especially not in their outmoded Mark IV.

And yet, Bartelborth's tank was already off. With orders to make his stand here, his intent was obvious: the company commander was laying an ambush.

Leppla led them through Cologne's financial district. Riding in his open hatch, Gustav searched for the reassurance of friendly forces. He expected to find German soldiers buzzing behind barricades or around command posts. But the shocking reality was that there were hardly any German troops at all. The few scattered ones that he *did* see peered from windows in ones and twos or stood smoking in doorways. Many were former policemen or firemen with no experience as soldiers. Of the city's Volkssturm militia—a force composed of the few, mostly older, men who hadn't yet been conscripted, only about 60 out of 600 had showed up to fight. And those who did were armed with outdated foreign rifles and no training.

And where were the Waffen SS, the military men of Hitler's SS army? A climactic, suicidal battle for a major German city seemed like the perfect stage for those who answered only to the Nazi Party, and who believed that a death on a battlefield was an honorable one.

Yet the SS was nowhere to be found in Cologne.

Ever since a July 1944 assassination attempt on Hitler's life by senior German Army officers, the rift between the SS and the army had deepened. Hitler himself now favored his SS units over the army.

And where were the city's Nazi overseers?

They, too, were long gone. After they had burned the papers that mapped out their heinous crimes, and changed from their uniforms into civilian clothes, they had fled in boats to save themselves. Their gauleiter had joined them after posting a manifesto urging Cologne's citizens to resist until the bitter end.

Yes, Gustav realized in that moment. He and his fellow tankers were on their own.

The Mark IV had gone about half a mile when artillery began falling. By then they had reached the district known as the Gereon quarter. Each blast tossed sharp rubble into the air. Lietuenant Leppla pointed frantically to a five-story building on the right, by the four-way intersection. "Over there!" he gestured. This was where their tank could deploy.

The Mark IV's walls closed in as Gustav shut his hatch cover. The tank had never felt so small. Rolf guided the driver as he backed the tank up. If the Americans came hurrying down the four-way intersection in a rush to reach the train station, they would drive right into their ambush. The men kept their guns aimed and ready. There was nothing left to do but wait.

"How many Americans are coming?" a crewman asked Rolf.

Rolf said he didn't know.

"What are our orders?" another asked.

"Fight them," Rolf said.

Gustav couldn't believe his ears. It was as if someone just wanted to be rid of them. Worse yet, Rolf wasn't resisting in the least.

In every burned building he came across in Cologne, Rolf must have envisioned his beloved home city of Dresden. During the British and American firebombing campaigns against Dresden, it was believed that as many as 25,000 Germans had been killed. Rolf had not received any mail from home, so he assumed the worst: his family was dead and his home was demolished.

For a man with nothing left to lose, fighting to the bitter end seemed like a good way to die.

No one came or went through the empty intersection in front of Gustav.

He fiddled with his radio, but every channel hissed with static. He checked his machine gun to ensure that the ammunition belt was secure. It would be useless against an American tank, but it made him feel better nonetheless.

A voice in his head kept asking: At this point, why keep fighting? Clearly, they were going to lose. Perhaps, Gustav thought, what mattered now was *how* they lost.

There was no way to end the war, short of overthrowing the Nazi leadership, an impossible scenario to envision. As one soldier posited after the war, "This had been an undiscussable subject due to the Nazis among us who still had the power to terrorize us even up to the last day."

With the Red Army preparing for its final assault just forty-five miles from Berlin, Gustav and other soldiers clung to a forlorn, naïve hope. Maybe if they fought hard enough, the Western Allies would seek a peace treaty. Maybe the Allies would offer terms that wouldn't destroy the German people.

If that possibility failed, all that remained was their duty—to their company, to the brigade, to the army, and to their people.

That morning, about a mile from Gustav's position, Buck's platoon of doughs took cover behind a series of empty storefronts.

A German sniper was firing at another platoon. Buck shuddered at every bullet crack. Before the sniper appeared, Buck's morning had been off to a great start. As A-Company departed aboard tanks, Annemarie and her father waved at him from the sidewalk. Buck's squad chided him mercilessly, repeating Annemarie's words from their first meeting: "Buck, first American I see!"

A-Company had been making steady progress toward the Gereon quarter. But then this sniper had struck, sending everyone scrambling for cover.

Lieutenant Boom had a plan: the platoon would help the doughs locate the sniper. If they split up, they could catch him. Boom reminded the men not to venture too far from safety.

Buck and two men from a sister squad posted up in the nearest building, an abandoned flower shop. Boom led Janicki and the others away, dispersing them up and down the block. The hunt was on.

Rising in unison, Buck and the two other men peered over the last jagged shard of glass left in the windowpane. Withered flower petals scattered across the floor. Buck wanted to see the sniper before anyone else. He peered at a crumbling three-story factory across the street. Its windows were dark.

To Buck's left, Private First Class Robert Morries was also searching as he swept his carbine from side to side. A short nineteen-year-old with deep bags under his eyes, Morries had quit elementary school after third grade to help his mother and sister run the family farm in Peach Orchard, Missouri.

"I see him," Morries whispered. From the direction of Morries's gaze, Buck understood that the sniper had to be hiding on one of the factory's higher floors. Morries raised his carbine and aimed it there. But before he could get a shot off, the German fired first.

The bullet zipped under Morries's trigger hand, entering his shoulder. The impact knocked him to the floor. Buck and the other dough hit the ground to hide. They hollered for a medic. Buck asked Morries if he could move.

"Barely," came the reply.

Staying low, Buck and the other dough pulled the wounded man behind a shelf. Morries's head came to rest on Buck's thigh. His dark eyes stared through Buck to the ceiling.

A medic arrived and went to work. Using scissors, he cut off Morries's shirt, which revealed a jagged black hole in his shoulder that was seeping blood. Buck cringed.

"How bad is it?" Morries asked. The medic said it wasn't pretty, but that the wound wasn't bleeding badly, either. The explanation seemed to comfort Morries.

The medic sprinkled sulfa powder and was reaching for a bandage when blood suddenly began spurting from the wound like a fountain. The bullet must have pierced an artery wall.

The medic compressed the wound to stanch the bleeding, but the bandage turned crimson in no time. As the medic reached for another bandage, Morries began coughing. "Raise him up!" the medic shouted. Buck lifted Morries, cradling him in his arms. The young man was turning pale at an alarming rate.

More blood shot into the air when the medic swapped bandages. Buck could tell that Morries was slipping away. Morries looked up at Buck, gasped one last time, and abruptly closed his eyes. He would never return to that farm to see his mother, Cinda, or his sister, Clara May, again.

The medic tossed aside the bloody bandages and departed in disgust. Buck was horrified by Morries's lifeless face, still resting on his knee.

The other dough, Private Richard Baughn, wasted no time. Buck joined him as he crept back to the ledge beneath the window. They were both more determined than ever to catch this sniper, and eager for the same thing: revenge.

Baughn's round, ruddy face was clenched with anger. A little older than Buck at twenty-three, Baughn was a former factory worker from Oklahoma, where he had left his wife and daughter in the care of his parents.

Baughn swung his M1 above the ledge and took aim. Buck popped up beside him, once again affirming his reputation: *Shorty thinks he's invisible.* With his heart pounding and the blood thumping in his eardrums, Buck searched the empty windows for the glint of the sniper's scope. His fingers wrapped around his rifle's hand guard. He was ready. But he couldn't see any trace of the enemy.

Buck's stomach sank when he realized his error. They'd never see the sniper because he was probably set back in the shadows. But Buck and Baughn were in the light—*he* could see *them*.

That instant, another crack split the air and Baughn spun to the floor. Buck dropped to the floor and lay there, panting. Baughn rose to his hands and knees and crawled toward the back door through Morries's blood, leaving a crimson streak behind him. He dropped to the floor short of the doorway. Buck screamed for the medic, darted to Baughn's side, and rolled him over. Baughn was gurgling blood.

"Where are you hit?"

"I don't know."

Buck unclipped the man's harness and spotted a hole on the left side of Baughn's neck where the bullet had entered. On the other side, a massive lump swelled and turned black with blood.

The medic returned and cursed at the sight of another wounded man. He examined Baughn's wound, looked at Buck, and just shook his head. It was that bad. The medic shouted for a stretcher bearer.

Baughn held a hand over his eyes as they carried him away. He'd die the following day, never to return to Oklahoma to reunite with his wife and child.

Buck wanted nothing more than to kill that cowardly sniper. This time, he was ready. Just when he was about to sprint back to his position, a voice floated into his mind with a competing thought: *Don't.*

Buck focused on the streak of blood that pointed from Morries's corpse like an arrow to the shop's exit. The sniper hadn't fired since shooting Baughn. Would there be a third target?

Buck wouldn't give the stranger the satisfaction.

He turned on his heels to go warn Lieutenant Boom and the others—maybe they could handle the sniper together? He was done trying to win the war alone.

Buck left the flower shop a different person from the one who entered.

He wasn't "invisible" anymore.

Several hours later, sometime after noon

The Pershing led the way through Cologne's shattered buildings. Clarence held his eyes to his periscope. A dark boulevard lay ahead of them. At the end of it stood the church with its twin spires. Buildings towered overhead, but now only ghosts watched from their ornate sculpted balconies.

The Pershing passed an arrow-shaped sign nailed to a tree. It pointed to the bridge. Earley consulted his map. They were just a mile away, he alerted the crew. The men remained silent, dreading the countdown. Their orders were not just to reach the bridge—but to charge across it and take the other side.

This was a job for an entire company, not just four tanks. It was a suicide mission. The enemy would take out the few remaining tanks as they lumbered across the bridge—if it didn't blow up beneath them, that is. Clarence yearned for the tank to go slower. The only thing awaiting them was certain death.

At one p.m., a distant explosion ripped the air. It was followed by the groan of crumpling steel.

When Earley saw a plume of gray smoke rising from behind the cathedral's twin spires, he knew exactly what it was: the Germans had *demolished* the Hohenzollern Bridge.

The Pershing stopped abruptly after the explosion. Inside, Clarence flashed DeRiggi a smile. Sighs of relief and outpourings of joy could be heard throughout the tank. Crews were also celebrating in Chuck Miller's tank and on down the line of their column. The suicide mission to the bridge was over, it seemed. They had been spared. Or had they?

Right then, Earley got a radio message from headquarters. The units were still ordered to reach Germany's sacred river. They were to keep going to the Rhine.

The crew groaned and cursed. The death march was still on. Earley reminded his men to remain alert, no matter what. After all, any German soldiers left behind had just lost their route out of Cologne. With their backs to the wall, they would probably fight for their lives.

Gloomily, Clarence gazed far and wide across Cologne as he scanned with his 6x zoom sight. Tall buildings had been smashed to pieces, as if a giant had lumbered through. With walls shorn away, he could see inside an empty office where employees had once typed. Scanning to the side, he saw the wallpaper in an apartment and a staircase climbing to a missing floor.

The buildings appeared deserted. But what about the street?

Clarence had been told that anything on wheels belonged to the German military.

With no need to distinguish between friend and foe, the rules of engagement were simple: *Shoot anything that moves.*

The Pershing held back in the shadows as the men plotted their next move.

Rolf was restless in the turret. He wanted to peek around the corner, but the five-story building to his right obstructed his view.

Where were the Americans coming from? Would it be from across the four-way intersection? Would they come in ones and twos, or in a huge wave?

There was only one way to find out. Rolf ordered the driver to bring the tank forward, just enough for him to try to catch a glimpse. Gustav tensed behind his gun. This sounded like a truly terrible idea. Still, the driver put the tank in gear, drove forward, and idled.

Above the turret, Rolf cursed and ordered a hasty retreat. He didn't like what he saw: a lone American tank.

"Did they see us?" his crew asked frantically.

Rolf wasn't sure.

"A Sherman?"

Rolf didn't have an answer for his men. The tank he had seen sure didn't look like a Sherman. In fact, it matched nothing familiar to him from the American arsenal.

• • •

Clarence cursed his bad luck.

He had turned the turret far to the right when he caught a brief glimpse of a German tank pulling out on his left. He had swung the 90mm gun toward the enemy, but the turret wasn't fast enough. The enemy tank had managed to quickly back-pedal from his view.

It was a German tank, there was no question of it. But Clarence didn't know what type.

Earley studied the area with binoculars. "You're sure?" he asked Clarence.

"Trust me," Clarence said. "He's hiding behind that building."

Earley radioed the Shermans to stay back.

Clarence set the reticle where he'd last seen the tank.

Try that again.

His index finger gently wrapped the trigger.

Shaking with terror, Gustav pressed an eye to his gunsight.

They were sitting ducks. Surely the American tank had spot-ted them.

Gustav angled his MG 34 machine gun toward the inter-section, as close to the enemy as he could get it. Across the street lay a pile of rubble—perfect cover for a bazooka man.

Gustav's scope was narrower than the width of his thumb, and the sight was scratched. He couldn't be sure, but he swore he saw rifle muzzles poking above the rubble. He fired a pan-icked burst or two. Green tracers cut the air above the pile, stir-ring up a halo of dust.

"What is it?" Rolf asked.

Gustav told him what he thought he saw.

"Then fire like you mean it!" Rolf said.

Gustav squeezed the trigger and swept the gun from side to side, sending a hail of bullets at the pile itself, hoping to shatter bricks and fling deadly splinters in the enemy's direction.

Green tracers weaved through the debris.

Clarence was miffed by what he was seeing downrange.

The Germans were firing a hose of green tracers at a pile of rubble. Either the enemy was spooked or this was an attempt to create a distraction.

Clarence wouldn't allow himself to blink. After all, the German tank could dart out at any moment and catch them by surprise. The rattle of the idling engine drowned out any other noise in his ears.

Sweat poured down the leather side flaps of his tanker helmet and beneath his wool shirt and jacket. No one moved or whispered. The intercom twitched with static.

Clarence was ready to fire at the drop of a hat.

Meanwhile, a black Opel P4 car raced toward the massive intersection. Its wheels bounced on the rutted street and stirred a swirl of dust in its wake.

In the passenger's seat rode twenty-six-year-old Katharina Esser.

Brunette locks draped her shoulders, and flat eyebrows framed her gentle brown eyes. She was dressed as if for a journey, wearing a red jacket and pants tucked into boots.

The third of four sisters, "Kathi" was a nurturer. Before the evacuations, she had cared for her sickly father and could be found in the park with her nieces and nephews, pushing them on their scooters. She worked at a small grocery store in Cologne's Old Town.

Forty-year-old Michael Delling, the grocery store's owner and Kathi's boss, sat beside her, gripping the wheel of the speeding car. He was permitted to use the car to get around the shut-down city, but strictly for business. As a grocer, he was considered an essential worker.

But today's was no pickup or delivery run.

Rather than awaiting liberation by foreign troops, Delling and Kathi were making a run for the bridge.

Either they hadn't heard the noise of the Hohenzollern Bridge's collapse, or they had and still harbored hope that it might be passable.

Clarence was peering straight across the intersection when the sudden motion took him by surprise. A black blur crossed into his sight line.

"Staff car!" Earley shouted.

Sure enough, a black car darted into the intersection at top speed. Instinctively, Clarence mashed the machine gun's trigger. The coaxial machine gun hammered, shattering the silence that had fallen over the tank.

Fiery orange bolts zipped downrange after the car. Near misses blazed past the car and skipped from the street, stirring the dust.

Clarence chased the fleeting target's tail end with the reticle. Just before his bullets could catch it, the car swung a hard left turn toward the German tank.

It was getting away.

Clarence reversed the turret's motion. He clamped the trigger, snapping a desperate whip of fire after the car. It veered out of control as his tracers cut the air.

Gustav flinched at the orange shafts of light that slanted in front of his tank.

"Get ready!" Rolf said.

Gustav gritted his teeth and gripped his machine gun. If it was the American tank, he would go down shooting.

Gustav clenched the trigger. The machine gun spat a steady stitch of green.

Green tracers interweaved with orange ones. The car drove through the flaming crosshatch. The rear window shattered before the car veered into the nearest curb.

Gustav released the trigger. Heat rose from the sizzling barrel, making his line of sight wavy. When the haze had cleared, Gustav peered at the scene with disbelief.

A black car was stopped and its driver was slumped over the wheel, dead.

Gustav was outraged. *Why would anyone drive through a battle!* Military or civilian, the person shouldn't have been there.

A door swung open from the passenger's side and a body crumpled to the street.

Gustav swore he saw a fling of curly brown hair.

A woman?

Clarence, too, saw the car's door swing open, but he couldn't see past the rubble. He wasn't sure if he'd hit the car or it had pulled over on its own. Besides, at that moment, he had more pressing concerns. He had seen the green tracers. The German tank was still there, lingering somewhere just beyond his sight.

Clarence faced a life-or-death decision. With orders to keep going to the Rhine, they couldn't just sit around waiting for the enemy. And yet . . . if they rolled forward, the German tank would surely get the first shot, an advantage that Clarence was reluctant to concede. He had to do something.

"Ears," Clarence said, which served as a warning to the crew that he was about to fire. He set the reticle low on the building, where he estimated the enemy tank was hiding.

With a deafening crack, Clarence blasted a warhead downrange. The shell cut straight through the building, leaving behind a smoking hole. Bricks tumbled down from a higher floor.

"No effect," Earley reported.

DeRiggi threw another shell into the breech and Clarence fired again.

No sign of a hit this time either, just more falling bricks. The building was obviously unstable after suffering damage in air raids. Clarence looked closer. A predictable pattern was forming after each shot, of bricks plunging from the building's higher stories.

The bricks. They were falling in the direction of the enemy tank.

Clarence fired a third time. "Keep 'em coming!" he urged DeRiggi.

Earley remained silent atop the turret. He could tell Clarence was up to something. But what, exactly? That remained to be seen.

Smoking shell casings piled up on the turret floor as Clarence repeatedly punched holes in the same wall.

Dust billowed from the building's ground floor. Clarence fired again and again. A pile of bricks cascaded down the façade. The entire structure was crumbling. A four-story wall wobbled before losing its support and falling backward. With a final well-placed shot, the upper floors of the building imploded in an avalanche of bricks.

Earley couldn't believe his eyes. Clarence had cut the building practically in half.

Gustav braced his hands over his head as he crouched in the darkness. The avalanche from the collapsing building had come crashing down. A trickle of bricks continued to slam the ceiling above him. Dust streamed inside, dimming any trace of light. The men hacked and coughed.

As soon as they had their wits about them again, the crew

flew into a panic. Surely the American tank was coming to finish them off.

The German driver backed the tank behind the collapsed building, trying to hide. The gunner tested the turret, but it made a grinding sound and wouldn't budge. There were probably bricks wedged between it and the hull.

Gustav tried to open his hatch. The cover wouldn't move an inch. He grunted and pressed harder. His arms quivered from the immense effort, but the hatch was weighed down by bricks. He was trapped. Again.

His breath quickened. The walls seemed to tighten. He put his shoulder against the cover and pushed with all his might. The bricks gave way and the hatch flung open. Gustav sucked in the fresh air and glanced wildly about. But since he wasn't sure where the Americans were, he quickly sank back into the tank and shut the hatch.

Rolf had emerged from the turret. "The bridge is gone," he called.

No. Gustav didn't believe it. He pressed the commander for answers. A civilian had told Rolf the news on good authority. Rolf and his crew had simply failed to hear the explosion over the engine's noise.

It took a moment for the enormity of the news to sink in. Normally quiet and obedient, Gustav felt a new sensation stirring—anger. Anger at his fellow German soldiers for looking out for themselves and leaving everyone else in a dangerous, even deadly corner. He began trembling.

Our own guys did this! They abandoned us!

One of the crewmen proposed a new course of action. He suggested that they back the tank into a cross street and let the Americans come to them. An ambush.

"What are we supposed to do," Rolf said, "throw bricks at them?"

The gunner reminded Rolf that they could still fire forward. Or maybe they could even get a side shot on an American tank.

Gustav couldn't believe it. They wanted to *keep* fighting? Even if they were totally overpowered and had no backup? Even if they were now left behind in Cologne, with no way to escape?

A third crewman was in agreement with the suicidal plan.

By now, Gustav was fuming. He'd just shot a car and might have killed innocent people. Fellow Germans. And now his crew was petitioning to trade their lives—and his—for the chance to kill some lone American tank crew.

"This is senseless!" Gustav blurted out.

A crewman snapped at him, reminding him of their orders.

There was no reasoning with the others, so Gustav spoke directly to Rolf. "What do we owe them anymore?" he said. "They sent us here to die!"

Rolf remained silent. He was waffling, having already resigned himself to an honorable death in his tank.

But it didn't matter. Gustav had made his decision. Yes, he valued his duty to his family, to his comrades, and to his countrymen. But he also had a duty to himself.

Rolf never issued an order to abandon the tank, but that didn't stop Gustav. He was finished being a pawn for Nazi

Germany. He flung open his hatch cover and made one last appeal to Rolf, his only friend left in the war.

"Come on, Rolf! Why get killed for nothing?" With that, Gustav tore off his headset and lifted himself from the tank.

Gustav bolted behind the tank to the nearest street corner but then hesitated. He was unsure which way to run or what to do next. Freedom was a fresh sensation.

Rolf peered out from the turret and spotted Gustav. In one swift motion, Rolf pushed himself up and jumped down to the street. Gustav braced himself as Rolf dashed after him. He wasn't sure whether his friend had come to punish him or join him.

"Let's go," Rolf said. He grabbed Gustav's arm and pulled him down a street in a new direction. A few civilians were standing in the entrance of a building, motioning for the duo to join them.

Gustav and Rolf ran toward the building for shelter.

Behind them, the Mark IV pulled a U-turn in the rubble and plunged into a cross street without them.

The tank—and the three men who chose to remain aboard— would never be seen again.

Clarence's plan had worked—the intersection was safely behind them.

He fixed his aim far beyond, in the direction of St. Gereon's Basilica, a Catholic church, ready for any threat that might come around the bend.

Doughs ducked around the fallen building, searching in vain for a buried enemy tank under the rubble. Clarence felt fortunate that he had seen the German tank at all. The thought of what would have happened had they just driven by it sent a shiver down his spine.

The Pershing idled behind the bullet-riddled black car that Clarence had shot at. Three medics rushed to the car. The driver was dead from a head shot, but there was someone else lying by the passenger side.

The medics rolled the victim over and Clarence swore he saw a flash of long, curly hair. But it happened so quickly, he wondered if his eyes had deceived him. He felt a pit open up in the depths of his stomach.

Did I shoot a woman?

His mind swirled with panic. Was she hurt badly? What was she doing there in the first place? Then, he remembered. This was Cologne. Didn't only Nazis have cars here?

To drive through a gunfight, the woman and her driver had to be running from something. Were they a pair of Nazi overseers who had waited too long to get out? Was he a general and she his mistress?

Clarence absolved himself of any guilt.

Whoever she was, she had to be one of the bad guys.

Behind the Pershing, Chuck Miller sat in his Sherman and peered through his telescopic sight at the crashed black car.

The medics had given up. It was hopeless. With grim looks

on their faces, they stood and stepped away, revealing the patient they had struggled to save—a young woman. One medic took a long coat from the car. He tenderly covered her up to the shoulders before departing to aid someone else in need.

The woman's face was turned toward Chuck. Her eyes were glassy and distant. She reminded him of one of his sisters, and he wondered if she was already dead.

Then, she blinked.

Chuck reeled back from his telescopic sight, horrified and guilt-stricken. It felt as if she had caught him looking, watching her die.

He couldn't tell his friend Clarence, he wouldn't, not with the darkest depths of Cologne—a place where no American crew wanted to go—still ahead. That man at the Pershing's gun was Chuck's best hope of ever reaching home again. Chuck had seen enough of this place to know it.

In the Fortress City, anything could be lurking around the next corner.

CHAPTER 16

THE MONSTER

Later that afternoon, around two p.m.
COLOGNE

A pair of Shermans crept down a narrow street, moving toward a bright light. The men inside could partly see the cathedral and its square at the end of the block. They could see some of the railroad station as well. Everything they'd fought for was finally within reach. But they weren't out of the woods yet. These last yards were treacherous.

The final push to the Rhine was really a job for the Pershing. The Super Tank had fallen behind after the fight at the intersection, though. So now the task fell to the Shermans of F-Company.

The plan was this: After F-Company seized the cathedral, the Stuart tanks of B-Company would make a run for the Rhine. Together they would share the glory as the conquerors of Cologne.

But first, they had to get past this street—which was blocked by a landslide of debris from a collapsed building.

The lead Sherman stopped beneath a street clock. Its hands

had frozen in the six o'clock position. The second Sherman pulled up parallel. From the lead tank's turret, Second Lieutenant Karl Kellner searched for a way forward.

If anyone might be worthy of reaching the cathedral first, it was Kellner. He'd already received a Silver Star for his actions in Normandy, France. But the road ahead was impassible. Kellner had no choice other than to call for a bulldozer tank. The triumph would have to wait.

Just then, a green bolt of German tank fire rained through the ruins of a building. It slammed into the gun shield of Kellner's Sherman, spraying shrapnel into the gunner's legs inside. Then came a second green bolt. Kellner's Sherman ruptured from the shell. Hatch covers burst open from turret to bow.

Desperate to escape the line of fire, the second Sherman veered backward. They pulled up behind a building, hiding from the assailant. The crew came pouring out.

Thin, steamy smoke rose from Kellner's Sherman. He emerged from the turret bareheaded. He dropped his rifle, falling to the engine deck. His left leg had been violently amputated at the knee. The stump was smoking.

Kellner rolled back across the engine deck before stopping at the edge. With only one leg to land on, it would be a long fall. Soldiers who were nearby rushed forward almost in unison to lend a hand. Together, they carried Kellner to safety before resting him on a pile of rubble.

Once Kellner's leg was elevated, a tanker removed Kellner's shirt and tied it around his thigh in an attempt to stem the bleeding. But this remedy was too little, too late. Kellner died in his fellow soldier's arms.

The U.S. Department of War would soon be wiring a telegram to Kellner's parents and his fiancée, Cecelia, to tell them that Karl had been killed in action, "somewhere in Germany."

Inside the turret, Kellner's loader lay in pieces. And his driver, Private First Class Julian Patrick, was dead at the tank's helm.

The smooth rattle of a German tank approaching from the square sent the survivors running.

The killer was approaching.

The Panther trundled past the cathedral. It stopped in the corner of the square, facing the derelict Shermans head-on.

The German tank had fired before emerging from the shadows, a way of staking its claim on the battlefield. The light revealed the tank's commander. Bartelborth stood tall in the turret. Without a bridge to defend, German soldiers were desperately swimming over the Rhine, using stray doors and planks as rafts to cross to friendly lines. But Bartelborth and his crew had chosen a different course. Inside the Panther, they had stayed to fight to the death.

One street over, the Pershing idled. Clarence and the crew followed the flurry of radio transmissions. The last they'd heard, doughs had been dispatched to pursue the enemy tank.

Earley told Clarence to assume command. He was going to investigate on foot.

"What?"

It was foolhardy. Clarence reminded Earley that there were no friendly troops ahead; the Pershing *was* the front line. But Earley couldn't be swayed. He wanted to see what they were up against with his own two eyes.

A shout from outside the Pershing rose above the engine's jangle. "Hey, Bob!"

Earley rose from the hatch and saw his friend Tech Sergeant Jim Bates, clutching a small motion-picture camera. With thick cheeks and dark hair, twenty-eight-year-old Jim Bates was a small, scrappy combat cameraman. Bates had filmed battles throughout the war, and he thrived amid danger. It was his fearlessness that made his films a cut above others'.

Earley lowered himself from the Pershing to greet his friend. "Jim, let's go down and see what we can see on that tank," he said. "I don't know what we're going to run into—we may never get back."

Earley and Bates headed forward. Bates brought his small camera along. They crept down the block through a no-man's-land. Propaganda posters decorated the buildings and walls. At the end of the street, on the left, the duo approached the German Labor Front Building, which was home to the nation's trade unions. Earley and Bates ducked inside. If they went any farther, the Panther might see them.

From the mezzanine-level windows, they saw it: two streets over, the yellow Panther idled in the corner of the bright square. Its gun was still, ominously, pointed directly at Kellner's destroyed Sherman.

And there, Earley saw his opportunity.

He laid out his plan to Bates: the Pershing would continue up the street, nose into the intersection, and blindside the Panther with a side shot.

"You get all ready for it," he told Bates. The idea that this feat could be captured on film was thrilling. "When you hear me coming . . . you'll know where I am."

As Earley went back to his tank, Bates took the stairs higher to position himself for the best-possible view of the daring attempt. He steadied his camera out the window and prepared to capture the action.

It was time to settle a longstanding question: Could an American tank finally stand on equal footing against a Panther?

The answer was long overdue.

Inside the Panther, the minutes felt like hours. The crew peered through their periscopes, searching for the enemy. The thrum of the engine drowned out their thoughts.

Second Lieutenant Wilhelm Bartelborth, Gustav's former company commander, had been fighting in tanks since 1941 and had even served a stint as an instructor. Maybe it was experience. Maybe it was instinct. But a sixth sense told Bartelborth that the Americans might come at him from an unexpected direction.

Leaving his Panther's hull facing forward, Bartelborth ordered the gunner to turn the turret to the right—toward an entirely empty street.

• • •

From his third-story window, Bates saw the Panther's turret turning toward him. Clutching his camera, he hit the floor, terrified. Had the German tank commander seen him? Cautiously, he raised himself up to take a peek below. What he saw filled him with dread: the Panther's super-velocity gun was aimed at street level—and facing the exact spot where Earley said he would pull out.

The tank had Bates trapped.

There was no walking out the front door. There was no time to warn his friend. Even if he screamed at the top of his lungs, it wouldn't do any good.

The Pershing was about to roll into an ambush.

The sound of the Panther reverberated through the empty streets. Buck and the rest of his platoon followed Lieutenant Boom toward its echo. One dough clutched a bazooka; another carried shells. The tank sounded close.

Boom led the men inside the nearest building. A shot fired from a window might be just the thing to knock the Germans off guard. Hopefully, they would never see it coming.

The squad ran through the empty building, bounding up its rubble-filled stairs. At each floor they came to, a dough darted to a window to survey their surroundings. And after each floor, the report was the same: "No Panther!" They still didn't have a shot.

Lieutenant Boom led the men higher.

As he chased the pounding footsteps in front of him, Buck's

mind was still back in the flower shop. By the time A-Company had converged on the building the German sniper had been hiding in, the man had escaped—thankfully without shooting anyone else. Janicki had tried to console Buck by reminding him, "It's not your fault. Your head was sticking up next to theirs."

But that wasn't the point.

Buck was angry with himself because he should have known better. He should never have gone back to that window a second time, let alone contemplated a *third* attempt. He had learned his lesson. If he was going to survive this war, it was time to start thinking like a veteran.

Before Buck and his crew knew it, they'd checked all the floors of the buildings. And still they couldn't see the German tank to shoot at. That was when they noticed the attic. It was the highest vantage point in the building. Someone would have to go up there—and that someone would have to be lightweight. Everyone expectantly turned to Buck.

Buck wanted to groan. He'd never escape the role of first scout now. He had never fired a bazooka before.

Boom motioned for him to climb up there.

"Fine," Buck said. He handed over his rifle. The Panther had whacked two American tanks and someone had to stop it, even though Buck wished it weren't him. Boom helped push him up into the attic space.

The bazooka had already been loaded when it was passed up to Buck. Buck armed the weapon and dropped to his belly. He shinnied forward while sliding the bazooka alongside him.

As soon as he propped open the window, the cacophonous noise of the Panther flooded the attic. From his perch, he was above the rooftops and eye-level with the cathedral.

Buck looked down on an empty street and cursed.

They were a block too far.

A sound rose from below. It was the mechanical noise of another tank approaching. Buck was horrified. This one was an American tank, moving forward toward the idling Panther. But he and the doughs hadn't destroyed the Panther yet. They needed more time. *Didn't anyone tell the men in the tank?*

Buck cringed at the noise as it came closer. It sounded like an American crew driving to their deaths.

Earley radioed instructions for the Shermans to hold back. The plan was simple. They would edge into the intersection and then it would be Clarence's show. The Pershing would handle this on its own.

"I'll go for a hull shot," Clarence volunteered. It was the largest target, so there would be less chance of missing.

"Shoot wherever you want," Earley said. "He's just sitting there like he owns the place."

Earley had cause for confidence. Even a 75 Sherman could knock out a Panther from broadside.

The intersection was fast approaching.

Across the turret, DeRiggi cradled a 24-pound T33 armor-piercing shell, poised for a speedy reload.

Clarence announced to the driver, Woody McVey, that he

was pre-positioning the gun. "Keep us on a line, Woody," he added. Then he lowered the reticle to where the enemy tank would be sitting and adjusted the 15.5-foot barrel.

And so, the two armored tanks blindly searched for each other. One, a Pershing with its gun pointed to the right, going up a street and preparing to breach its corner. The other, a stationary Panther with its gun targeting the very intersection the Pershing was heading toward.

McVey fed the tank more gas. The Pershing quickly gained speed.

Clarence set his eyes to the periscope for the widest possible view. *Don't miss.* The way Clarence saw it, it came down to them or his tank family. And with his family's lives in his hands, he wasn't taking any chances.

From inside the Pershing, Smokey Davis saw the Panther first. The crew hadn't known that the enemy tank was sitting right there in the intersection, bathed in light. Smokey cried out in terror, helplessly.

McVey panicked. He stomped on the gas, sending the Pershing lurching even farther into the intersection and harm's way.

The crew gasped.

Clarence's heart seized as the Panther slid into his sights. Between the rubble and the dangling streetcar lines, all he saw was the black hole of its muzzle.

Inside the Panther, Bartelborth saw the dark, blurry vehicle leap from the shadowy street. The green tank was low and sleek, with strong frontal armor. This was no Sherman, he realized. Then how could it possibly be the Americans?

"Stop!" Bartelborth screamed to his gunner. "That's one of ours!"

Clarence had no time to aim. There wasn't even time for the tank to stop. There was no time for anything. The reticle rested on the Panther, and that would have to be good enough.

Clarence fired. The 90mm's muzzle flash illuminated the shadows.

Earley saw it all from his perch above the turret.

An orange bolt streaked like a flame, then punched into the Panther's engine bay. Sparks flew, followed by a crack that sounded like lightning. Dust swirled from the rubble. Behind the cloudy tentacles came flames licking from the Panther's engine.

The commander's hatch slid open, releasing a gush of smoke from the Panther. The German commander wiggled free from the turret and jumped to the ground. The driver rolled over his side of the hull to safety.

Inside the Pershing, Clarence couldn't even tell if he had hit the Panther. The 90mm's blast had stirred up so much dust that the Panther appeared to be just an outline, pointy and threatening, with its gun still angled at him.

"Another T33!" Clarence demanded.

DeRiggi slammed another shell into the breech. Clarence shifted his aim forward. His finger squeezed the trigger. Through the dusty gloom, another burst of sparks split sidelong from the Panther. The tank had been struck.

"Hit!" Earley yelled.

The holes in the Panther's hull began glowing with light. A fire was rapidly spreading along the length of the tank—from the rear to the front.

A disoriented German crewman pushed himself up from the turret and flopped over the Panther's side. Another dove from the loader's rear hatch with his uniform ablaze. They all scattered behind the wall of the tank.

Meanwhile, inside the Pershing, Clarence called for another armor-piercing shell. Was this butchery? An excessive use of force? The Panther's gun was still pointed at Clarence and his crew. If a German crewman reached the trigger in his last gasp, he could still kill them all. Clarence would not let that happen. The dust was settling, and this time he took aim. He lowered the reticle to the Panther's wheels and hull.

His finger crushed the trigger. In a blinding flash, the shell punched through the Panther's heart and straight out the other side with the sound of a metallic slice.

This time, Clarence saw it all.

A volcano seemed to surge from the turret. The front hatch covers blasted open, and flames stood where men once sat. The fire soared twice the height of the tank as it roared like a blowtorch. Clarence swore he felt heat around his eyes.

All three shell holes in the Panther's flank glowed and pulsed as fire consumed the tank's interior. The gunner's optical sight flickered at Clarence like a cyclops's eye.

From above, Earley had seen enough: "Driver, reverse!"

The engine growled as the Pershing rolled backward into the shadows. The turret smelled harsh from the empty shell casings.

DeRiggi opened a hatch and tossed them out. One. Two. Three casings clanked on the street.

The Pershing stopped. The crew listened. Clarence sat back from the periscope, still stunned by the previous forty or fifty seconds of furious action. *Did that really happen?*

DeRiggi, Smokey Davis, and McVey sat quiet, in awe of Clarence's abilities. Earley sank into his seat and leaned forward to catch his breath as if he was going to be sick. No one had been more shocked at the sight of the Panther's barrel than he was.

Earley laid a hand on Clarence's shoulder.

After some time, Clarence broke the silence in the tank. "That was close," he said.

"Really close," DeRiggi agreed.

Clarence returned to his periscope, scanning for threats. Over the rooftops, the Panther's smoke rose like ash from Mount Vesuvius.

It was about three p.m. when a figure emerged from the German Labor Front Building before making a mad dash toward the Pershing.

It was the cameraman, Jim Bates. He shouted up to Earley, "I think I got it!"

"What?" Earley responded quizzically.

Despite the 90mm's shock waves rattling his camera, Bates had filmed the duel between the two tanks. He needed just one last shot: a picture of the Pershing's crew.

"It'll take less than a minute," Bates promised.

Earley checked his surroundings. The other three Shermans had pulled up behind the Pershing. He figured it was safe enough, so he gathered the young men. Behind them stood pitted columns and blown-in windows.

Bates began filming.

McVey looked past the camera, his eyes casting a faraway stare. Smokey chomped a cigarette. Earley looked nothing short of disturbed. Bates told him to tip back his helmet—the shadows were hiding his face. DeRiggi squeezed a tight grin and Clarence cast a hesitant smile.

True to his word, Bates capped the camera's lens just shy of a minute after he started filming.

The tankers could go back to war.

The four American tanks were rolling toward the remains of the Hohenzollern Bridge. The Pershing and the three Shermans searched for any remaining signs of the enemy.

Nothing. The murky Rhine streamed around the ramshackled bridge. The train station nearby was cold and cavernous. And the cathedral was now the headstone to a lifeless city.

Earley made the call at 3:10 p.m. His patrol had reached Germany's sacred river. "Any further and we'll be swimming."

Before he could release the Transmit button, the crew erupted in shouts of joy. Clarence and DeRiggi, McVey and Smokey, everyone whooped and hollered and looked for one another to shake hands. During his crew's celebration, Earley remained above the turret, still tangled in the emotion of their close call.

Clarence sat back in his seat, stunned.

Cologne was theirs.

Later that evening

Soon after fleeing their tank, Gustav and Rolf had found their way to a nearby building to hide out in. There were others hiding out too, mostly locals. People were chatting nearby, expressing their relief that the war would soon be over. The locals had shared their bread and schnapps with the tankers to calm their nerves. Still, Gustav remained on edge. It was only a matter of time before the Americans searched this block and found them. And then what?

The wait was torturous. What worried Gustav the most was the Panzer Wrap uniform that he wore beneath his camouflaged coveralls. Like many Wehrmacht tankers before him, the black uniform and silver skull patches on the collar— which resembled those of Hitler's SS—now made him a target. Would his captors confuse him with an SS man and shoot him on sight?

Gustav thought of tearing off the skull emblems but stopped short of doing so. It could be worse if the Americans thought he was hiding something. He hoped his captors would know the difference between the uniforms.

Gustav remembered how his family had treated "their" prisoner of war. Because of manpower shortages in Germany while the men were away at war, every farm in Gustav's region was assigned a POW laborer. One day, a young Russian appeared on the family's doorstep. He had a shaved head and still wore his Red Army uniform on his slim frame.

Gustav had worked his family's fields with the Russian. Each night, after a long day of toil, authorities would collect the POW to take him back to his prison camp. But first, the farmer's family was to serve him supper.

The Nazis had a strict rule: POWs could not, under any circumstances, eat at the same table as the farmers "hosting" them. But Gustav's mother, Mina, wouldn't have it. The young Russian was as hard a worker as the rest of them. So, each night she prepared a side table, complete with a full set of cutlery, just in case the authorities came knocking. And each night, the young Russian dined at the same table as the family.

Now, in the cellar, Gustav, Rolf, and the others heard shouts from the street. Someone went to investigate. The Americans were approaching. Rather than endanger the local people by their presence, Gustav and Rolf knew it was their time to surrender.

"Bubi." Rolf stopped Gustav at the top of the steps and wished him luck, for whatever the future held for him.

Outside, twilight had settled across Cologne. In the fading light, Gustav and Rolf raised their hands in a sign of surrender. Two American doughs cradled rifles across the street. As they approached their captors, Rolf spoke in English. The effect was disarming, and the Americans relaxed. They searched the Germans' pockets and took Gustav's compass.

The doughs passed Gustav and Rolf off to an American

intelligence officer who spoke German. The officer asked them how many tanks the Germans had remaining in Cologne.

"Three tanks in the center," Rolf said. That was all he knew.

At this point, there was nothing to hide. Throughout Cologne, in a seemingly endless trickle, German soldiers were emerging from hiding places. Others would wait for the Allies to find them. Among the crew in the Panther that Clarence had destroyed, Bartelborth had suffered leg wounds and his gunner had burns on his face. A third crewman lay nearby in a charred uniform. He appeared to be dying but would ultimately pull through. The remainder of their crew was missing.

There, in the abandoned building, an American officer asked Gustav and Rolf for their *Wehrpässe,* or soldier's identification booklets. The officer thumbed through Gustav's before glancing up at him. "So you belong to the 'Fire Department of the West'?"

Unsure of how he should react, Gustav just smiled and nodded. At Gustav's response, the officer's demeanor flipped like a light switch. He punched Gustav in the side of the face. Gustav staggered from the blow and came back nursing his cheek. This time he remained tight-lipped.

The doughs led Gustav and Rolf to the ruins of the Gereon Hotel. It was serving as a makeshift holding space for some of the 326 Germans who would surrender to Spearhead that day. There, the men sat in a corridor, opposite a guard with a flashlight.

That night, Gustav's mind felt haunted. The same images from earlier that day replayed over and over. A car door swinging open. A woman's hair unfurling. He still couldn't figure out what she was doing in the middle of a battle. It made no sense but troubled him regardless.

Had he shot her? Or had the American gunner?

Perhaps he'd never know.

And perhaps that was for the best.

CHAPTER 17

THE CONQUERORS

That next morning, March 7, 1945
COLOGNE

At the crack of dawn the following morning, Clarence sneaked toward the cathedral. Throughout yesterday's battle, he'd gazed at its jagged façade from his turret. Now, he wanted to see what lay within.

The towering spires looked majestic in the light of a new day. Clarence crossed the church square. Entry into the cathedral was forbidden right now. No one guarding the front doors, though. Cautiously, he walked inside.

The stained glass had been removed, the pews were gone, and rubble lay where people once had prayed. But even in the cathedral's diminished state, when the sun streamed down on the altar, it was a humbling sight.

Clarence removed his cap.

There was one last item that he wanted to cross off his list. He had to see the city he had helped liberate.

After climbing 500 steps to the top, Clarence gazed over the ruined city from the northern spire. He simply spoke to God, offering thanks for bringing him through his journey this far.

• • •

Word of the American triumph over the Panther traveled quickly. Every newsman wanted to talk to the heroes of Cologne. Later that morning, war reporters encircled the Pershing. The frenzy was highest around Clarence.

One journalist was writing a segment about the defeat of the Panther called "Killing a Monster." Everyone's questions boiled down to "How did you defeat it?"

The honest answer was that Clarence didn't know. All the attention made him nervous. The Panther had had them cornered, but for some reason the German gunner didn't pull the trigger. The victory was a mystery to Clarence. But how could he tell them that? "It was him or me. I just shot first," he told the reporters.

In the course of the interview, someone asked, "What are you looking forward to when this is over?"

Clarence and his comrades often dreamed about where life would take them after the fighting was over. Before the war, Bob Earley had been a machinist in an aircraft factory, but now he dreamed of owning a quiet farm in Minnesota. Chuck Miller simply wanted to buy a car. And Clarence, who had never had much growing up, dreamed simple dreams.

He harbored no illusions about the future. He told them he just wanted to get a factory job when he returned home. He hoped he might someday become a manager, so he wouldn't be subject to someone else's orders for the rest of his life.

That answer didn't satisfy the newspapermen. When the reporters pressed him, Clarence reminisced about an even simpler pleasure. "I just want to get this thing over with," he said, "so I can get back to roller-skating at Graver's."

That answer gave everyone a chuckle.

Later that morning, Clarence followed Smokey across the cathedral square. He had to hustle to keep up. The bow gunner was practically running.

Smokey and DeRiggi had caught a whiff of something lootworthy across the square in the Dom Hotel, a renowned, fancy place. DeRiggi was already there.

Clarence's pace slowed as they passed by the now-destroyed Panther on their way to the hotel. Even though the fire had finally gone out that morning, the tank still looked like a glowing ember—black and charred on top and orange everywhere else.

Smokey powered past the derelict tank without a second thought. But Clarence gave its burned-out shell a wide berth. A "coffin on wheels" in the words of the cameraman Jim Bates, it had only one man—the radio operator/gunner—dead inside. But Clarence assumed the worst. He believed the entire German crew had died in there but wouldn't dare take a look to confirm his suspicions.

That could have been us. Clarence shivered at the thought.

When they reached the once-palatial Dom Hotel, it was in ruins. An entryway of classical columns stood intact, but bombs had scooped out several floors. The roof's Byzantine domes had been hammered into new shapes.

Clarence followed Smokey down into the basement. The

temperature dropped as they descended; then came jubilant voices and sounds of breaking glass.

Clarence and Smokey stepped into a vast wine cellar with walls like a castle's. Everywhere they could see was stacked with bottles of wine that stretched from floor to ceiling, and a flurry of Easy Company tankers were going rack to rack, shuttling bottles into wooden cases as fast as they could. They wanted to grab as much as they could before officers arrived and ruined the fun.

Clarence joined in. His boots crunched broken glass and stuck to patches of a syrupy liquid as he waded through the cellar.

A religiously devout tanker lamented that they were stealing. But his laments didn't stop him from filling a crate of his own with bottles.

Upstairs in the hotel, Clarence opened the door to a suite and set his full case of alcohol aside. Exhaustion had taken him by surprise. The hotel bed was strewn with debris from the ceiling, so he collapsed on a couch. The cathedral filled his view through a massive shattered window.

After more than 221 days in combat, Clarence didn't care what happened next. He would do what he was told and go where he was sent. But that didn't stop him from believing the rumor that he—and many other men in Easy Company—had heard.

The war might end here in Cologne.

During the First World War, the Germans surrendered when the battle lines hit the fringes of their empire, *before* the fighting could reach the heartland. Was it too much to hope that Europe's Second World War would end here, nearly three hundred miles from Berlin?

Clarence closed his eyes.

Only time would tell.

The sun was setting that evening as Buck emerged from an air-raid shelter by the train station. A gray BMW motorcycle, outfitted with a sidecar, roared down the street in his direction. The bike pulled to a halt in front of him.

Bob Janicki sat behind the vibrating handlebars. After some mechanical tinkering, Janicki had brought the ex–German Army bike back to life. A pair of goggles was set high on his helmet. It was time for a test ride.

"Hop in!" he shouted.

Buck hedged. He was unarmed. What if they ran into German soldiers? And besides, riding in a seized vehicle was forbidden.

Janicki dismissed Buck's concerns. He had seen his young friend looking troubled and sad. "Don't you want to go back to that fräulein's house?" Janicki asked. It would be a quick trip, he promised. No one else would know. It would be their secret. Buck relented and hopped into the sidecar. Janicki handed him two bottles of looted wine. "For you and the fräulein," he said with a mischievous smile.

"Oh, jeez!" Buck settled in and held on tight.

The motorcycle's engine whirred through Cologne's empty streets. The few German civilians who remained stared from the sidewalks in a state of bemusement. Grinning, Janicki shifted gears and gave a hoot. His eyes were wide and bright behind his goggles. Buck was amazed to finally see the real Bob Janicki.

And he knew why Janicki was suddenly so joyful. A promotion. Word had trickled down that Janicki would become a half-track driver in two weeks. From here on out, he'd be sitting pretty. Janicki would drive the squad into battle, then wait around for their return. But it was so much more than just a promotion. It was a ticket to what Janicki wanted above all else: to make it home to his wife in one piece.

Every bomb-blasted street looked exactly the same. Numerous times, Janicki pulled over and Buck hopped out to ask Germans for directions. He'd show them Annemarie's address on the back of her photo, and the civilians would give directions by hand signal. They seemed eager enough to help the Americans, and for a moment, it was almost as if there had never been a war at all.

A *Yank* magazine reporter labeled these citizens of Cologne the "Who? Me?" Germans.

"When you talk to them about the misery they have brought on the world and on themselves their reaction is: 'Who? Me? Oh, no! *Not me.* Those were the bad Germans, the Nazis. They are all gone. They ran away across the Rhine.'"

That generalization might have overstated the case, especially in the city of Cologne.

During the elections in 1933—before Hitler seized power—44 percent of Germans across the country voted for the Nazi Party. However, in Cologne, the vote was 33.1 percent in favor of the Nazis. About two-thirds of the city's populace voted against the regime. And that was before Cologne's citizens had weathered a brutal decade living under the shadow of the Gestapo.

The Nazi Party's secret police were still executing people in Cologne—including a fifteen-year-old local, a Russian POW, a Polish slave laborer, and seven others—four days before the Americans reached the city.

When Buck and Janicki finally arrived at the address on the back of the photo, Annemarie's father, Wilhelm, opened the door.

The man greeted them warmly but didn't come out. He hadn't forgotten the young American's crush on his daughter.

Buck played their only ace card in hopes of breaking the ice. He smiled and raised both bottles of wine. It helped. Wilhelm invited them in.

Upstairs, the family was in the middle of a party. One of Annemarie's aunts was celebrating a birthday with family and several neighbors. Annemarie was overjoyed to see Buck. She threw her arms around him and they embraced.

Wilhelm took the men's helmets. Annemarie's aunts served them cake and beverages. For the first time in ages, Buck felt at home among friends.

At one point in the party, Annemarie fetched a candle and led Buck away for a "tour" of her father's dental office so the two of them could be alone. Janicki gave his friend a wink as he departed. A little romance would surely improve Buck's mood.

Annemarie proudly led Buck around the office, opening drawers and picking up dental tools. Once this had been her grandfather's barbershop, where wealthy clients would stop each morning for a shave while they smoked cigars and drank coffee with cognac.

Annemarie confided that she had once worked side by side with her mother, Anna. Buck remembered seeing her in the photo album, but not in person, and asked the indelicate question. Was Annemarie's mother still alive?

Annemarie's mood turned somber. But she told Buck what she knew.

It started with a rumor in September 1942. In those earlier days of the war, all young men had to serve six months in the Reich Labor Service, building fortifications and tending to the West Wall. And it wasn't just the men; young women were drafted too.

Annemarie's teacher told her female students that when they reported to the Reich Labor Service, they would have to bear a child for the Führer. They wouldn't need parental permission, and the party would raise the babies for them.

Horrified at the prospect of having a child for the regime, Annemarie told her mother. When an officer in the Reich Labor Service came to the office for dental work, Annemarie's mother asked him point-blank about the rumor. Was it true?

The Gestapo provided a definitive answer.

For simply asking the question, they arrested Annemarie's mother, imprisoned her, and put her on trial three months later for making a "false assertion that could indeed damage the nation and the reputation" of the Nazis.

The punishment could be cruel. Would she be sent to a concentration camp? As Cologne's Jewish population was being deported to ghettos and extermination camps in the east, the Gestapo was sending its remaining enemies to Buchenwald and Theresienstadt.

The worst didn't happen, in this case. Annemarie's mother was spared by a judge. He freed her on the grounds that she had merely sought an answer from a Reich Labor Service leader, without spreading the rumor publicly.

But even though she escaped the camps, irreparable damage had been done. Annemarie's mother was so traumatized by her treatment at the hands of the Gestapo that the family had no choice but to commit her to a psychiatric asylum. She hadn't come home since.

Buck comforted Annemarie when she started to cry. Now he realized why she had been so happy to see him. He and his fellow Americans had liberated her from the people who had destroyed her mother.

Maybe some of the sacrifices he'd witnessed were for something after all?

Together, Annemarie and Buck headed back to the party. Perhaps, now, they had each other to rely on.

• • •

There was a heavy bang on the front door. The partygoers quieted down.

One of Annemarie's aunts went downstairs to investigate. She returned in a hurry. Three American MPs had arrived to search the house. Buck cursed. Under the nonfraternization policy, they could bust him for "cohabitation" with a German woman. The punishment was a fine of sixty-five dollars, which was five dollars more than his monthly salary.

But there was a way out.

Annemarie followed as her father quietly led Buck and Janicki to a fire escape behind the house. It was almost dark outside. Everyone had lost track of time. Buck paused to steal one last moment with Annemarie as her father and Janicki descended the fire escape. She kissed him quickly.

"You'll come back?" she asked.

Buck knew it was unlikely that he'd see her again at this juncture of the war. But he didn't want her to think he would abandon her by choice.

"I will, someday," he said.

Tears streamed down Annemarie's face, but she understood. Their time together was spent. Buck's hand slipped from hers before he climbed down the fire escape.

But Janicki's borrowed motorcycle was missing. It had disappeared from the alleyway. The MPs must have found it, triggering their search of the house.

After saying goodbye to Annemarie's father, the doughs took off running. They dashed through the dark streets, back toward the cathedral. Buck looked repeatedly over his shoulder.

The city was much more menacing at night than it was during the day.

"I'm sorry I fixed that motorcycle up," Janicki said at one point.

"I'm not," Buck said. "I just wish we went earlier."

The duo was halfway through an intersection when an American voice yelled, "Halt!"

Buck and Janicki froze. They had stumbled upon a checkpoint. There was probably a .30-caliber machine gun aimed at them from a corner building, with a trigger-happy GI ready to light up the intersection.

The American gave the sign of the day, then waited for the intruders to give the countersign.

"We don't know your signs!" Buck shouted. His voice was unmistakable, high and Southern. A pair of GIs approached with flashlights. Buck explained the situation and the unfamiliar GIs gave a laugh before letting them proceed.

After five hours on foot, Buck and Janicki slipped into the air-raid shelter sometime after midnight. Safe in the warm bunker, they regaled their buddies with tales of how they had survived at least five checkpoints. The stories screeched to a stop when their squad leader barged into the room.

"Sorry, fellas," he said, "but I had to report you as 'missing.'" The report was already with the company clerk and would be in the officers' hands by morning.

Janicki nearly collapsed with anguish, and Buck knew why: his friend's promotion—the ticket home to his wife—was in jeopardy.

Heads would roll.

Several days later

Whenever he wasn't on duty, Clarence went wandering through the city like a tourist. That morning, he moved slowly through the backstreets, headed back to the tank. The deserted streets seemed innocuous in the light of midmorning. But when he turned a corner near the train station, he knew immediately that he was in trouble.

Five or so young German children were sitting on the staircase of a ruined building. They perked up at the sight of an American soldier.

A young woman watched over them from the front doorstep. Clarence didn't think she was their mother; she was too young to have that many children already. Some of the children were probably orphans.

The kids flocked to Clarence's side. He wasn't surprised by the attention—this happened everywhere a GI went in Cologne. The kids kept pace with him and tugged his sleeve, begging him for bubble gum. Clarence cringed. He wasn't supposed to talk with them. Even contact with children was forbidden under the fraternization ban. On top of that, typhus was spreading through Cologne's lice-ridden air-raid shelters and medical clinics. American troops had been warned of the disease.

But the children were there, right in front of him, hungry and desperate.

Clarence stopped and searched his pockets while they bounced with excitement. He felt empathy for them. They were pale from living underground, having spent more of their lives in wartime than he had. Their eyes hinted at a psychological trauma that Clarence couldn't imagine.

"The fear of airpower is so deep in them that you will see little children with their heads buried in their mothers' aprons shuddering, or peeping fearfully up at the terrible skies," wrote one reporter.

Clarence's childhood hadn't always been easy, but he'd never worried for his life.

The only things he had in his pockets were cigarettes, and he couldn't share those with children. He squatted down to the kids' level and broke the bad news to them in German. "I'm sorry, guys, but I don't have any gum."

The kids' faces sank, but they weren't buying it. Certainly every American soldier carried gum. Thinking that Clarence was holding out on them, they turned on the charm even more.

Clarence directed the kids toward the young woman, asking her to explain things to them. But before he could clear up the situation, the throb of an engine drew everyone's attention. An American jeep slowly turned the corner.

Clarence cursed under his breath. The jeep pulled over and two MPs hopped out. Full of fear, the children bolted to the young woman's side.

An MP sergeant approached Clarence and opened his pad. He eyed the 3rd Armored Division patch on Clarence's sleeve and asked for his documents.

Clarence tried to make his case, but the MPs weren't buying his explanation. They'd caught him red-handed, talking to a German woman with at least five kids tugging at his sleeves. The sergeant noted his name and serial number before announcing that Clarence was getting reported for fraternization.

Satisfied that they'd done their duty, the MPs drove away.

The kids were still watching from behind the young woman. Clarence gave them a little wave and resumed his trek. There were worse fates that could have befallen him. The fine wouldn't pinch his pocket too badly. He had been warned and he had learned his lesson. It was just embarrassing for a former candy salesman.

Next time he came back this way, he wouldn't be caught without a few packs of gum.

Soon after, United States of America

The postal carrier dropped mail through the slot of a two-story home in suburban Kansas City. A slender, gray-haired woman picked it up.

Hattie Pearl Miller's quiet eyes hid behind wire-rim glasses. Raising Chuck and his six siblings had aged her far beyond her fifty-seven years, but she still wore cheerful floral dresses when she did her seamstress work from home.

To honor her sons, she kept their photos above the fireplace— Chuck in his army green, and his older brother, William, in the tropical uniform of the Army Air Forces.

Among the ordinary mail, one envelope in particular drew Hattie's attention. It bore the return address of her sister, Beth, who lived in Washington, D.C. Inside was a newspaper clipping from the *Washington Post* accompanied by a short, handwritten note: "Is this our Chuck?"

A quick glance at the clipping gave Hattie cause to fret. "Nazi Tanks Excel Ours, Troops Say," the headline declared above a photo of a smoldering Sherman tank. Chuck had hoped that his mother would be proud when she saw his name in the article by Ann Stringer, but instead, the story terrified her.

"Don't talk about the superiority of American tanks to men of this 3rd Armored unit," Stringer had written. She went on to describe the slaughter at Blatzheim, observing, "In one field alone, this company lost half its tanks."

Hattie might have cried as she read the quotes from Bob Earley and her son, disparaging their Sherman tanks, but she never admitted this to Chuck. She wasn't the only one dismayed by the news. Supreme Allied Commander Eisenhower had sent an inquiry to General Maurice Rose, commander of the 3rd Armored, to ask if the claims were true, and Rose had backed up his tankers. But by then, the damage was done. The story had been printed from coast to coast, and the families of countless tankers were shocked by the headlines.

"American Tanks Not Worth Drop of Water, Crews Say."

"U.S. Tanks No Good in Battle, Say Crewmen After Losing Half of M-4 Machines."

"American Tanks No Good, Assert Troops in Reich."

But there was a curious sidebar in the clipping that Hattie held. To counter the negative fallout from Stringer's article and any public outcry, the army had rushed forth an announcement of a new American "Super Tank." It was a machine that the assistant secretary of war called "one of the strongest weapons of the war . . . the most powerful tank we have ever built."

The Pershing.

The juxtaposition was strange—a blurb hailing a new tank

within a story disparaging the older models. But whatever a Pershing was, it offered a glimmer of hope for the distraught families back home.

Hattie set aside the clipping. The article had said that Chuck was in Cologne. She opened an atlas and located the city on the Rhine. Chuck was still a long way from Berlin. Hattie was no military tactician, but the map spoke volumes. There was only one direction that her son could travel—deeper into the heart of Nazi Germany.

She would pray for Chuck and the boys, and prepare herself for more news she didn't want to hear. If things were as bad as Stringer's story suggested—half the tanks lost in one field—the worst might be yet to come.

CHAPTER 18

THE BREAKOUT

About a week later

FISCHENICH, GERMANY, FIVE MILES SOUTH OF COLOGNE

The scent of the Rhine was in the air. It was morning, and finally felt like spring. The men of Easy Company lounged outside their tanks in a small, grassy field surrounded by trees. While other GIs were swimming, fishing, and kayaking in the Rhine's cold waters, Easy Company was holding a riverside party. Almost everyone was drinking. Some drank from canteen cups. Some straight from the bottle. Tankers strolled past to shoot the breeze.

Clarence, DeRiggi, and the crew all laughed and drank around the Pershing . . . all except for Earley. It was possible that he was the only sober man left in the field. There was no telling how long this party would last. But Earley would let his platoon enjoy the downtime while they could.

Cologne had not been the end of the road that many had hoped it would be. American troops had already crossed the Rhine, deeper into Germany. Soon it would be Spearhead's turn to do the same.

A tank crew from B-Company drifted through the gathering, searching for Clarence. The tank's driver, Harley Swenson, and his gunner, Phil Dest, had something to say. Back in Cologne, they had been one of the Stuart crews ordered to prepare for a mad dash to the Rhine. They were certain that if it hadn't been for Clarence, the Panther would have killed them. They assured Clarence that he had saved their lives, and for this, they were forever grateful.

Clarence was uncomfortable with the attention. He didn't feel he had truly bested the Panther as everyone thought. He had run through countless scenarios but still couldn't figure out why the German gunner had held his fire. "I didn't save your lives," Clarence joked with the Stuart crew. "I saved my life and yours were along for the ride!"

The Stuart crew laughed as they raised their glasses in his honor, and Clarence grudgingly accepted their tribute. He wasn't about to spoil their celebration by revealing the truth about the Panther: he had just gotten lucky.

Later that morning, a jeep pulled up next to the Pershing. "Smoyer?" the driver behind the wheel asked.

Clarence ambled forward. Captain Salisbury wanted to see him.

"Oh, shit," Clarence said. How was he going to fake sobriety in front of the captain?

Earley thrust a canteen of water into Clarence's hand and made him chug the contents. Clarence racked his foggy mind, trying to discern why the captain had summoned him.

"Don't talk any more than you have to," Earley advised.

Clarence dropped into the jeep's passenger seat and gave a sloppy salute.

This wouldn't be pretty.

An aide ushered Clarence into Salisbury's office, which was on the first floor of a German farmhouse. The captain was seated behind his desk, scribbling away on paperwork. His curly hair was neatly clipped and his uniform was pressed. Clarence saluted and remained standing uneasily.

Salisbury looked up. His commanding stare fixed squarely on Clarence. "I never realized what a great gunner you were until you knocked those chimneys off," he said, referring to the firing demonstration in Stolberg. "It made me proud."

Clarence breathed a deep sigh of relief. He wasn't in trouble after all.

"Then you got that Panther in Cologne and you did the unit proud," Salisbury added. The captain informed Clarence that he had been recommended for the Bronze Star.

Clarence was shocked and honored.

Salisbury took a written report from the desk and waved it in front of Clarence.

"And then you go and do this."

Clarence's mind raced. *What did I do?*

Salisbury read the MP's report, which detailed how he had caught Clarence fraternizing with a German woman and her kids. Clarence couldn't believe his ears. After he had led Easy Company up through Blatzheim, *and* across the apocalyptic cityscape of Cologne, the captain was holding a tiny, harmless offense against him?

He tried to explain himself. Salisbury was unmoved.

"I can fine you," he said, "or give you KP."

The dreaded Kitchen Police.

Clarence's blood began boiling. Being assigned to the potato peelers in the rear of the formation was supposed to be a punishment. It was intended to be emasculating and degrading.

Clarence couldn't bottle it up any longer. "Sir, KP sounds like a vacation to me."

Salisbury was blindsided by his display of defiance. He reminded Clarence that they'd given his crew the best tank in the battalion. They were *lucky* to have the Pershing.

Clarence couldn't let that go. Earley, DeRiggi, Smokey Davis, and McVey never had a chance to be candid with their captain, so he would speak for them all.

"Yeah, and because of it we're always the first over the goddamn hill," Clarence said. "Whenever we turn a corner, we don't know if it's going to be our last."

Salisbury held himself back. He couldn't afford a rift with a top gunner like Clarence. Not when the company was days from crossing the Rhine.

After having spoken his mind, Clarence remembered his place. Salisbury was still his company commander.

"Sir," Clarence said calmly, "one of these days we're going to end up dead in a ditch."

Salisbury's stance softened. He asked if Clarence would like a transfer to another crew in the rear. After all he'd done, he deserved a breather. Salisbury was offering Clarence nothing short of survival.

"I'll stay up front with the guys," Clarence said. He would never leave his family, even if it meant saving himself. He told Salisbury it would be nice if there were a few more Pershings, so the crews could take turns leading the way.

Salisbury agreed. The Pershing would be in demand, now more than ever.

"There's a big drive coming," Salisbury said, "that's all I can tell you." He crumpled the report, threw it in the trash, and told Clarence to go sober up.

Clarence saluted and left.

He had just talked himself out of a Bronze Star, but that wasn't as important as what he'd achieved. He had spoken for the crew. Even if nothing changed, the captain had heard them, loud and clear.

Clarence had made sure of that.

About a week later, March 26, 1945

A spring shower fell late that morning as the armored column raced through a misty forest. Task Force X sped along a dirt road, traveling deeper yet into Germany. The Pershing set the pace.

Three days earlier, Spearhead had made the leap across the Rhine. By now the First Army, the Third Army, the Ninth Army, and the British forces had all crossed the river. The British and the Americans were racing to beat Russia's Red Army to Hitler's doorstep. "This was the beginning of the big push," the 3rd Armored history recorded. "There was victory in the air and it was contagious." Anticipation was high.

From above the Pershing's turret, Earley and DeRiggi eyed their surroundings. In the bow, McVey drove with his hatch open. The men were soaking wet from riding in the rain. The forest felt foggy and mysterious. Cold black streams gushed with snowmelt as winter thawed. The Germans were out there—but where?

"Sooner or later somebody is going to get the first shot," Clarence told Earley, "and we're not going to be around here anymore."

Earley agreed. But what could they do? The lead tank would always be the first target.

It was a bitter pill for Clarence to swallow. *It's just a matter of time.*

Behind the Pershing rolled a Sherman. Janicki and his team rode with their legs dangling over the sides of the tank. Janicki was miserable. The higher-ups had torn away his stripes for breaking curfew and rescinded his promotion to half-track driver. He was right back to fighting on foot. But he never blamed Buck— the motorcycle had been his idea alone.

Buck hadn't gotten in trouble at all. He was already the low man on the totem pole and couldn't be demoted any further. Instead, Lieutenant Boom had awarded Buck a pass to a rest facility in Viviers, France. He was there now, enjoying three days of hot food, clean sheets, and all the movies he could watch.

Janicki and the rest of the squad were envious. But everyone knew Buck deserved it. As first scout, he'd kept them safe on the road to Cologne and in the city itself. They'd rely on him again after his break.

The forest road ahead curved to the right.

About a hundred yards on, a roadblock made of logs stretched across their path. It was a strange sight in the otherwise empty woods. Earley halted the Pershing and the column of Shermans behind them. He needed to assess the situation. DeRiggi squinted and studied the curious roadblock. So did the doughs from other tanks.

And all the while, the enemy was watching them.

High above the rocky rise, eight German antiaircraft trucks—used to shoot at enemy planes—were parked in the misty drizzle. In each truck bed was a Flak 38 cannon. Gunners swung the cannons toward the American column. They stomped their firing pedals. Rhythmic thumps split the air as cannons shot forward.

Inside the Pershing, Clarence shrank in his seat as a flurry of shells shattered against the turret. Earley ducked inside and slammed the hatch just in time. But DeRiggi wasn't quick enough. The loader fell to the turret floor amid a spray of crimson, writhing and clutching his face. His blood sprayed the white interior.

Clarence rose to help his friend, but Earley stopped him. "Stay on the gun!"

• • •

Directly in the line of fire, Janicki and the doughs didn't stand a chance.

A rain of glowing red shells the size of golf balls came down on them. Explosions rippled across the tank's flank. Doughs pressed themselves flat against the engine deck, but the shrapnel found them anyway.

The sizzling steel pierced smoking holes left and right. A direct hit landed against Janicki's left leg. All he saw was a flash of sparks and a haze of blood. When he looked down, his leg was hanging by a thread below the knee.

His stomach lurched. Clutching his wounded leg, he rolled away from the fire with the others, across the blistering engine deck and over the side of the tank.

Janicki was a fighter. It wasn't his day to die.

Inside the Pershing, Earley desperately wrestled with DeRiggi in a furious attempt to save his life. DeRiggi was thrashing and Earley was trying to stick him with a syringe of morphine.

Shrapnel had torn a hole in the side of DeRiggi's face. His screams tortured the others. Clarence's chest heaved. His friend was bleeding out, but there was nothing he could do to help.

The shell bursts against the armor sounded like someone was trying to break in with a sledgehammer. Clarence had to act.

No one had a shot at the enemy, and men were suffering. Five tankers had head wounds and ten doughs were injured, most with leg wounds. They had to get the injured men to safety.

Clarence alerted Earley: headquarters was calling for a retreat. But Earley had his hands full with DeRiggi, so he told Clarence to take command of the tank.

Clarence leaped to the commander's position, plugged into the intercom, and stood to see what was behind him, using a periscope. He summoned a calm voice and called for a reverse. Without a rearview mirror, McVey, the driver, would steer blind. Clarence told him to go steady. He would be his eyes.

CHAPTER 19

THE AMERICAN BLITZ

Three days later, March 29, 1945
ABOUT FIFTY MILES FARTHER EAST

The pack of Spearhead vehicles stretched along the highway as far as the eye could see. Tank after tank, more than 150 vehicles were all headed in the same direction: Marburg, Germany. "This show looked like the beginning of the last rat race in Europe," noted one GI.

Ominous storm clouds lingered in the sky, with only a few cracks of blue shining through. The convoy roamed through broad valleys bordered by evergreen forests and a crumbling castle. The scenery reminded some men of their hometowns back in places like Wisconsin and Minnesota. Others took in the sights like tourists.

It was midmorning and they had been on the go since six a.m. Easy Company's Task Force X had relinquished the lead position for a change. This time, it was tagging along behind Task Force Welborn, which was named for its colonel, Jack Welborn.

In the middle of the pack, the crew inside the Pershing drove with their faces buffeted by the wind. Atop the turret, Earley occupied one hatch. Clarence stood in the other. A white silk scarf fluttered from Clarence's neck. He had found a parachute hung up in a tree and fashioned it into a scarf, perfect for a moment like this. Standing there amid the howling motors, Clarence couldn't help but grin. He was relishing the speed of the formation, a sensation only possible when no one was shooting at him. And there was something else that sent his spirits soaring.

There was the feat that they were attempting.

Eisenhower's headquarters had its mandate to end the war by targeting "the heart of Germany." But where exactly would that be? There were two candidates: Berlin and the Ruhr Valley.

For the Americans, capturing Berlin before the Russians got to it would be a symbolic, political coup. The Ruhr, on the other hand, would represent a strategic military victory. The Ruhr was the source of 80 percent of Germany's coal and 66 percent of its steel. If they could isolate the Ruhr from the rest of Germany, the enemy's army would not survive.

Given its strategic importance, the choice was clear. The higher-ups issued orders, and at first light, Spearhead began another one of its legendary mad dashes, to the Ruhr Valley.

But this time, they wouldn't be charging into trouble alone. As the 3rd Armored plowed north, the 2nd Armored—known as "Hell on Wheels"—would swing south. With luck, the army's two divisions would team up near the German town of Paderborn to "slip a steel wall around the great industrial Ruhr." This would show the Germans: *It's over.* Their army would be surrounded *and* overpowered—and there would be nothing they could do about it.

There was just one hiccup: getting there. Depending on the route, Paderborn lay more than a hundred miles away. To pull it all off, Spearhead would have to make one of the longest, fastest drives of the war. It would be an American "blitz." But if it worked, it would get them straight to the heart of Germany.

A course was set for Paderborn. General Rose spread Spearhead across four parallel roads. As his division rolled forth, Rose radioed the task force commanders to offer a bounty for capture of the Nazi leadership: "One case of Scotch for dead or alive Guderian, Himmler, Kesselring, or Dietrich—one bottle for Hitler."

Rose issued the challenge over unsecured radio channels in hopes that the dispatch would be intercepted by the Germans and the words carried back to Berlin.

He wanted Hitler himself to hear the voice of Spearhead.

The ride felt like it might never end. Everyone felt stiffer by the hour. Eventually, Clarence sought comfort by sitting on the turret floor. There was nothing new to see outside anyway, just an endless parade of Sherman tanks.

On the other side of the breech rode a short, dark-haired kid named Mathews, who had been brought in to replace DeRiggi. Clarence liked him already. He was quiet and capable, although he lacked DeRiggi's pluck. DeRiggi had survived—that was all the crew had heard after they laid him in a ditch where medics were caring for the wounded. Clarence hoped he'd see him again.

To pass the time on the way to Paderborn, Clarence reread

his mail. The words bounced on the page before his eyes as the floor vibrated beneath him. One particular letter from his mother brought a smile to his face every time.

At the urging of friends and family, his parents had gone to the movies. His mother had worn her best dress, and his father had ditched his laborer's jacket and boots in favor of a suit. They went to the theater specifically to see the newsreels that ran before the main feature.

And there they saw Clarence on-screen. They had never been so proud.

The Bates film that showed the Pershing's duel with the Panther was everywhere. Theaters across America were showing the gritty tank battle, transporting audiences closer to the fighting than they'd ever been before. It culminated with a steady pan of the Pershing crew, which featured Clarence standing in the middle, staring impassively at the camera.

Bates would later receive the Bronze Star, in large part for his film work in Cologne. Earley would receive one too, for leading the takedown of that Panther. Clarence knew that no such award was in the cards for him, but he was okay with that.

He was simply amazed at what his parents had done in order to see him on the big screen. They'd gone to the movies for the first time in their lives.

Buck Marsh, back from his break in France, sat in a half-track behind Easy Company, fiddling with a single-burner stove that he'd set on the floor to hard-boil some eggs. Four of his buddies' seats now stood empty in the compartment behind him. Janicki—his left leg soon to be amputated—was on his way to England. Others were still in a field hospital recovering from their injuries.

Meanwhile, Private First Class Byron Mitchell and others were telling a shocking story to anyone in the half-track who would listen: they had been captured by Germans and forced to dig their own graves—until a German tank commander had appeared and spared their lives.

"We were lucky he was a good guy," said Byron, who seldom had much to say.

Buck listened to the amazing story, relieved that his Easy Company buddies had been saved. And yet, he felt somewhat distracted. Poor Janicki, he thought. Buck found relief in the one bright spot in the whole awful situation: at least Janicki was going home to his wife.

As the convoy plunged deeper into Germany that afternoon, the tension mounted. Through his periscope, Clarence kept an eye out for any and all potential threats.

A German vehicle burning by the side of the road drifted into view. At the sight of the convoy, most German soldiers scattered from their guard posts. They were astonished to see American armor in the region. No one had taken a shot at Easy Company yet. It was only a matter of time.

Whenever Clarence returned to the turret, Earley seemed to be poring over the same piece of mail—a letter that his girlfriend had sent him. But no matter how many times he read the letter, the message didn't change. She had found someone else, another man who hadn't gone away like he had. Earley was heartbroken.

Clarence would take his seat and pretend he didn't notice. It was a conversation that he had never had and didn't know how to handle.

Meanwhile, Clarence's sister regiment, the 33rd Armored Regiment, was positioned at the spearhead of Task Force Welborn. As one crew were stretching their legs, a jeep pulled up beside their Sherman.

Corporal John Irwin, a rookie gunner, saw an unfamiliar figure in the jeep's passenger seat.

"He had a crew cut, stiff graying hair, a serious, handsome face, and a big frame," Irwin recalled. "He looked up at us and touched a forefinger to his brow in salute and said, 'My helmet's off to you men—keep it up!'" Irwin still had no idea who the man was until his buddies razzed him for not recognizing General Rose himself.

Rose was beaming for a reason. His division was on the verge of driving farther in a single day than any other unit in military history.

Night fell over the German countryside as the column rolled forward.

Chuck Miller dozed in his seat to the whir of the Sherman tank's engine. As Chuck slept, his tank's driver followed the taillights of the Sherman ahead of them. Under the cover of darkness, the threat of violence felt magnified. The smell of burning wood singed the air. That was because German soldiers had set villages ablaze with tank shells.

From the turret of the Sherman, a pair of headlights came into view. Sounds echoed in the dark. Just then, three motorcycles emerged from the shadows. They kept pace with the Sherman before pulling ahead of the tank. At the sight of them, the tank's commander, Red Villa, nearly leaped from the turret. The motorcycle riders wore gray rubberized trench coats and German helmets.

Suddenly, Chuck felt himself being shaken awake. He swung the tank's cannon leftward, but all he could see was darkness.

"Thirty-caliber," Commander Villa said. "Fire, right where you are!"

The machine gun's bright flame blinded Chuck as he stood on the trigger. Glowing tracers zipped into the dark and—in a flash—illuminated a slice of the road.

Chuck had aimed too high, but it was enough to get the job done. He missed the first two motorcyclists but managed to spook the one bringing up the rear.

A shower of sparks burst at ground level as the motorcyclist spun out. He hadn't been hit, but the fire flying overhead had made him lose control of his bike. Chuck let off the trigger as the tank roared past the fallen German.

Shortly thereafter, the convoy halted for the night at 9:50 p.m., but Chuck couldn't fall back to sleep.

He wouldn't stop shaking for the next hour.

• • •

As the sun rose the next morning, March 30, 1945, the convoy powered along a high, curvy road. In the Pershing, Earley spoke into the radio as he guided Smokey. To the right, the road dropped off to a wide valley. It was a tight fit for the tank, offering no room for error. But Paderborn couldn't be far now.

Throughout the company, drivers' arms had cramped badly. One reported that his rear was so bruised from sitting for extended periods that he "took to kneeling on the floor of the turret, just to relieve the pressure."

It was a price to pay to make history. It was official: that endless drive had been "the greatest one-day advance in the history of mobile warfare," according to the 3rd Armored unit history. One task force had even gone 102 miles. As a whole or in parts, Spearhead went farther through enemy territory than any German, Russian, or British unit.

It began like any other refueling stop.

The convoy edged to the side of the road. The tanks shut down and the crews climbed into the daylight.

Clarence paused atop the turret. The view was as good as any scenic overlook he'd ever seen. But something wasn't right. His eyes settled on sharp lines that stood out in the middle of their natural surroundings. He rubbed his eyes and looked closer. These lines were almost the same size as tanks. He dropped into the turret and swung the gun to the right, setting the reticle on a target. His 6x zoom sight would give him a closer look.

They *were* tanks. It appeared that some column had begun to pull from a forest and had stopped. Perhaps to consult a map? They looked like light tanks, maybe Stuarts or the division's new M24 Chaffees.

Clarence shouted to Earley.

Earley raised his binoculars but couldn't discern their identity.

"I'm pretty sure they're American," Clarence said.

Earley radioed Salisbury and reported that Clarence had eyes on tanks, possibly friendly forces.

Salisbury replied quickly. Too quickly. "There's no troops of ours down there, fire on them."

Clarence was aghast. "I can't knock out our own tanks!"

Earley was torn. Whoever the tanks were, they were in enemy territory. But Clarence didn't waver. Earley stalled and pleaded for Salisbury to reconsider.

"Goddammit, I told you they aren't our tanks!" Salisbury said. "Fire!"

On any other day, Earley would have resisted. The stoic commander generally landed on the moral side of any argument. Logic usually won out for him over the hot tempers of the war zone. But Earley wasn't acting like his usual self that day. The crew's father figure was worn down physically and emotionally. Recently, he'd received a letter from his girlfriend, saying she'd found someone else. The war, the long drive, and the news from home were taking their toll on him. So, it wasn't really Bob Earley speaking when he gave Clarence the command: "Well, you heard him—fire."

Earley sank into his seat. He couldn't bear to watch.

Clarence turned and looked him straight in the eye—*Are you serious?*

"Want them to put us in chains?" Earley said.

Clarence returned to his zoom sight with his jaw clenched in frustration. He worked the hand crank, inching his aim leftward. He squeezed the trigger. The 90mm gun blasted the shell with an ear-piercing crack.

He counted down the time until the tracer made impact. A splash of dirt burst from the road ahead of the lead tank. Clarence had missed—intentionally.

Hatch covers flung open and crewmen came pouring out. The men frantically waved colored panels toward the shooter to identify themselves.

They're Americans, all right!

They were probably scouting ahead of the other task force.

"That would have stayed with us!" Clarence snapped at Earley.

Earley leaped to his feet and raised his binoculars. He muttered in astonishment before getting on the horn to give Salisbury the news. "Well, Captain," Earley said, "looks like they *are* our tanks."

The only response from Salisbury's end was a stunned silence.

Several hours later, the convoy descended into a world of trouble.

The column had stalled about eight miles south of Paderborn. They could hear fire crackling. Panzerfausts thumped in the distance. SS men were firing from a ridge, and Task Force Welborn was bearing the brunt of the fighting.

Through his periscope, Clarence saw traces of the battle raging ahead. He was thankful to be seated right where he was, nestled in the idling line of tanks. The landscape outside looked cold and unwelcoming, with dull green fields and thin trees.

An awful truth had spread from vehicle to vehicle in the convoy by then: Paderborn wasn't just a name on the map along the way to the Ruhr. It was much more than that. Paderborn was the "home port" for the armored forces of the Third Reich. The "Nazi Fort Knox," as GIs would call it.

Every German tanker spent a stint in training there. The German Army's elite tank training base was at Paderborn, as was the SS's armor school. In fact, the SS would lead the fighting to come.

To defend Paderborn, the SS had assembled SS Panzerbrigade Westfalen, a mixed battle group of troops from the SS, the army, the air force, and Hitler Youth. Even battle-scarred instructors from both tank schools would be coming out to fight.

Spearhead had put itself deep behind enemy lines, deeper than ever before, and that worried Clarence. This was tank country, after all.

German tank country.

CHAPTER 20

THE FATHERLESS

That night, March 30, 1945
SEVEN MILES SOUTH OF PADERBORN

Deep in the darkness of Böddeken Forest, Clarence and the crew stood horrified alongside the Pershing. Other Easy Company tankers lingered around their mounts nearby.

They couldn't look away from the terrible sight that stretched above the treetops. Over the Paderborn countryside, the clouds were glowing red.

The bark of German tank guns roared through the woods.

Chaos was reigning just a mile to the north, but there was nothing Clarence and his crew could do. Easy Company was forbidden to go forward to help. Until the higher-ups could get a handle on the situation, no one else was to enter the frenzy.

In its haste to reach Paderborn that night, Task Force Welborn had forged ahead, leaving Easy Company and Task Force X behind in the forest for the night. Task Force Welborn was in trouble—it was unmistakable. And now Clarence's crew and the others were too far away to help.

Americans were dying out there.

A mile north

Task Force Welborn had indeed driven into an ambush. German guns were thundering from seemingly every direction. Vehicles ruptured. The enemy gave no sign that they were about to let up.

General Rose and his entourage abandoned their vehicles and jumped into a roadside ditch. Tankers and doughs followed, seeking cover. Only a few men were able to return fire, using small arms.

There was no going forward. In front of the American column, ten German tanks blasted away. There would be no retreat, either. Behind them, another five German tanks shot down from a hilltop. The woods were a killing zone too. The tree line blinked with small-arms fire. SS infantry were stationed at both ends of the route.

With nowhere to run, all that remained for most of the Americans was to hide.

Rose and his entourage flattened themselves against the walls of the ditch. The general gripped a Thompson submachine gun, while the others clung to pistols and carbines.

SS Panzerbrigade Westfalen had struck the convoy with deadly efficiency. Enemy tank shells whizzed overhead. The German tanks pumped shells into every vehicle in the column. Only Colonel Welborn and some of his Shermans had escaped. The Germans had splintered the rest of the American column by blasting vehicles at both ends—which trapped everyone else in the middle.

American tank crews jumped from flaming hulls. Squads of

doughs tumbled from their half-tracks, screaming, burned, and bleeding. Men darted into the fields and hid from the enemy behind haystacks.

Several tankers made a run for it. Unfortunately, their escape route sent them running toward their general. Rose climbed out of the ditch and caught the fleeing men by their arms, pushing them back toward their tanks.

The general was desperate to turn things around. This night was supposed to be the triumph of his career, the climax of his division's record-breaking drive. Beneath his raincoat, he was wearing riding breeches and polished boots. He had abandoned the safety of commanding from the rear, opting to ride with his lead task force. He had even brought a stenographer along with him to keep a record of the moment when his division reached Paderborn.

With his crowning achievement ruined, new priorities took hold. Now he would fight just to see another day. The vehicles that Rose's entourage rode in on—three jeeps, two motorcycles, and a Greyhound armored car—were close at hand. Two of the jeeps were equipped with radios. If he could get to them, Rose could radio headquarters for backup.

On Rose's command, two drivers braved the enemy's fire to maneuver the jeeps into the ditch. It worked. A soldier handed him one jeep's handset. On the line was his headquarters.

"Smith," Rose said, "send somebody to close up this column. We have been cut."

Enemy shells were hitting targets at an alarming rate, as if they couldn't miss. One of Rose's jeeps exploded on the road.

Then, a shell felled a tree just behind the column. Now there was no way out. No remaining hope of retreat.

Through the light of the burning vehicles, Rose and his men saw a wedge of enemy tanks plowing through the field. They were coming to finish the job.

"We're in a hell of a fix now," Rose said to a colonel at his side.

The German tankers fired flares into the air to illuminate any remaining resistance. German voices could be heard screaming commands over the hissing flames and the roar of motors. They rammed the lead American vehicles off the road and fired flares into their open compartments to destroy whatever, or whoever, was left inside.

German tanks snarled closer. Some of Rose's entourage thought they should make a run for the woods. The general disagreed. He wanted to team up with Colonel Welborn, who had found refuge in a place called Hamborn Castle. The castle was about two miles away from Rose's current position—a difficult, but passable, trek.

Rose and his entourage ran for their vehicles. They would try for the castle.

Two colonels piled into the lead jeep, Rose leaped into a second jeep, and men ran for the Greyhound. Rose insisted that they leave the motorcycles behind because they were too noisy.

General Rose's loyal driver darted to the front of the jeep and ripped off a red license plate that identified the vehicle as the general's. Engines surged, and the entourage peeled to the right, dropped into the field, and raced forward.

German tracers zipped through the flames and chased the getaway vehicles while American radio waves echoed with voices trying to reach Rose: "Big Six, come in Big Six!"

The next morning, around eight a.m.

Easy Company was finally unleashed to lead a rescue party. In the clear light of day, the Pershing led Task Force X from the Böddeken Forest.

As the forest opened up, Clarence pressed his eyes into his periscope. Gray smoke drifted over the fields like fog. He searched far and wide, hoping that there might still be time to save someone, anyone.

The crew remained silent as the Pershing neared the carnage.

They were too late.

As many as thirty-seven American vehicles lay strewn along the road like broken toys. Tanks and half-tracks, jeeps and trucks, everything was burned and many were still smoldering.

The destruction spread before them would soon be known as the Welborn Massacre.

Clarence was shaken. He had never seen so many of their own vehicles destroyed. And he had certainly never expected such an outcome at this stage of the war—when America was supposed to be on the verge of winning.

With his face held tight to the periscope, Clarence swept the turret from side to side. His aim slowed across the hills. The Germans might still be watching.

"You seeing this?" It was the replacement loader, his voice trembling. "You seeing this?"

"Shut up!" Clarence snapped. "I'm looking for the gun that's pointing at us!"

Earley restored the peace. Everyone was emotional. The last thing they could afford was to turn on one another.

The Pershing pulled up to a crossroads.

Satisfied that the enemy had vacated the area, Clarence resumed scanning for survivors.

To the left, the decimated American column stretched for several hundred yards. Derelict Shermans lay frozen in confusion with their turrets pointed haphazardly in different directions. Bullet-ridden half-tracks leaned into ditches. Torn canvas flapped from trucks. Many vehicles were destroyed. Nine Shermans. Twenty-one half-tracks. A Stuart. A pair of jeeps and trucks.

A dead tanker lay nearby. His arms, legs, and head were all gone, and all that remained was a torso with skin that had been roasted red from the heat of his burning tank. He no longer looked like a man at all. It was no way to die.

Clarence felt his stomach turn and had to sit back from his periscope before he lost it. After a moment, he regained his composure and resumed scanning.

At the lead of the ghostly column lay an abandoned Pershing, damaged by a shell strike. It was pointed toward the road that ran uphill to Hamborn Castle. It was a rare tank to behold on any European battlefield, and to see a Pershing grounded in defeat was even more shocking.

Maybe it hadn't been fast enough to keep up with the escaping Shermans. Maybe the Germans had targeted it specifically. No one would ever know.

Clarence felt a cold, hollow pit in his stomach as he gazed upon the mangled spearhead of Task Force Welborn. A pattern was forming, at the forefront of every advance.

Meanwhile, doughs were coming from the opposite direction. Buck and the men of A- and B-Companies waded through grass littered with old shell casings. Buck covered his mouth and nose against the sickening scent of burning rubber.

Up close, the carnage was even worse. The enemy tanks had rammed aside or flattened anything on wheels. Doughs from Buck's sister company, F-Company, had been riding in these vehicles. And many hadn't escaped. In the back compartment of one half-track, several doughs were dead in their seats, still being consumed by the fire.

Small groups of men in uniforms emerged from the tree line. They were tankers and doughs, many in a state of shock after hiding all night in the cold woods.

Rather than waiting for the enemy to stomp each and every trapped vehicle, most of the men of Task Force Welborn had bailed from their machines before the German shells could reach them.

Doughs discovered the motorcycles that had belonged to Rose's bodyguards, abruptly abandoned on the road. But what had become of the general?

That morning, a reconnaissance patrol set out from Hamborn Castle in search of the answer. Along the way, they came upon a jeep that had been smashed against a tree. It looked as if a boulder had rolled down into it.

The heavy footprints of German tanks were everywhere.

The night before, Rose and his escape party had been nearly in the clear. They had bypassed the burning column and returned to the road. Against all odds, they'd left the ambush behind them.

But just when they thought they were finally safe, a tank appeared on the road, headed straight for them. The colonel at the wheel of the lead jeep was relieved. The tank was broad, with a long barrel. It looked American, like a Pershing under Welborn's command.

"That's one of Jack [Welborn]'s new tanks," the colonel said to his passenger as they passed.

From the passenger's seat, another colonel looked over his shoulder and caught sight of the tank's two exhaust stacks. German exhaust stacks. "Holy shit! It's a Tiger!" he shouted. "Get off the road."

The jeep jumped from the road and fled cross-country.

Rose's jeep was the next vehicle to come face to face with the shadowy German tank. Rose's driver also tried to veer to the left, but before he could make a clean escape, the German driver swerved the nearly 70-ton beast into the Americans' path and rammed Rose's jeep against a plum tree. The Greyhound behind Rose's jeep tried to pass the collision but didn't make it far. It was quickly stopped by more German tanks up the road.

Rose, his driver, and an aide emerged from the jeep with their hands held high. The outline of a German tank commander stood in the tank's turret clutching an MP 40 machine pistol.

The enemy commander screamed rapid-fire orders. His voice was harsh and guttural. Rose spoke Yiddish, which has similarities with German, but he couldn't decipher their words.

"*No versteh,*" Rose repeated. "I don't understand."

Maybe the German commander was demanding their pistols, Rose's driver suggested. Rose agreed. It was a small price to pay for their lives. Rose's aide removed his shoulder holster and set it on the tank. Rose went next. He unlatched the belt from around his hips. Then he let the belt and pistol fall to his feet.

Rose brought his hands up to eye level and was raising them farther when the German's machine pistol crackled to life. A spurt of flames split the darkness. Witnesses heard the German fire three more bursts and saw the general's helmet spin through the air.

When the German commander moved to reload, Rose's driver and aide bolted into the dark.

The two sergeants from the reconnaissance patrol found their general dead in front of his jeep. He lay on his back, with fourteen bullet holes in his body.

His pistol lay at his side, and his helmet, punched with bullet holes, lay nearby.

One of the American sergeants removed a blanket from Rose's jeep and wrapped his body in it. He and his fellow sergeant each lifted an end, and together they half carried, half dragged the body of their fallen leader up to Hamborn Castle.

Hardened fighting men were reduced to tears when they realized what the bundle held. Mourning fell over the troops. A soldier in the headquarters company put it best: "We felt like he was one of us."

Thirteen men had died and sixteen had been wounded from Task Force Welborn during the day and night of the massacre. But it was this fourteenth body that rattled the division most deeply.

That same night

In darkness, Buck led four doughs to a long line of American tanks. He was looking for a place to sleep. Other doughs had pitched tents, but Buck wasn't taking a chance on the weather. He had his eye on a particular tank at the left end of the line. It was wider than the others, offering more room to stretch out between its tracks.

He rapped the tank's hull with the butt of his rifle to draw someone's attention. Bob Earley leaned over the side and looked down from the turret.

"Mind if we sleep here?" Buck asked.

Earley was fine with it. He said he'd wake them if the tank had to move unexpectedly.

Buck crawled underneath the tank and his charges followed.

Lieutenant Boom had promoted Buck to assistant squad leader. Boom had even given him a fire team of rookies. The doughs following Buck were new replacements, who had been sent to fill empty seats. They were his responsibility now.

The men spread blankets over tarps before lying down side by side between the walls of wheels. The low ceiling made it feel like they were camping in a cave, but the ground was warm from the machine's engine. They could hear hammering and wrenching noises from the barns in a nearby village. Mechanics were readying the tanks for battle.

The rookies fell easily asleep, but Buck's mind was restless. At dawn they would attack the "Nazi Fort Knox." This time, he'd have to fight with rookies hanging on to his belt. They reminded Buck of himself when he first arrived in the company—which didn't exactly inspire confidence.

There was Clyde Reed, one of thirteen brothers and sisters. He'd been a sheltered kid, and the first thing he said when he met Buck was that he "didn't want to have to kill anybody." There was Dick Schneider, who was known as a picky eater. There was Stan Richards, slender and quiet, who acted like his M1 rifle wasn't actually that heavy. And there was Luther Jones, the eldest of the bunch at thirty-one; he would summon any passerby to show off photos of his children back home in West Virginia.

These men weren't ready for the intensity of an armored clash, and Buck knew it. Lying there, he worried about the choice he would have to face at dawn. How could he keep himself safe—and his men? When the bullets started flying, whom would he choose?

Inside the very same Pershing that Buck was sleeping under, Clarence prepared to sleep. The crew was taking turns on watch duty, and it wasn't his shift yet.

Clarence removed his seat back and laid a wooden board from his seat to Earley's. He scrunched a blanket up into a pillow, turned off the ceiling light, and lay back while he rested his feet on the gun mount.

Word had circulated around the company that the Germans had never searched Rose's body. Apparently they didn't know they'd just killed the highest-ranking American to die by enemy fire in the European theater—and a father.

Just before the trek to Paderborn, a newspaper reporter had asked General Rose what he was going to do after the war. The reporter had quoted Rose replying: "I have a son . . . He's four years old now, and I don't know him. We're going to get acquainted, and that's going to take a lot of time."

Now General Rose's son, Mike, was fatherless. And so was Spearhead.

Beyond the sorrow that was sapping the division's morale, Rose's death was proof of Clarence's worst fear: *It's just a matter of time.*

No one was untouchable.

Rose had often put himself at the forefront of the action. He had been the exception to the rule, the glimmer of hope for Clarence and any man who repeatedly faced the enemy.

No matter how bad the scrapes were, if Rose always landed on his feet, so could any GI. But that belief died when they laid the general's body on the dining room table in Hamborn Castle.

That was what leading got him.

That was what it got Paul Faircloth as he ran toward the wounded men at Mons.

Or Lieutenant Charlie Rose, killed at Hèdrée a week and a half after his son was born.

Or Sergeant Bill Hey, who hit a mine at Grand-Sart but didn't turn back.

Or Karl Kellner, the former grocery clerk who fell within sight of a cathedral.

Leading had gotten them all killed.

And come dawn tomorrow, Clarence would be leading again. The men had been briefed. Tanks had been fueled and racked with ammo. The Pershing would lead a task force against SS Panzerbrigade Westfalen in Spearhead's last major fight of the war. Surely the enemy would target the tank out in front of the others, the one with the biggest gun.

Trapped within the Pershing's cold steel walls, Clarence felt like it was the night before his own execution. He reflected on his twenty-one years of life and pondered the hereafter as he counted down the hours.

The hatch was right there in the ceiling above his face. He could walk out, flee, disappear, and get to live the rest of his life. Or he could stay and let fate carry him to his ending.

There in the darkness, Clarence searched for the answer to the riddle of the American tanker:

Why would any man saddle up for this?

CHAPTER 21

FAMILY

Easy Company greeted the dawn hesitantly. Dark clouds hung low. A few thin beams of golden sun dotted the distant hills and woods. The long line of tanks stretched to the east; two other task forces were alongside them.

Toward the end of the line, Clarence nervously smoked a cigarette in the Pershing's commander's position. It was around 6:15 a.m. Earley was away at the last briefing. Clarence's white scarf was tied around his neck in preparation for battle. He took long drags at the cigarette. Nothing could calm his anxiety. There was no escaping the sight in front of him.

The Pershing's gun pointed the way to Paderborn.

Two miles away, the old German town stood out amid the surrounding darkness. Five days earlier, an RAF (Royal Air Force) air raid had stomped across Paderborn's white houses and shattered its Gothic cathedral. Some areas were still smoldering.

But Clarence's concerns were far more immediate.

Easy Company was positioned to attack Paderborn's rail yard, where empty trains were parked. It was on the fringe of the town. Their orders were to take the rail yard, then hold it until reinforcements came to relieve them. From a tactical perspective, the rail yard was a tanker's nightmare. Enemy armor could hide behind abandoned train cars or use its long lanes of tracks and platforms as a shooting gallery.

Even getting to the rail yard would be a battle in its own right. Easy Company would first have to cross two miles of treacherous fields that were so pocked with bombs they looked like the surface of the moon. And then the company would have to punch through a tidy row of houses with slate roofs.

Unlike other civilian homes that Clarence had seen, these had no bedsheets unfurled from the windows—the signal of the occupants' surrender. And that in itself was worrisome.

By now, Clarence could sense the enemy even where he couldn't see them. SS Panzerbrigade Westfalen was just out there, waiting. He could feel them. As he burned through cigarette after cigarette, he couldn't shake the thought: *Why? They know it's over, why don't they just let this end?*

A rumble over his right shoulder drew his attention. Had F-Company finally come?

There was a gap between Easy Company and the next task force down the line. Many of Task Force X's troops—including F-Company's Shermans and two companies of doughs—still hadn't reached the line of departure.

Instead of F-Company, four M36 Jackson tank destroyers appeared. The M36s—each armed with 90mm guns—had come to provide fire support for Easy Company's attack. The firepower would come in handy. It was all but guaranteed that Easy Company would face enemy tanks.

The Sennelager base, the "Nazi Fort Knox," lay on the other side of Paderborn. Spearhead wouldn't be going there, though. This time, the enemy would be coming to them. The German armor schools at the base were deploying twenty-five tanks—a lot, considering that Germany had only around two hundred operational tanks and armored vehicles in the entire Western theater.

"Mount up!"

The men of A-Company moved to their tanks.

Doughs climbed up, hoping for a ride to the rail yard.

"Mind if we come aboard?"

Clarence looked and saw Buck and his four rookies waiting behind the Pershing. They assumed he was the commander.

Clarence didn't mind. He flicked away his cigarette and descended to give the doughs a hand.

"Scooch forward," Buck advised the rookies, "or you'll fry your butts." Clarence chuckled at the sight of the four rookies shimmying away from the grates over the radiator.

Just then, Earley came back from the briefing. Clarence wondered what the official update and orders would be. He leaned over to get a good look at Earley, trying to judge his level of anxiety. It was worse than he thought. Earley's pipe was vibrating between his chattering teeth.

Clarence would spare the crew and keep this observation to himself.

"Where's F-Company?" he asked.

Earley shook his head. That half of the task force was late, he said. And the attack couldn't wait for them.

Clarence cursed. F-Company was supposed to secure Paderborn's airfield—and whatever forces were still stationed there—on the way to the rail yard. Now, Easy Company would have to drive right past them.

The battalion chaplain, a tall, fit, white-haired man wearing purple vestments over his shoulders, approached the Pershing.

"How about a blessing?" he asked the men.

Earley was eager to receive one. He shouted inside the turret, which drew the crew from their hatches.

The chaplain took his place before the tank and removed his helmet. Clarence and Earley removed their headwear as Buck and the young doughs crowded forward to hear.

"I just want you all to remember that it's Easter," the chaplain said, "the day when life conquered death."

Easter! Amid the frenzy of preparing for battle, Clarence had totally forgotten about the holiday. He bowed his head alongside his fellow soldiers. The chaplain prayed aloud. When the blessing was finished, the chaplain wished the men a safe journey and moved on to the next tank.

A hush settled over the tankers and doughs.

Clarence watched men come down from their Shermans and assemble in front of their tanks while others stood in place as the chaplain worked his way down the line. Some men took a knee; others bowed their heads as the chaplain's blessing cut through the silence.

Clarence was struck by the sight of the staggered ranks of men ascending to their Shermans, silhouetted by the sun rising behind them.

He had always fought for his family. It had always been just the five of them—Earley, Smokey Davis, McVey, DeRiggi, and him—against the Germans. But on Easter 1945, Clarence saw the bigger picture for the first time.

His family was more than just the men in his own tank.

Hatch covers slammed up and down the line. It was time to go. Clarence turned to the doughs to offer some parting advice.

"Guys, when I fire you're going to get a hell of a scare, so just hold on tight."

Buck thanked him for the warning.

Clarence dropped inside the turret.

The field ahead of him held nothing but death. Yet, Clarence was exactly where he wanted to be. Paul Faircloth, General Rose—they had all made a choice. And that morning, Clarence had too: *We've got the biggest gun, we belong up front.*

As soon as his watch showed 6:30 a.m., Earley gave his commands. The Pershing's engine roared to life. Off it went toward Paderborn. The next in line, a Sherman, paused for about ten seconds before it launched forward. Ten seconds later, the next tank took off. And so on down the line.

Rather than going in a straight line, the tanks cut a "left

echelon" slant across the field. That way, each crew could guard the flanks of the tank next to them.

Perhaps the war's last great victory lay ahead of them. Paderborn was the link between the German forces in the Ruhr Valley and the rest of Germany. Everything—road traffic, rail traffic, communications—flowed through Paderborn. And the town could be the escape route for the Ruhr's 370,000 German troops—unless Spearhead got there first.

If the division could take Paderborn and link up with the division known as "Hell on Wheels," the "steel wall" would be complete. They would be the victors in the "largest encirclement battle in history" and the Third Reich would be doomed.

But first they needed to get to the Paderborn rail yard.

Buck held on to the turret for dear life. Trees blurred past, and he noticed that they were already bearing spring blossoms. On his right, tanks charged forward with their guns leveled. Doughs rode along with their legs dangling over the sides. The formation sped past one shell hole after another. Buck shouted, "Hang on!" to his rookies as they were violently jostled by the tank's movement. The obstacles slowed the Pershing down, but not by much.

As the tanks chugged past, enemy soldiers rose from shell holes, clutching Panzerfausts. If the war was really all but over, SS Panzerbrigade Westfalen hadn't gotten the memo.

Just then, a faraway Sherman exploded. Its doughs were

tossed into the air by the force of its rupturing fuel and ammunition.

A dough on a neighboring tank leaped to the turret. He blazed away with the machine gun, seeking revenge. But his defiance was brief. A Panzerfaust whizzed up from a shell hole and slammed the turret, blasting him to the ground with a fatal head wound.

Doughs fired back from their perches. Buck pressed himself against the turret and blasted away at the enemy. The rookies, following his lead, joined in the firing.

Accuracy was impossible. Tanks were bouncing over the pockmarked terrain. Within a few seconds, any Germans they saw in the craters were far behind.

Another Panzerfaust struck a Sherman's left track. The tank fell out of formation, its driver either dead or wounded at the controls. Stunned doughs fell off the sides and fled the crippled tank, which was still rolling haphazardly. If they didn't carefully time their scramble to safety, they would be crushed.

The Pershing slowed further to prevent the formation from disintegrating. Buck rose from his crouch to peek at their progress. Despite the resistance they'd faced, they were more than halfway there.

But they weren't in the clear yet.

Suddenly, dozens of glowing red orbs sprang up and arced toward Easy Company. A Luftwaffe (German air force) flak regiment had turned its 20mm flak guns on them.

Across the company, doughs made themselves small. Buck and the rookies flattened themselves on the hot engine deck as the orbs descended upon them. The orbs picked up speed. The shells targeted a Sherman near the airfield, blasting a dough off the back. One driver rode his Sherman into a shell crater to avoid getting hit. With a metallic crunch, doughs were flung headlong over the turret. A radioman picked himself up and limped for cover. A shell felled him mere feet from safety.

The red hose of orbs swept far and wide and zoomed toward the Pershing. Buck clutched his helmet as shells landed in front of the tank, showering him with dirt. A hit smacked the Pershing's side, tossing a wave of sparks over Buck and the rookies.

Buck crawled forward to the left side of the turret so only his legs would be exposed.

"The hell with this!" a rookie shouted. Gripping a handle on the left side of the Pershing's hull, the rookie jumped to the ground and ran alongside the tank, carrying his rifle in his other hand.

Another rookie followed his lead and dropped down from the tank as well. Yet another followed soon after. Before Buck knew it, all four rookies were running alongside the tank. He remained flat where he was, watching.

The glowing orbs stopped hosing across the tanks.

Buck lifted his head. What had crimped the Germans' fire?

Earley was silent as he rode head and shoulders above the turret. Suspiciously silent. Far behind him, command had made up for F-Company's absence by dispatching an "assault section" of three Shermans to storm the airfield.

Clarence could only endure it for so long. "How are we looking, Bob?" he asked.

"Not good," Earley replied.

Only about six Shermans remained in formation, and there were wide gaps between them. A long trail of derelict tanks stretched in their wake. Easy Company had been whittled in half. And the fighting was just beginning.

A green bolt rocketed toward them. A violent strike of steel on steel sent Earley ducking for cover. Down the line, a Sherman was stopped cold in its tracks. The shot was terrifyingly precise. Shouts of alarm filled Clarence's earphones.

Easy Company plowed forward as more green bolts, cracking like whips, zipped through the ranks. A ricochet struck a tank and spun skyward. Muzzle flashes were seen coming from the east side of the rail yard. Shermans fired blindly in that direction. One crew turned back. Another lurched to a stop after absorbing a heavy hit. The crew rolled from their hatches before a fountain of flames overtook the turret.

The platoon leader of the M36 tank destroyers radioed a warning: they had seen enemy tanks. The M36 crews reported seeing a Tiger and what looked like a Panther and two self-propelled guns. The Germans were firing from the northeast, where they were hidden in the rail yard. Clarence's blood ran cold at the news.

Earley hunted for a target with his binoculars but couldn't see one. Clarence grew increasingly frustrated. The only things he saw were the shadowy rail-yard buildings.

Orange tracers soared over Easy Company from behind like

flaming arrows. Over Earley's right shoulder, the M36s were firing back.

Clarence followed the flight of the tracers as they landed in the rail yard's shadows.

With the shells pointing the way, he took aim at the space between buildings. There was little point in firing without seeing the target. The reticle was bouncing, which made it hard to fix his aim. Besides, these German tank commanders wouldn't be intimidated by a near miss.

Clarence's finger tightened on the trigger.

Whoever the enemy was, and wherever his shells would land, none of that mattered to him. He had a message for the Germans at the rail yard: if he was going to die here, it wouldn't be sitting on a full load of ammo.

The Pershing's 90mm belched one earsplitting roar after another. Buck gripped a ring alongside the turret and held on, his ears ringing and his lungs struggling for air. His vision wavered through watering eyes. And the worst of it was that there was no anticipating the next blast. It could come at any moment.

We're never going to make it! he thought.

The Pershing's crew must have been thinking the same thing. And yet the 46-ton tank surged forward, kicking clumps of grass in its trail. The neighboring Shermans went to full throttle as well.

"Get up here!" Buck shouted to the rookies.

Setting his rifle aside, Buck leaned over, keeping one hand on the turret ring, and helped lift a rookie up and over the tank's spinning road wheels. He then grabbed a second, and a third, until just one rookie remained on the ground.

The last rookie was flying alongside the speeding tank even though he kept a grip on the handle. Each time he got his feet beneath him, he lost his footing. With the other rookies' help, Buck managed to pull him back aboard.

Earley rose from the turret and shouted at the distracted doughs: "Prepare to dismount!"

The Pershing slowed to a stop fifty yards from the row of houses—still dangerously within a Panzerfaust's range.

Clarence saw nothing but trouble through his periscope. The enemy had dug foxholes in the front yards of the houses, and there was movement at ground level. Helmeted heads rose up for a peek. In the background, German soldiers darted between houses. Clarence brought the coaxial machine gun to life with a press of the trigger. And just like that, German troops shrank from sight.

"Tell the doughs the yards are full of them!" Clarence said.

Earley ventured outside for a quick look before returning. "Too late, they're off," he said. "Watch your fire!"

Buck and his fire team surged ahead on foot. Meanwhile, the Pershing held back. The area was too risky for tanks until Buck and the other doughs cleared the houses.

A German machine gun sent green snaps of fire across the yards from a house down the block. Buck dropped to the lawn.

Two rookies hit the dirt next to him. The other two rookies didn't get the message and went charging headlong into the yard.

At that moment, a realization struck them. There were foxholes all around them. Foxholes full of German soldiers. The rookies froze with stunned expressions as bullets tore the air around them.

"Get down!" Buck shouted.

One rookie ran to the nearest foxhole. A German looked up at him with hands raised in surrender. The rookie motioned frantically with his rifle: *Out!* The American jumped inside as soon as the German climbed out the foxhole. Facing the choice of surrender or being run over by American tanks, the enemy chose the first option.

The other rookie disappeared into the nearest foxhole.

Another Sherman pulled up to the right, delivering Lieutenant Boom with his headquarters squad. Buck was relieved to see that Boom had caught up.

With three or four men, Boom charged the house from which the enemy machine gun was firing. They kicked in the door before disappearing inside. After a few moments, the enemy machine gun went silent. When he reemerged, Boom motioned for Buck and the others to join him.

Buck shoved two of his rookies to jump-start the shell-shocked doughs. He then called another rookie from his foxhole with a shout.

Buck stopped in his tracks as he ran through the yard. He was one rookie short.

He located the missing rookie in a foxhole to his left. The inexperienced dough was standing face to face with a German Wehrmacht soldier. The two boys, about the same age, were clutching their rifles to their chests and shaking in their boots.

Buck motioned for the German's rifle, grabbed it by the muzzle, and tossed it away. Then he reached down and hauled the rookie out by the collar, leaving the German behind.

The rookie's feet were moving so slowly that Buck had to drag him forward. Buck plunged into the house, pulling the rookie inside behind him.

CHAPTER 22

COME OUT AND FIGHT

That same morning
PADERBORN

Buck felt an immense sense of security inside the house, as if he had left the war behind him. He caught his breath while the rookie he had rescued steadied himself against the wall.

The inside of the house was buzzing with activity. A dozen doughs were bustling around. Boom deployed lookouts.

Buck discovered a white Easter cake sitting on a table. He was amazed that no one had touched it.

The front door flew open and A-Company's commander—a bespectacled captain named Walter Berlin—entered, followed by other doughs. Buck was glad to see Captain Berlin; the man always had a steady, calm manner that Buck respected.

A worried look settled across Berlin's long face as he took a radio call. He handed the headset back to his radioman and asked, "Anyone know if our Pershing got in?"

"Yes sir, we rode in on it," Buck said.

Berlin was relieved. Two German tanks had been spotted. They were near the buildings where the M36 tank destroyers had been firing earlier. If they came any closer, the Pershing would be desperately needed.

The attack would go on.

The captain briefed Lieutenant Boom on the assault plan. Behind the house sat the railroad yards. There was a switch house in the yards, which would be the perfect place for the men to keep watch. Boom was tasked with taking twenty men to secure the switch house. Once they succeeded, friendly tanks would move forward.

There was no time to waste. Buck checked his ammunition and turned to his fire team. The four rookies were standing so close to one another that they could have fit on a sofa.

Buck warned them to watch their spacing when they went outside. "If there is a German machine gun and you're clustered, you're going to be their first target."

The doughs streamed out the back door of the house. The platoon sergeant led the men toward the switch house, about a hundred yards away. Meanwhile, Lieutenant Boom stayed behind to brief the tank crews on A-Company's plan.

It was strangely quiet as the men entered the rail yard. Buck and the doughs charged forward, unaware of just how alone they were. Buck glanced back at his rookies. They had taken his advice to the extreme, keeping a wide berth—twenty yards or more—from one another. If the gap between two doughs narrowed, each would frantically wave the other away. At any other place or time, Buck would have found humor in the spectacle.

The two-story brick switch house lay ahead. Buck and several doughs burst inside with their rifles leveled. The first floor was windowless and mostly empty. Through the grated metal floor above, they saw that the second story was empty as well. The building was clear.

"*Hilfe!*" A German voice moaned for help. "*Hilfe!*"

Outside, a dough discovered a badly wounded German soldier. They carried the man inside and laid him on the concrete floor. Buck cringed at the sight when a medic lifted his shirt. The man's stomach was torn open. It looked like a bullet or shrapnel had hit him across the gut.

The German begged for water with an outstretched hand. Buck uncapped his canteen, but before he could give the enemy water, the medic stopped him: "He's going to die, but the water will only kill him faster." The German laid his head back and started moaning again as the medic tended to him as best he could. It pained Buck to cap his canteen. Even if it wouldn't help the man, he wanted to offer the German some comfort in his final moments.

Buck held the rookies back while three veteran doughs pounded up the metal stairs to keep watch. From their higher perch, the veterans gazed down onto a train station in view.

There was movement below.

A scope flashed in a train car about thirty yards away. That was when a German sniper lifted his rifle to his shoulder. The Americans ducked just before a bullet punched through the glass of the switch house, splintering the top of the window frame. The three veterans lay flat on their stomachs above, cursing after their close call.

The staccato tap of bullets drew everyone's attention. Bullets were splattering against the outside of the switch house. Glass shattered and rained from the second-floor windows. Machine-gun fire hit the bricks.

The Germans were mounting a full-blown counterattack.

Lieutenant Boom bolted breathlessly into the switch house. German soldiers were pouring from the train station and advancing toward them, he reported.

The doughs had fought the Luftwaffe and the German army that morning. But the enemy outside was clearly a different breed of soldier, the type who would pin himself in a train car with little chance of escape. The type who wore the lightning-bolt runes of the SS.

Boom moved toward the staircase with his eyes locked on the broad windows. He was determined to take charge and hold the switch house as ordered.

Buck grabbed his sleeve. "Please don't, Lieutenant. That sniper's just waiting."

Boom shook free and turned to face Buck. "I have to see what we're up against." He flashed a nervous smile and continued up the stairs, brushing past Buck. Buck was overcome by dread. He knew Boom. And he knew what Boom was about to attempt. A hush fell over the first floor. Everyone looked up except Buck, who couldn't bring himself to watch.

Boom raised his carbine to his shoulder as he turned the corner at the top of the stairs. With the body of a basketball star, he was a lanky target.

Buck flinched when the shot rang out. Boom crashed backward to the floor and his carbine and helmet rattled.

Buck glanced up in disbelief. A man ran to the top of the stairs and returned shaking his head. Lieutenant Boom was dead, shot through the throat. From there, the bullet had probably hit his spinal cord. He'd never had a chance.

Buck slumped against the nearest wall, his helmet scraping brick. He buried his face in his hands, overwhelmed by a swirl of grief, fear, and anger. He had tried to stop Boom from giving the sniper the satisfaction.

Buck returned to his senses and found the rookies looking to him for guidance. He dried his eyes and wiped his nose. All of their lives were on the line now. Their shelter was being chewed apart. Bullets continued to splatter the building. Bricks shattered into clouds of red dust.

Over the racket of gunfire, Buck could hear the platoon sergeant radioing Captain Berlin. "Sir, we can't make it back, it's too hot!" he said.

Buck's mind cycled through their options for escape. But from what he could gather, A-Company didn't have the manpower to send a relief force. Air support couldn't help them either. A flight of P-47s was arriving above the clouds but couldn't descend because it was too foggy to see.

Buck's mind cycled through their options for escape. *Where are our tanks?* he thought. Then, he remembered. For the tanks to advance, the doughs were first to have gained observation over the tracks. And that hadn't happened.

Buck's stomach sank at the realization. The armor that had

brought them in wouldn't be coming to their rescue. That simply wasn't part of the plan.

The doughs in the switch house desperately needed tank support. So far, only Easy Company had reached Paderborn to help. And how many of *their* tanks had made it in? The division had committed three task forces to the attack. Salisbury's tank was unable to continue because of mechanical problems, and another vehicle was also out of commission. So the officers had passed command to the last platoon sergeant still standing.

Bob Earley.

Earley had heard the pleas over the radio. He couldn't just sit there and listen to the doughs in distress, regardless of what the plan had been. "We're pushing on the railroad," he announced over the radio. "Anyone who's left, fall in with us."

The Pershing rolled forward with Earley standing head and shoulders above his hatch.

A 76 Sherman pulled out beside them, with Red Villa in the turret and Chuck Miller at the gun. Farther down the line a second 76 emerged. Its gunner was Clarence's friend Private John Danforth, a twenty-eight-year-old Texan built like a football player.

Three tanks. Three crews. It was all that Easy Company could muster.

Side by side, each tank moved slowly as they approached the switch house from behind. At the sight of American armor, the enemy's fire slackened. Their foot soldiers crouched, trying to take cover.

Each Easy Company tank gunner kept an eye on a different sector. Clarence covered the left flank of the formation. Chuck Miller aimed forward. Danforth held down the right flank.

The tanks had barely edged over the first tracks when Danforth saw trouble.

"Tank!" His commander broadcast the alert over the radio. "One o'clock, behind the station."

Everyone halted. Earley swung his binoculars.

An enemy tank peeked out from behind the train station across the tracks. Its gun was pointing toward the switch house. Was this an opening for the Americans to land the first shot? They hoped so.

Danforth's 76mm barked.

Sparks leaped from the German tank downrange. Danforth had delivered only a glancing blow. The enemy tank threw itself into reverse and slipped from sight.

Everyone groaned and cursed. It was a bad miss.

The chatter cut out abruptly.

The enemy tank was not alone.

A second German tank rolled forward from the same position, trying its luck. Chuck Miller was waiting for it. Chuck's Sherman spat a length of flame. The tracer shell struck the enemy tank. But it ricocheted skyward—another strike that failed to penetrate.

The second German tank retreated without firing a shot. Where it was going next was anyone's guess.

Earley radioed Task Force X from the Pershing, announcing: "At least two enemy tanks here . . . our shots bounced off."

Clarence had seen enough. *Now we've got two pissed-off German tanks!* If they were going to fire, they needed a weapon that would kill. He swung the 90mm toward the station and set the reticle where the enemy tanks had been.

"I've got my gun on the spot," Clarence told Earley. "Tell the guys to watch the flanks."

Earley radioed directions to the others. But it was too late. Danforth's tank had already sent out a green lance of tracer. The clash of steel going through steel rippled through the rail yard. The sound raised the hair on the back of Clarence's neck. Was Danforth okay? His eyes drifted. A slap on his right shoulder brought him back to reality.

"Three o'clock!" Earley shouted. The shot had originated from the far end of the station.

Clarence swung the gun farther right and took aim. The German tank had already vanished from sight.

Clarence shivered. *This guy's good.*

From his perch outside, Earley watched as Danforth and his crew abandoned their tank. Some of them limped, but they had all made it out alive.

It was time to get back to business.

"Bob, watch the right," Clarence said. "He knows this place better than us."

Earley agreed with Clarence's assessment.

Villa came over the radio, sounding shaky. *What now?*

The choice was in Earley's hands. They could retreat—

though that might embolden the enemy to follow them and swarm the switch house. Or they could stand their ground.

Earley didn't hesitate to make his decision. The Pershing and Sherman wheeled to face the train station, side by side, with hulls pointing forward. They stopped. Each could cover only about half of the battlefield, but this was better than running away.

With one tank, they could never do it.

With two, they just might be able to hold.

It was as if someone had rung a bell, announcing it was time to attack Easy Company tanks. Bullets cracked and zinged against the turrets. When the machine guns joined in, a shower of sparks flew over the tanks' open hatches. A sniper's bullet clanged the hatch cover. Earley dropped inside to take shelter. German soldiers were gunning for the tanks' commanders. Machine guns blinked rapidly from their hiding place at the train station.

With his eyes pressed to the periscope, Clarence didn't know where to begin. Flashes were coming from every direction. He steadied the reticle on a train car. His finger hovered over the coaxial trigger as he waited for a German soldier to reappear.

Then, he remembered. He could still reach them.

His finger wrapped the main gun trigger, and the 90mm spat out an armor-piercing shell. The train car shattered on impact, which sent a cloud of red minerals—and whatever remained of the enemy soldier—skyward.

The new loader, De Riggi's replacement, slammed home a fresh shell. Clarence shifted his aim and another train car popped.

Each red cloud that Clarence sent billowing into the sky doubled as a smoke signal to the enemy—"Come out and fight!"

Smokey's bow gun sprang to life as it fired orange tracers. Clarence joined in, and now two orange hoses poured downrange. A third followed, and a fourth joined the party as Red Villa's tank added its firepower to the mix.

The four orange streams weaved and crisscrossed one another. The noise from the multiple guns blended into one long rip that sounded like tearing fabric.

A blurry yellow shape flying through the air caught Clarence's attention. It fell directly in front of the Pershing before it burst with a blinding flash. Clarence reeled back as shrapnel smacked against the tank's armor. He recognized that explosion all too well. It was fire from a Panzerfaust.

Clarence returned to his periscope. Outside, cinders were still raining down, and another Panzerfaust was approaching. A warhead soared over the distant train cars like a football, then landed with another flash. Moments later, more warheads followed, leaving thin trails of black smoke in their wakes.

Villa's tank drove forward, trying to escape the line of fire. Clarence tracked the smoke trail to the opposite side of the tracks and realized that it came from a residential neighborhood. It was there that enemy soldiers were darting onto a narrow footbridge, firing, then retreating out of the line of fire, shielded by boxcars.

Clarence raked the footbridge with machine-gun fire repeatedly. But despite his efforts, the Germans refused to surrender. Several daring souls dashed forward, gripping a Panzerfaust. Most were felled by Clarence's fire, but a few managed to launch shots in his direction.

With every Panzerfaust that streaked toward the Pershing, Clarence grew increasingly desperate. Sooner or later, the enemy would land a direct hit.

Someone had to destroy the footbridge the Germans were standing on.

Clarence had a plan in mind, but it was risky. It required a high-explosive shell.

Shrapnel clattered against the Pershing's armor. Inside the tank, it sounded like a hailstorm was hitting a tin roof. The Panzerfausts were landing closer and closer to their position. Clarence had to act. "HE!" Clarence called.

The loader retrieved a silver-tipped high-explosive shell and slid it into the breech. The seconds ticked by slowly. Finally, the breech closed with a clang. Clarence was in business.

He settled the reticle on the center of the bridge as his finger tensed against the trigger. It was just then, right as he was about to squeeze the trigger, that he saw it: a Panzerfaust warhead flying straight at him, in what seemed like slow motion.

Clarence gasped. All he could do was watch. At the last second, the warhead dipped. A white flash filled his periscope as the explosion rocked the tank. The overwhelming force raced straight down the 90mm's barrel, causing the gun to discharge without Clarence's even touching the trigger.

A flaming ball of gases escaped the breech and rose toward

Earley. The commander howled in pain as the flaming ball seared the side of his face. The turret turned dark with smoke. McVey and Smokey were screaming.

Clarence bent over, heaving for breath.

"We're on fire!" Earley shouted. "Bail out!"

Clarence turned just in time to see Earley's boots abandoning the turret. Sunlight poured inside when the loader threw open his hatch and climbed up and out. Clarence scrambled back through the turret and snatched a Thompson submachine gun from its rack on his way out. Even if he had to abandon the tank, he wasn't going down without a fight.

He felt the breath of passing bullets hot on his face as he emerged from the commander's position. He dropped to the engine deck, then rolled off the back of the Pershing before he fell hard to the ground.

Earley and the loader crouched in a ditch behind the tank. They waved Clarence toward them. Bullets nipped at Clarence's heels as he ran to safety, sliding feet-first into the ditch like a baseball player going for home plate. Smokey and McVey were missing. Clarence peered over the ditch and searched for his friends.

A murderous flood of green machine-gun tracers was still splashing the Pershing. Both men were frantically crawling beneath the tank, trying to get out.

"Come on!" Clarence shouted, waving them toward safety.

Smokey and McVey made a run for it. As they hurled themselves toward the ditch, tripping and tumbling to the edge, Clarence and the others pulled them inside.

Smokey lay on his back and cursed a blue streak at the sky.

Earley and the others racked rounds into their pistols. Clarence worked the action of his Thompson. They might have to shoot their way out of this tight spot. He glanced over the top of the ditch before a snap of German bullets sent him diving back down. Green tracers kicked up the dirt just inches above his face. They pinged off the steel rail tracks like fireflies.

Earley gritted his teeth, saying nothing. Clarence's chest felt tight with dread.

Meanwhile, Chuck Miller, Red Villa, and their crew were still fighting in their tank. Their turret fired in every direction out of sheer desperation. They wouldn't stand a chance alone. They couldn't defend themselves from all directions, and when the enemy advanced with Panzerfausts, the last tank would go silent.

Pinned in his shallow grave, Clarence feared that the end was near. *It's only a matter of time.* It was a mantra Clarence had recited, an acknowledgment of his circumstances. Now his time had come.

And the Germans realized it as well. Everything lay in plain view.

A Pershing, abandoned and smoking. A crew, pinned like rats. The enemy must have called their command center to the north and urged them to send in the big guns—to "Strike them now!"

That was the only explanation for what was to follow.

CHAPTER 23

THE GIANT

That same morning, April 1, 1945
PADERBORN RAIL YARD

Buck kept the rookies close by his side. Together, they crouched deep in the shadows of the switch house.

The Germans were closing in on them. In the words of one eyewitness account, the building was being "shot to pieces."

The wounded German was still pleading for assistance, addressing Private Danforth and his battered crew, who sat against the wall with pistols across their laps.

One of Buck's rookies wanted to make a break for it, back the way they'd come. But Buck kept him from bolting.

"You'll just get cut down!" Buck said.

Out there, death was everywhere.

From the ditch, Clarence saw it too. The Germans' focus had shifted. They were crossing the tracks toward the switch house, stopping only to fire their weapons.

The enemy's plan was apparent: First, subdue that strong

point. Then, silence the last functioning tank and end the brave stand of Chuck Miller, Red Villa, and their crew.

Clarence took aim over the top with his Thompson. If the Germans wanted to get to Chuck, they'd have to get past him first. As Clarence surveyed his field of fire, his eye settled on the Pershing.

Wait a second.

The tank was still idling in place, with its gun aimed. The smoke had stopped rising, providing him with a clear view of the damage.

My God.

Clarence saw cause for hope.

He had *thought* that the Panzerfaust had hit the Pershing's barrel. But no, they'd only hit the muzzle brake at the *tip*. That was the only damage.

Clarence drew the crew's attention over the clash of battle— "I think that gun can fire!"

Everyone crept over to take a look at the tank. Earley squinted. It was risky. If the gun barrel was fractured, that meant a shell could get stuck—which would send the blast back into the turret.

Clearly, they couldn't hold the Germans off for much longer. Time was running out.

"The tube looks okay," Clarence said, trying to sound sure.

"That's a heck of a gamble," Earley said. If they were wrong, the mistake could wipe out the entire crew. "Are you certain?"

All eyes turned to Clarence. "No," he said. "But we have to try something."

"Let's go, then," Earley said, leading the way to the Pershing. He climbed aboard and crouched behind the turret. Clarence and the others followed in a mad dash.

Across the rail yard, the German troops aimed rifles and machine guns at the Americans. Bullets dinged against the Pershing as Clarence and the loader dropped inside the turret. Earley slammed the hatch cover behind them.

Under the Pershing, McVey wormed his way to the escape hatch. He pulled himself up and into the tank. Smokey was lagging behind, though, and struggling to catch his breath.

"Put us up there with Red," Earley ordered.

The Pershing rolled toward the lone fighting Sherman as McVey fed the engine some gas. No one had noticed Smokey's empty seat.

Unable to pull himself inside, the bow gunner was being dragged forward on his back as he gripped the escape hatch with all his might beneath the moving tank.

"Stop, goddammit!" Smokey screamed into the hull.

McVey heard him, looked over, and realized that Smokey was missing.

The tank screeched to a halt, allowing Smokey to pull himself inside. Once he was safely on board, a tempest of curse words flooded the intercom.

Earley asked what had happened. Clarence fought not to snicker as Smokey explained.

Earley radioed Villa. His voice was all business. "We're back," he said. "They got us down, but not out."

Villa welcomed the crew's return, relieved.

Soon after the Pershing had started rolling, Clarence asked Earley to stop. He had spotted German machine guns near the station.

He called for a high-explosive shell.

The loader threw a fresh shell in. The breech snapped shut. Clarence's finger hesitated against the trigger. Firing was a heck of a gamble. If the barrel was fractured, they wouldn't survive to figure out they'd been wrong.

Earley opened his hatch to look around with his binoculars.

It was then that he heard them: the unmistakable sounds of metal squeaking on metal, and steel tracks slapping the ground. The raspy snarl of an engine accelerating. Earley glanced over his right shoulder. The noise was originating from about fifty yards *behind* them.

Something was moving straight in their direction.

"Tank!"

Clarence heard the call and felt Earley's heavy grip on his right shoulder, the signal to turn the turret. "Five o'clock," Earley said.

Clarence couldn't believe his ears. *Five o'clock?* Someone was practically behind them. He turned the turret so hard to the right that he nearly broke the pistol grip.

"What is it?" Clarence asked.

Earley replied with the word that every American tanker dreaded: "Panther."

All of a sudden, Clarence felt cold.

Earley's muttering certainly didn't help. "Faster, faster, faster." Earley held on above the rotating turret, powerless to do anything but watch. There was no need for binoculars anymore. The Panther was that close, and it was ready to fight. From Earley's vantage point, though, something didn't add up. The Pershing was the closer target, and yet the Panther's gun was pointed all the way to the rear: toward Villa's tank.

The Germans must have received a radio call warning them that the Pershing was abandoned. And that the Sherman was the one ripe for the picking. But that was ten minutes ago. Things were different. Now, the Pershing had risen from the dead.

And the Panther had taken notice.

Inside the enemy tank, the crew was likely urging their gunner to shift his aim to the Pershing, the tank with a gun turning toward them. Sure enough, the Panther's gun began swinging left while the Pershing's gun swung right, the two guns turning toward each other like gates closing. Someone wasn't going to drive away from this.

Clarence held his eyes to his periscope. Then, he remembered: they had the wrong shell loaded. A high-explosive shell was locked in the breech. This shell was the right firepower needed to take out a machine-gun nest. But it wouldn't dent a Panther.

Gotta clear the gun! Clarence thought in a panic. "Ready an AP!" he yelled to his loader.

The loader lifted a black-tipped T33 armor-piercing shell from the ready rack, anticipating a shell change.

"Not yet," Clarence said. "On my call."

A shell change would take time, and Clarence didn't have a second to spare. He'd have to do it differently from the way any instructor would teach in gunnery school.

Above the turret, Earley kept silent. He could sense that

Clarence must have a plan. If he didn't, they were all already dead.

Clarence gripped the wheel that controlled the gun's elevation. He waited for his first glimpse of the Panther. After a moment, it appeared out of the corner of his eye. Clarence spun the elevation handwheel counterclockwise, using every ounce of muscle.

Outside the tank, the 90mm gun dipped. The turret kept turning until it reached the Panther. The 90mm roared and the HE shell slammed the ground in front of the Panther, kicking cinders and dust in the enemy tank's face. For a moment, the Panther disappeared behind the cloud.

Inside the turret, Clarence angled the pistol grip.

"Now!" he shouted.

The loader slammed the AP shell into the breech. Spinning the elevation wheel, Clarence returned the 90mm to its level position. He set his eyes to the periscope.

The huge Panther reappeared as the cloud of dust settled down. Its gun was still turning, its black muzzle hole searching for him.

Clarence's finger crushed the trigger.

The 90mm spoke with an earsplitting crack. A blinding flash illuminated both tanks. The 24-pound shell went spinning through the air at 2,774 feet per second and covered the distance in a blink.

A screech of sparks blasted from the Panther's front armor. The shell had bored through more than five and a half inches of steel—and it kept going into the tank's guts.

"Hit!" Earley shouted with elation. The loader locked another shell in the breech.

Clarence's finger hovered over the trigger in a rare moment of indecision.

Wait.

As the dust settled around the enemy tank, he could see figures—the Panther's crew. They were leaping from the turret. The driver was opening his hatch. There was a gaping black hole in the Panther's armor between where the driver and the radio operator had once sat. The driver flopped over the side of the tank and fled to the rear.

Clarence peered through the periscope sight. Instincts took over. An enemy soldier was downrange, a man who, mere moments before, had tried to kill Clarence and his crew.

The German driver disappeared behind his tank, then reappeared. He might have been injured or in shock, because he staggered and dropped in the road. Clarence fixed his eye to the 6x zoom sight and set the reticle on the man.

At that exact moment, the German turned and stared back at the Pershing. The zoom sight brought his face close, as if Clarence were standing a few feet away from him. The driver was young, with brown hair. His eyes welled up with despair as he realized his mistake.

Clarence balanced the power of life and death in his index finger. With a few pounds of pressure, his coaxial could wipe one more enemy soldier from the earth.

Those were his orders, after all. This was his duty, too.

But Clarence hedged.

Fighting to the end. Killing to the end. That was what *they* did, the Germans he'd been fighting all these months.

And he wasn't about to become someone like them.

Clarence nudged the pistol grip to the left. The 90mm slid off the man and stopped, its muzzle brake bobbing like a nod.

It was a signal. The Panther was out of the war and that was enough for Clarence.

The German driver's eyes changed. He stood up and ran away in disbelief.

The Pershing's shot reverberated across the rail yard. German soldiers could see their Panther sitting there frozen in defeat. And they could hear the rattle of the two American tanks that were still standing.

The enemy stopped advancing. Their fire tapered off. There was nothing left to win here. As if pulled by puppet strings, the German forces retreated across the tracks and into the residential neighborhood on the other side.

Meanwhile, the Pershing's engine shuddered to a stop in front of the switch house. It parked near the abandoned Panther. Villa's tank pulled up beside the Pershing. Both American tanks were speckled silver by bullets or shrapnel.

But relief had finally come. F-Company's Shermans had secured the rail yard with two companies of doughs. They had claimed ninety-three German prisoners of war in the process, before continuing their sweep into town.

"It was disgusting to watch how the Third Reich died," wrote a German sergeant afterward. "None of its leaders came to the foxholes to defend it . . . as they had promised. They all abandoned their posts and fled, afraid of being held responsible, or cowardly died by suicide."

Clarence came down from the turret and joined his crew as they examined the hole in the muzzle brake. Another inch to the side and the Panzerfaust warhead would have landed in the barrel itself. His gamble to fire the gun had been riskier than even he had imagined. But it had paid off.

Still shaken by the ordeal, Earley puffed away at his pipe. He had never seen anything like Clarence's first shot, a deliberate miss. Later on, he wouldn't hesitate to tell him so.

If Clarence had called for a shell change as soon as he realized that the wrong ammunition was loaded—as gunners were trained to do—he would have condemned himself, and his entire crew, to death. But luckily, Clarence had never been formally trained as a gunner. His own instincts had been enough.

Red Villa's crew gathered around the Pershing and its tankers. Chuck Miller approached Clarence with a wry smile. "I hear you missed with your first shot," Chuck said.

"Yeah, but not the second!" Clarence said.

Chuck laughed and hugged his friend tightly.

A chain of exhausted A-Company doughs slogged out of the switch house without looking back. Buck lingered inside long after everyone else had departed.

Lieutenant Boom's eyes were closed, but Buck took a knee

alongside his body and spoke to him as if he were still alive. Buck told Boom that everyone had made it, and thanked him for keeping them safe.

Boom would be buried in the Netherlands American Cemetery, near the grave of General Rose. His name would appear in his hometown paper one last time, but not in the sports highlights column where it usually could be found. This time, the article would include his name, a photo, and a caption: "Makes Sacrifice."

Afterward, having returned to A-Company's headquarters— the home with the untouched Easter cake—Buck settled his eyes on a curious sight: a knocked-out German tank down the road that looked as if it were frozen in motion.

Byron and the rookies went to investigate it.

It was a Tiger I, Germany's most legendary tank of the war, a monstrous machine that looked as if it had been chiseled from a block of stone. Its interlacing wheels were wrapped in tracks that stood chest-high on Buck. Byron circled the Tiger, looking up at it in awe. The rookies climbed aboard.

A commotion to the left of the Tiger drew Buck's attention. An Easy Company tank crew was pushing a German tank crew against a brick wall. They were looking for one man in particular.

A rough American tanker who, like Buck, came from the Deep South singled out the German tank commander, throwing him down to the ground. He then began kicking him over and over again. The German's crew watched, powerless to intervene.

Buck cursed. Hadn't there been enough violence already? He told the rookies they might want to look away.

Buck and Private First Class Byron Mitchell moved in behind the angry American crew. Buck expected to find SS runes
on the German's collar but saw only silver Panzer skulls. The
man was a Wehrmacht tanker, probably the commander of the
Tiger.

The rest of the American tank crew encouraged the abuse.
Buck shot Byron a look that asked: *Is it worth interceding?*
Byron shrugged in response.

Maybe the tankers had lost a buddy that morning? It had
been a rough one. Doughs and tankers, everyone had bled taking the rail yard. A-Company had suffered seventeen casualties
and Easy Company fifteen—not to mention their five tanks destroyed and others disabled. For the next two years, Shermans
would lie rusting in the fields of Paderborn.

The aggressive American tanker drew his 1911 pistol. He
turned red as the pistol shook in his hand.

"You don't need to do this," Buck suddenly said aloud. Even
the tanker's own crew agreed with Buck. From his knees, the
German commander removed his peaked cap and pleaded for
mercy.

Byron saw something and began shaking his head—No, no,
no. He couldn't take his pale blue eyes off the German commander's face. It was a face that was burned into his memory.
He'd recognize it anywhere.

The rough tanker shucked a round into the pistol, but before
he could make a move, Byron thrust himself between the gun-
man and his target. It was an audacious move. There was no
telling what this enraged Southern man was capable of. Byron

took a closer look at the German before turning to face the incensed American.

"Don't shoot him," Byron pleaded.

"What the hell, boy?" said the tanker. "Are you a Kraut lover?"

"This fellow saved my life," Byron said, "and if you'll get that damn gun out of my face, I'll tell you about it."

The tanker uttered a harrumph of disbelief but lowered his pistol all the same. Buck felt a wave of relief wash over him.

Byron explained how he and some other doughs had been captured. They had been forced to dig their own graves when a German tank commander—this same man—had driven past, seen what was happening, and prevented their execution.

Buck was floored by his friend's revelation. He remembered the shocking story; Byron had once told the crew back in the half-track. And what a coincidence: *This* was the German guy who'd saved him?

Buck stepped to Byron's side with palms raised. "He's telling the truth," he said.

The American tanker's eyes shot back and forth between Buck and Byron. "Are you sure this is the same Kraut?" he asked.

Byron was certain and turned the question back on the tanker. How could he forget the man who had saved his life?

The tanker almost spat as he holstered his pistol. "Get him out of my sight before I change my mind."

Byron pulled the German commander toward his fellow prisoners. The American tank crew moved on. Buck and Byron lingered with the prisoners until someone came along to claim them.

The German commander laid a hand on Byron's shoulder. "Thank you," he said in English.

Byron gave the man a nod.

As Buck and the doughs returned to headquarters, Byron was as white as a sheet. He sat on the curb, his lip quivering. He buried his face in his hands as all the emotions he'd bottled up came flooding out.

Buck gave his friend some space.

As Buck and the squad readied for the next round, Panzerfausts could be heard bursting in Paderborn. The enemy was creating a distraction, so that the last of SS Panzer Brigade Westfalen could escape. But the worst was over.

The rail yard was now theirs. So was the airfield. And it was only a matter of time until Paderborn would be theirs as well.

A radio call would soon go out: "Spearhead to Powerhouse." At 3:45 p.m., the tankers of Spearhead would unite with the tankers of "Hell on Wheels." Together, they would complete that "steel wall" around the Ruhr.

The prize? More than 325,000 German troops—including twenty-six generals and one admiral, all trapped inside the "Ruhr Pocket." It would be a greater blow to the enemy than the loss of Stalingrad in Russia or the defeat in Africa.

Soon enough, news spread that the army had decided to rename the Ruhr Pocket. It would be known as the "Rose Pocket," in honor of General Rose.

And from Paderborn, Spearhead would head eastward. There, they would come face to face with the crimes of the Nazi regime. Two task forces would liberate the Dora-Nordhausen concentration camp, releasing slave laborers from across Europe, including Jewish prisoners transferred from Auschwitz. Meanwhile, Clarence's task force rammed down the walls at the nearby copper mines of Sangerhausen, liberating five hundred British and Russian POWs.

As for Berlin, the men of Spearhead would never lay eyes on the German capital. General Omar Bradley estimated that the battle for Berlin could cost 100,000 American casualties. The top officers would stop Spearhead at the Elbe River, sixty-six miles from Berlin, leaving Hitler to the Russians.

But all of that was to come.

Buck went from one rookie to the next, checking their ammo levels and finding them disturbingly low. Shaking his head in bewilderment, he harangued them for being unprepared: Were they expecting the Germans to share?

If his old classmates had voted again that day, Buck would no longer be elected the "Boy with the Best Personality."

He'd become something better.

The Panther attracted Clarence like a magnet. He approached the German war machine slowly. Its armor was pitted from earlier scuffles and heavily scarred.

Clarence felt the jagged shell hole. His shot had gouged right through the Panther's breastplate, revealing a thick, dark core.

Clarence climbed aboard. He looked behind the tank in the direction its driver had fled. But the street was empty.

Above the hull, where the radioman/bow gunner would sit, Clarence took a knee. He had seen all but one member of the Panther's crew come pouring out in the aftermath of his hit. He had to know.

He lifted the hatch cover.

Below, a young German tanker sat dead in his seat. He was fair-haired, with light eyes that remained open as if he were only dreaming and would wake up soon.

Clarence didn't cringe at the sight of the man he'd killed. He didn't lose his stomach. He didn't even look away. He just wished he could speak with his fallen foe. He'd ask him one simple question: *Why?*

Why fight to the last hour, to the last breath, to try to kill him and his friends? The war was lost. *Why didn't you just let this end?*

The enemy's mind-set was one he'd never understand. There was no sense in trying.

Clarence focused on the black holster at the man's side. He reached inside and drew the German's pistol. It was a Walther P-38, stamped with Nazi proof marks and all. Clarence wiped the pistol on his coveralls and stuffed it inside his tanker jacket.

It was his by right—he had fought for it.

He'd once been a loader, but not anymore.

He was a tank gunner now.

Clarence shut the hatch.

CHAPTER 24

GETTING HOME

Nine months later, Christmas Eve 1945
MOURMELON-LE-GRAND AIRFIELD, FRANCE

Mourmelon-le-Grand was a transition camp for American soldiers who were either leaving Europe or beginning their tours with the forces occupying defeated Germany. On Christmas Eve, its base canteen was in full swing. It looked like a beer hall, with a high wooden roof and garlands draping the walls. Conversations buzzed. American soldiers sat together in groups, chatting and eating. A military band played holiday tunes on a stage. Snow flurries streaked the windows. Gustav carried plates of piping-hot doughnuts as he moved between tables. He wore a green American training uniform stitched with black letters: *PW*, an abbreviation for "prisoner of war."

Dinner had ended and it was time for dessert. Gustav delivered the doughnuts—plain, with a dusting of powdered sugar—to a table of GIs. The Americans were appreciative. Other German POWs poured coffee from stainless steel pitchers, and the smell flooded the room.

Gustav's specialty on the kitchen crew was making doughnuts. He was paid eighty cents a day. He had sent his family a postcard through the Red Cross, so that they knew he was alive. He had survived the *Endkampf,* and that was all that mattered. The resistance in those first five months of 1945 had cost Germany more than 1 million fighting men—25 percent of those who died during the entire war—not to mention the 3 million troops marched into Russian captivity. Of those unfortunates, 1 million would never return.

When he was first captured, Gustav hadn't thought he'd survive a week.

From Cologne, he and Rolf had been transported by train across Belgium. They rode huddled against the cold in an open-top train car with about fifty other POWs. If a prisoner even glanced over the side of the car, an American guard would fire warning shots from a machine gun.

Halfway across Belgium, the train stopped. The POWs were served soup, cruelly without bowls or utensils. Gustav and the others used their caps as bowls, but the soup quickly soaked through the fabric.

News of the train carrying German POWs spread through villages along the route. At one point, Gustav and Rolf saw Belgian civilians waiting with bricks in their hands as the train passed. *This can't be good,* Gustav had thought. Just like that, bricks came raining down upon them from above. Gustav and Rolf covered their heads. Thanks to the train's momentum, the bricks missed Gustav's car and landed in the car behind them, killing several POWs.

The assault was repeated at the next overpass. And the one after that.

The Germans were separated upon their arrival at the camp.

SS men went one way, Wehrmacht soldiers another. Ranks were further separated, and Rolf bade Gustav goodbye with a nod. Gustav hadn't seen his friend since.

The Americans were unprepared for the vast numbers of prisoners they'd taken. And besides that, Americans treated Germans not as fellow soldiers or as human beings—but as nothing more than war criminals. The POWs' food rations were painfully meager. They were typically allotted a single loaf of bread, per day, split among ten men. POWs became sickly from malnourishment, often to the point of death. After the war ended, Gustav discovered an explanation for the hostility. He and other POWs were herded into the camp theater and shown a film reel taken inside a concentration camp.

Since 1933, the Nazis had told Gustav and other Germans that concentration camps were prisons for society's degenerates. But the film showed a different reality, one far worse than anything Gustav could have imagined. It was sickening to see the sadistic cruelty and violence inflicted on Jews, as well as on Slavs, Gypsies, people of color, and individuals with disabilities. Gustav buried his face in his hands. While he had been fighting on the front lines, the Nazis had been committing genocide.

Gustav eventually found sympathy where he least expected it. He was assigned to the kitchen crew, where he struck up a friendship with an African American GI while he cleared the men's trays after meals. Gustav was puzzled that white and black Americans sat separately. His new friend explained segregation, which itself was steeped in the same kind of racism that was part of the Nazi ethos. His new friend explained segregation this way: "You are Prisoner number 1, and we are Prisoner number 2!"

When Gustav cleared the Black GIs' trays, he found something curious—morsels of food untouched in the corners. A smear of peanut butter. A slice of fruit. Some crackers. Gustav devoured the leftovers when his guards weren't looking. The black GI flashed Gustav a wink and other Black soldiers gave him a nod. The leftovers were no accident.

Their generosity would pull him through.

That had been nine months ago. Now, the Christmas party was swinging. As Gustav collected empty plates to refill them with doughnuts, he noticed his guard going from prisoner to prisoner.

Was something wrong?

To each POW, the guard whispered a message, and the POW abandoned whatever he was doing to head back to the concession counter. The guard approached Gustav and told him he could visit the chow line. Gustav didn't understand.

"Everyone gets the same tonight," the guard said— commander's orders.

Gustav swore he was dreaming.

The food in the chow line was plentiful. As Gustav moved from station to station, the cooks—his fellow POWs—filled his tray high with turkey and all the trimmings.

At the end of the line, he faced a choice: Beer? Or a bottle of cola?

Other POWs had taken seats at the end of a table of GIs, but Gustav hesitated. *Is this permitted?* he asked himself.

The GIs didn't seem to mind. Neither did the guards, who had turned their attention to the band. So, Gustav took a seat and experienced his first bite of turkey. It was meaty and marvelous. The cruelly small rations of the last few months made it taste even better.

Gustav had chosen the cola. He had never drunk a carbonated beverage before. As he carefully popped the cap, the cola hissed. He took a sip and nearly coughed from the carbonation.

It was the single best sip he'd ever taken.

A hush fell over the canteen as the American bandleader drew everyone's attention with a tap on the microphone. GIs lowered their coffee cups and POWs' forks hovered over their suppers.

The bandleader asked the audience to sing along to the next song with them. The song was "Silent Night," an Austrian Christmas song composed in the early 1800s.

The bandleader translated the title, so the Germans would understand him—*"Stille Nacht."*

Gustav was surprised. The Americans wanted them to sing too?

The music began filtering through the canteen.

At first, only American voices carried the tune.

Silent night. Holy night.

Gustav looked to the POWs at his sides. A few joined the Americans in singing.

> All is calm—*Alles schläft.*
> All is bright—*einsam wacht.*

With each verse, more German voices joined the chorus, and the two languages blended throughout the cavernous room.

Gustav found his voice and sang along.

As the song continued, Gustav's eyes moistened with tears. He dabbed at them, but tears kept slipping despite his efforts.

The sound of everyone singing together told him it was true.

The war was really over.

Two months later, February 1946

Gustav walked the empty road as the sun set at his back.

The last miles were the longest. And the hardest.

A fierce, cold wind swept across northern Germany.

He carried his belongings in a small sack over one shoulder. His boyhood home sat in the middle of the British zone of occupation. It was the British troops who had delivered him to the nearest city. Now, he was free.

Gustav walked the remaining fifteen miles home. After the time he'd spent as a prisoner, freedom felt unnatural to him. It was overwhelming and strange, like an itch he couldn't quite scratch.

He had stayed at Mourmelon-le-Grand as a volunteer, working up to the day the camp closed. He had even inquired about emigrating to America.

Gustav was apprehensive about coming home. There were too many questions. What would tomorrow hold? How could he just resume his life as if nothing had happened?

Part of him wished he could keep walking forever.

The Schaefer family was finishing their work in the fields for the day when they saw him coming. They dropped their tools and ran toward him. Gustav's father bounded among them. By some miracle, the Russians had released him from captivity because of his age.

Gustav's face lit up as he embraced his family—it had been two years since they'd been together. Since last he'd seen him, Gustav's brother had grown taller than Gustav. His grandmother and grandfather wept as they held him. Gustav's mother pulled him by the arm toward the house. She declared that they would celebrate that night with a ham, schnapps, and bread with slabs of butter.

As his mother entered the house, she flipped a switch. The sight was wondrous.

Lightbulbs illuminated the entire room.

Gustav marveled at the spectacle of his boyhood home cast in brightness. That summer his family had invested their meager savings and had a power line attached to the house.

Gustav couldn't stop smiling as he examined the new lightbulbs up close.

Here, the darkness of the war felt far behind him.

CHAPTER 25

THE LAST BATTLE

Thirty-seven years later, winter 1983
FORT MYERS, FLORIDA

Clarence Smoyer pedaled his three-wheel cruiser bike down a path with an easy, calm rhythm. Beside him, dunes rolled down to the white sand of Fort Myers beach.

Clarence was sixty, balding, and tan from head to toe. He had embraced the Florida lifestyle, wearing just the essentials— shorts, boat shoes, and sunglasses. Amid this paradise of blue skies and towering clouds, he had found peace. His wife, Melba, rode a matching bike at his side.

Just a few weeks after Clarence returned from the war, he'd bumped into Melba—the young admirer who had sent him the homemade fudge when he was in combat—at his local skating rink. She was eighteen and petite with cherubic cheeks and gentle eyes. She often wore a bow in her curly brown hair. They were married within a year and had lived a wonderful life ever since.

Clarence had retired as supervisor of an industrial cement plant earlier that year, and the couple now split their time between a mobile home in Florida and another in Pennsylvania, where their two daughters lived.

And they roller-skated. They brought their skates along in the trunk of their green Rambler station wagon whenever they made a road trip. They belonged to a skate club in Pennsylvania and would travel to "Old Timers' Nights" at rinks that still played live organ music. Melba could skate backward, but Clarence struggled with his coordination. The only way he could pull off what seemed to come so naturally for her was when Melba steadied him by the hands.

Clarence held on and didn't look back.

In these, his golden years, the war seemed far behind him.

Twelve years later, November 1996

Clarence emerged from his trailer in Palmerton, Pennsylvania, on a cool fall morning. The Forrest Inn trailer park was neat and tidy, tucked beneath a canopy of trees.

Clarence walked toward a bank of mailboxes at the park's entrance. Every day for the past week, he'd checked the mail obsessively, hoping it would come.

Today was the day. It had finally arrived. The package was just the size of a book, but even holding it made him nervous.

Melba was out running errands, so the trailer was quiet. Clarence unwrapped the package, revealing a VHS cassette entitled *Scenes of War*. For fifty-one years, he had waited to see the contents of this tape. By the time Clarence had returned from Europe, Jim Bates's film of the fighting in Cologne had disappeared from theaters and was nowhere to be found.

Until now.

A war buddy had sent a letter alerting Clarence to the tape's whereabouts. Apparently, Bates had held on to a personal copy of the film and had recently donated it to his local library in Colorado Springs, Colorado. The library had produced a documentary using the footage. Clarence wasted no time ordering a copy.

But now, with the tape in his hands, he was having doubts.

Is this a bad idea?

For fifty-one years, he had waged an epic battle of will. If a war movie played on TV, he'd skip over the channel. When fireworks popped on the Fourth of July, he'd shut the windows. No 3rd Armored Division license-plate holder would be found on his car. That way, no one would ask questions or figure out the truth: the wounds were still there.

Clarence could still blink and see Paul Faircloth lying upside down on the bank as blood gushed from the stump of his leg. Even all these years later, he imagined the torso of the tanker at the Welborn Massacre. And he saw the events at Blatzheim, where an entire crew had to work together to remove a dead buddy from their tank.

Despite his misgivings, Clarence inserted the VHS tape into the player.

It's just nostalgia, he told himself. *It's harmless.*

After all, his parents had seen this film back then. So how bad could it be?

Clarence pressed Play. Bates's black-and-white film flickered as the documentary began.

Clarence watched a dough advancing through the streets of Cologne, firing a machine gun from the hip. A narrator gave a play-by-play in a pitchy voice while an orchestral soundtrack stoked the tension.

The cathedral's spires loomed large.

The footage showed the Pershing idling, pursuing someone or something.

Clarence watched eagerly. It was like opening a time capsule.

A massive four-way intersection appeared on-screen. Clarence recognized this place. The Gereon neighborhood was on the other side, where the German tank had taken cover behind a building. Bates steadied his camera on the spot where the enemy tank had been, hoping to catch another glimpse. Instead, he filmed something totally unexpected, a dramatic event that took Clarence by surprise once again, all these years later.

A black Opel P4 car suddenly raced into the intersection from the left, driving wildly.

Clarence edged forward in his seat—he remembered this.

Machine-gun tracers chased the car. Misses skipped from the street like stones off the water. Puffs of dust—the sign of hits—leaped from the car itself.

The film flickered. . . .

The fighting had ended on-screen and the setting had changed. Bates was tagging along as the doughs secured the opposite side of the intersection. He turned his camera on the bullet-ridden car that had come to rest against the curb. American medics had already found one victim—a man who lay dead behind the wheel, killed by a bullet to the head. His identity had become known in the intervening years.

He was no Nazi general fleeing justice, as Clarence had thought at the time. The driver was Michael Delling, the owner of a grocery store. He was just a civilian trying to escape the carnage that surrounded him.

Clarence stared at the screen, dumbstruck by what he was seeing.

The film flickered. . . .

On the passenger's side, the medics tended to the second victim. The young woman lay on her back against the curb. Her eyes were closed and she was barely breathing.

Clarence watched in horror. Back then, he had only seen the flash of her long, curly hair and had wondered if his eyes were playing tricks on him. Now there was no doubt.

A medic opened the woman's jacket, revealing a light-colored sweater with embroidered flowers. The medic checked for entry or exit wounds. When he lifted her sweater, he discovered that her pale skin was streaked with blood.

Clarence hadn't seen any of this back then. He had been too busy maintaining a lookout for enemy tanks. He had not seen the look of defeat on the medic's face after he bandaged the woman's wounds. He had not noticed the man checking for a pulse before tenderly lowering her hand. The car had shielded Clarence from the heartbreaking details, but it hadn't impeded Jim Bates from keeping his camera rolling so people on the home front could see the tragic face of war.

The film flickered. . . .

Two of the medics moved to rejoin the doughs, while a third remained with the wounded woman. The remaining medic retrieved a briefcase from the car before placing it under the woman's head to serve as a makeshift pillow. Next he found a jacket to drape over her like a blanket. Curled in the fetal position, the woman gazed into Bates's lens with glassy eyes.

She was dying, and there was nothing anyone could do for her. But as the documentary revealed, that didn't stop the medic from trying to make her last moments a little less painful.

Inside the briefcase resting under her head were her letters, photos, and a certificate attesting to a degree in home economics. She was an innocent young woman, a grocery clerk named Kathi Esser who would die soon after Bates lowered his camera.

Clarence lurched forward and turned off the TV.

He stared at the black screen in disbelief, his chest heaving as the thought took hold: *Did I kill her?*

A decade later, 2006

Clarence had never imagined that in his eighties he would fear the dark. Nighttime had never frightened him as a child, but now he lay awake at Melba's side, afraid to close his eyes.

A full night's sleep was now an exception to the rule, ever since he had first laid eyes on the Bates documentary. In the few hours he did get, Clarence often dreamed that he was wandering around Cologne on foot, trying to get to safety. But every sound or shadow that he chased led him back to the black car, where he found Kathi dying on the curb all over again. Every time he came across her body in his dreams, he would bolt wide-awake, soaked in sweat.

It was unlike any traumatic memory of the war that he'd experienced. This wasn't some dusty, lingering memory from

1945. This guilt was fresh, born the moment that her face appeared on his television screen.

And the torment wasn't restricted to the dark of night. It often spilled into daylight. On any given day, Clarence would sit on his couch, listless from lack of sleep. His hands trembled. He was irritable, disheartened, and depressed.

And he suffered in silence. Melba was by his side, typically curled around a pillow, but the spark had vanished from her eyes. She was in the grip of Alzheimer's. Sometimes she recognized Clarence's face. His voice still had a calming effect when she became agitated. But after sixty-one years of marriage, she had forgotten his name.

Clarence was faltering and he knew it. He had promised Melba he would never place her in a nursing home, but her care consumed what little energy he had. It was only a matter of time before his fatigue led to sickness and sickness claimed him, too. If he was going to be there to care for Melba until the end, Clarence knew he had to fix himself, somehow.

The past could destroy the present—he had seen it happen before.

When Captain Salisbury, Clarence's company commander, had returned home from the war, he had finished his degree at Yale, attended Columbia Law School, and gone on to become a lawyer at a prestigious New York firm.

In late November 1950, he spent the weekend at his parents' mansion on Long Island. He played tennis on Saturday and dined with his mother and his father, a general retired from the National Guard, on Sunday.

The following morning when his father opened the garage, he was floored by a rush of exhaust fumes. A car had been running all night long in the garage. Inside was his son.

Clarence's commanding officer had committed suicide at thirty years old. No one had seen it coming. When the press came calling, his father hinted at the contents of a note left behind. As one reporter wrote, "General Salisbury said that since the war his son had been increasingly depressed over the battlefield loss of friends."

After surviving more close calls with German shells than he could count, Captain Salisbury had been stalked and cut down by the unseen killer: the mental toll of war.

About five years later, 2011

Clarence paced through the sterile hallways of the VA hospital in Wilkes-Barre, Pennsylvania. He'd been here so many times by now that he knew the corridors by heart.

Before this, a VA psychiatrist had diagnosed his symptoms and told him the name of the demons that kept him up at night: "PTSD." Post-traumatic stress disorder. His psychiatrist had prescribed an antianxiety pill and another for depression, which would help him sleep. The medications masked his pain, but no dosage could erase his guilt. So his psychiatrist urged Clarence to try another approach to treat his problems.

As Clarence neared the conference room's open door, upbeat conversation poured forth from within. A group therapy session was about to begin. A collection of strangers—mostly Vietnam War veterans and some of the new generation who had fought in Iraq or Afghanistan—were gathered inside.

Clarence slowed his step and paused outside the door. He had forced himself to come this far, but now he was wavering. The men in there were all younger than he was. Why would they want to hear about the problems of an old man? Especially when the wounds of their wars were still so raw.

It was embarrassing for him. He was a World War II veteran—he wasn't supposed to have PTSD. His peers had all sorted out their problems six decades ago. And they'd done it without needing to sit in a circle with strangers, hadn't they?

If that was what they did, then that was what he would do.

Before he could second-guess his decision, Clarence resumed walking, straight past the open door.

With a notepad in hand, Clarence scoured Bates's film for clues.

He had acquired the original uncut footage from the National Archives and now watched it over and over again, searching for an explanation as to what really happened that day so long ago.

Maybe it wasn't his fault? Maybe someone else had shot Kathi and her driver?

The film showed several doughs carrying the same type of machine gun as his. Clarence tracked their movements from frame to frame, pausing to take notes.

What about Smokey? Smokey Davis, in his role as bow gunner, had been aiming down the same field of fire. And so were three more Sherman tanks behind them.

Clarence played the film in slow motion, tracking the tracers' trajectory to discern the truth: Did the bullets that killed Kathi really come from his gun?

But his hunt for answers was inconclusive. No matter how many times he watched the film, it showed only the same frustrating narrow slice of the battlefield.

If only he could talk to someone who had been there. But Bates, Smokey Davis, Earley, and the rest of the crew had all died of old age by then. Chuck Miller was still alive, but that day he had been parked behind the Pershing and hadn't seen the car dart into the intersection and come under fire.

Then, out of the blue, an idea struck Clarence. An epiphany. There *was* someone else, another man with his finger on the trigger that day.

The German.

Clarence had seen the green tracers the enemy had fired, even though Bates's film had failed to capture it. But by the time the Pershing drove past the collapsed building, the enemy tank had slipped away. Clarence had always assumed that someone else had finished the job that he'd started and bagged the enemy tank around the next bend. But what if he was wrong?

What if the German from that tank *had* survived?

What if he was still alive?

More than a year later, March 21, 2013

On a cold winter afternoon, Clarence stood in front of the Cologne Cathedral once again.

A biting wind rustled through the vast square. If the clouds overhead had suddenly burst with flurries, he wouldn't have been surprised. Clarence flipped up the collar of his gray U.S. Army running jacket. A combination of nervousness and cold kept him fidgeting. He had fought here at this time of year, long ago, but he had forgotten how frigid Cologne could be.

With his back turned to the cathedral, Clarence studied the people who crisscrossed the square. Cologne on a Thursday was far less deserted than the setting in his nightmares.

The square was full of activity. Businessmen strode past on their way to the train station. Nuns filtered through the cathedral's double doors. Tourists snapped photos of the spires.[1] Clarence was looking for a fellow World War II veteran, but not just any veteran. A German veteran.

With the help of a journalist, Hermann Rheindorf, Clarence had found him: the last living German tanker from the three crews who had fought for the inner city. And the German had agreed to meet Clarence. Here. Today.

But where was he? Their agreed-upon meeting time had come and gone twenty minutes ago.

Had the German veteran had second thoughts? Was Clarence crazy for ever thinking it could work? Clarence was eighty-nine. Senior citizens just didn't attempt things like this.

He had left Melba in their daughter Cindy's care and traveled four thousand miles to a foreign city just to talk to someone about something that had happened sixty-eight years ago. And to top it off, that "someone" happened to be the man who had been trying to kill him.

"Hey, Clarence!" A high-pitched Southern voice called his name.

---

1 Clarence allowed this author to accompany him, to record the dialogue and events as they played out.

Buck Marsh approached Clarence from a side of the square, where he had been helping to keep an eye out for the German veteran.

Buck, now eighty-nine as well, had recently retired from his construction company and still looked the part of a CEO—he wore small glasses, and a sweater vest beneath his jacket. He and Clarence had reunited and become close friends in 2006, after Buck had hosted Clarence as the guest of honor at an A-Company reunion.

Buck sidled up to Clarence. "Any sign of our guy?" he asked.

"Afraid not," Clarence said.

A third American veteran approached Clarence from the other direction. Now eighty-eight, Chuck Miller moved with a cane but hadn't lost his telltale squint and wry grin.

Chuck's hair was thick and white now. He wore a yellow Spearhead ball cap littered with pins in the style of many veterans. But Chuck wasn't just any veteran.

He was "Major Miller" now.

Back when the Cold War was heating up, Chuck had reenlisted in the reserves and gone on to command a tank battalion. He always credited Clarence as the greatest tank gunner he'd ever known.

Chuck took his place with the others. "Well, any luck?"

Clarence shook his head in defeat. "What if he walked right past us?" he said.

Buck and Chuck reassured Clarence that there was no way that could have happened, not with the three of them maintaining a lookout. Cologne was a busy city, they said. The German was probably stuck somewhere in traffic.

The three men stood in silence, rubbing their hands together against the cold.

Clarence hoped he hadn't dragged his friends all this way for nothing.

When Clarence had asked Buck and Chuck if they would go with him to Cologne, they had asked, *When do we leave?* Their enthusiasm took him by surprise.

In their minds, Clarence had kept them safe through some of the worst battles of the war. This was their chance to repay him. Besides, from what they could tell, this was a journey that their friend needed to make.

After coming home from the war, Buck and Chuck had done one thing that Clarence had not. They had faced their trauma.

While attending Auburn University, Buck spent afternoons on the sun porch discussing the war with a fraternity brother, the budding author Eugene Sledge, who had fought as a Marine in the Pacific.

As soon as Chuck returned, he bought himself a present—a new Studebaker—then set out on a road trip with his brother, who was also a veteran. On those desert highways on the way to California, Chuck told his brother all about the horrors he'd seen.

Talking. That was what had healed them—and that was what they hoped might help Clarence now. And Clarence was thankful for their encouragement. Frankly, he was amazed that his friends had dropped everything to join him on this long shot of a journey.

Buck had a wife, Wanda, and a beautiful lake house in Auburn, Alabama, where he fed the ducks each morning and spent days volunteering at his church, mowing the lawn in the summer. And when Chuck wasn't helping run his legion post and serving as treasurer of the local cemetery, he and his wife, Winona, were grandparents back in Missouri.

Yet, both men had come so far and showed no signs of quitting now.

So Clarence would wait in the cold, windy square as long as it took. This was his last chance at healing, even if the reality might be difficult to accept: only his enemy could save him now.

Chuck looked up abruptly. "I see him," he said.

"That's gotta be him," Buck concurred.

Clarence followed their eyes to the city side of the square. There, a diminutive older gentleman stood with his arms tucked timidly behind his back.

Gustav Schaefer looked as lost as they did.

Now eighty-six, Gustav wore his black winter jacket open at the collar, his shirt and tie peeking out. His white hair was neatly combed. He glanced from side to side, hoping he hadn't missed the Americans. His glasses' dark transition lenses hid worried eyes.

His son, Uwe, had driven him, and they had hit heavy traffic during the four-hour trip, which made matters even worse. After all, he was here to meet the American who had brought a building down upon his tank. And even though his former enemy had seemed friendly in his letter, he'd also mentioned bringing two comrades along with him.

What will they be like? Gustav wondered. *And what have they come all this way to talk about?*

• • •

"That's him, all right." Clarence moved toward the German vet-eran. After all the thought that had gone into getting here, he was now operating on instinct.

Buck and Chuck held back. Their role was complete—this was Clarence's show now.

Gustav saw the American approaching from the cathedral side of the square and moved hesitantly in his direction.

The American was intimidating, a far taller man than Gus-tav had expected.

Clarence moved faster with each step he took toward Gus-tav, like a train picking up speed. He felt a knot forming in his throat and feared he wouldn't be able to speak. When they were still many feet apart, a nervous grin spread across his face and he reached out an open hand to his enemy.

A smile appeared on Gustav's face as he extended his hand to meet Clarence's.

The American and the German shook hands and kept shak-ing while extending greetings to each other. Although one spoke German and the other English, they understood each other perfectly—Clarence remembered enough German from his boyhood, and Gustav had picked up some English during his POW days.

Clarence leaned close to Gustav's ear with something to say. "The war is over and we can be friends now."

Gustav nodded, visibly relieved. "*Ja, ja, gute,*" he replied.

Gustav had been thinking the exact same thing.

• • •

In a nearby hotel bar, Clarence and Gustav sat side by side, sipping beers as they talked. For the next two nights, Gustav and his son would stay at the same hotel as the Americans.

Buck and Chuck hovered nearby as Clarence asked Gustav—through an interpreter they'd hired—about his life after the war.

Gustav said he had been so accustomed to sleeping on wooden planks covered with straw in the POW camp that he slept on the floor alongside his bed for the first week after he came home.

With his family's farm in good hands, Gustav found work and spent his life operating bulldozers and, later, Caterpillars, converting marshland into farmland.

And these days? Gustav said he lived on a small ranch within sight of his boyhood home. Since his wife, Helga, had died in 2006, he passed his time with a new hobby: Google Earth. Seated at his computer, he spent most days exploring the world using the satellite imagery program to travel without leaving the comforts of home.

He had already looked up Clarence's house and had questions about the things he saw. What kind of car did Clarence park outside? How was his home decorated inside?

Clarence chuckled at the line of questioning.

As the men became more comfortable, they discovered a shared sense of humor.

"Did you have a bathroom in your tank?" Clarence asked Gustav. "Because they forgot to put one in mine."

"Yes, we did," Gustav said, "in the empty shells!"

"We had a chargrill in the Pershing," Clarence said. "And a refrigerator."

Gustav nodded, playing along. "We also had a refrigerator," he said, "but only in wintertime!"

Buck and Chuck roared with laughter from the sidelines.

Several beers later, after both Buck and Chuck had departed, Clarence and Gustav's conversation took a somber turn.

Clarence revealed that his nightmares of Cologne still woke him in the night. "I can see her in my dreams," he said. "The woman from the car."

Gustav knew exactly whom Clarence meant. A decade earlier, he had stumbled across the same film as Clarence, while watching a documentary about the battle on television.

Gustav admitted that he, too, had lingering nightmares, but his played out differently. In his dreams, he was trapped inside his tank and all he could see outside was the shattered car and Kathi Esser lying wounded on the sidewalk.

Clarence leaned close and spoke in a hushed tone. "Did you ever tell anyone about what happened?"

A deep frown settled across Gustav's face. "Who would have understood?" he asked.

Clarence knew the feeling all too well.

With little to do but to wait for their friend, Buck and Chuck ventured from the hotel on a side mission of their own.

Both men wore their collars raised against the cold as

they stepped out of a cab onto Eichendorf Street in a stately neighborhood of northern Cologne. Buck led the way toward a house on the corner while Chuck—who had come along simply out of curiosity—followed.

"Maybe she'll be sitting on the front porch, waiting for you?" Chuck joked—"Without any teeth."

Buck chuckled at the thought.

The duo stopped across from the cream-colored stone house numbered 28. Even after all these years, it still had the same impressive carved window flourishes.

In Buck's hands was the sepia-tone photograph given to him by Annemarie Berghoff. The address she had written on the reverse side had guided him back.

Buck had always wished he'd handled things differently.

After losing Lieutenant Boom at Paderborn, Buck made no attempt to return to Cologne, as he had assured Annemarie he would. He was just twenty-one then and wanted desperately to go home.

Only in his old age did the thought occur to him: How many times had she run to the door when someone came knocking, thinking he was back, only to be disappointed? He wished he'd at least written to inform her of his change in plans.

And now he found himself wondering, with a hint of guilt: *Did she have a good life?*

Buck had asked his wife, Wanda, if while he was in Cologne he could investigate what had become of Annemarie, and Wanda was understanding—she supported anything that would bring closure for Buck.

Sounds of hammering and buzz saws echoed from the house's side door. Contractors were hard at work inside, dividing the single-family home into separate apartments.

It was now or never.

Buck waded inside while Chuck lingered at the doorway.

No stranger to a construction site, Buck located the building engineer on a familiar stone staircase. The engineer spoke English, but because of confidentiality laws he couldn't reveal the name of the home's owner.

Buck was crestfallen, but he understood. He gave the engineer his business card and the name of his hotel, just in case the engineer encountered the owner.

Deflated, Buck stepped outside and into the cold. He had waited too long.

Bundled in winter attire, Clarence and Gustav shared the city sidewalk the next morning as if they were simply two old buddies headed to the bus stop.

Clarence wore a yellow Spearhead ball cap, while Gustav wore a black beret. Their noses were red from the cold, but their spirits were high with the zest of a fresh start.

The boulevard to their right was mostly free of traffic. People shuffled past the veterans sporadically, wearing long jackets and knit caps. Exhaust puffed from taxis idling at the stoplights.

Buck and Chuck had stayed behind at the hotel so Clarence and Gustav could complete their journey alone, just the two of them. It was time to confront their past.

Gustav and Clarence worked their way toward a familiar massive intersection that was awash with light.

Gustav's face was tight with concentration. It had been sixty-eight years since he had last been in this neighborhood—could he even find the street again?

Suddenly, his face lit up with recognition. There it was.

He directed Clarence's attention across the boulevard. On the corner was a building with a pub at ground level. It was bordered by a quiet cross street lined with apartments.

Gustav explained the meaning of this place: it was where his tank crew had retreated after they spotted the Pershing. Before Clarence demolished the building and the bricks came tumbling down, that is.

Now, the building he had destroyed years earlier had been rebuilt. Clarence marveled at its new height. The building was tall again. It was as if nothing had ever happened.

Revisiting the memories sent a shiver running down Gustav's spine. "Back then I wasn't as afraid as I should have been," he said. "But in discussing it now, I am afraid for my eighteen-year-old self!"

Gustav revealed that during postwar reunions of his brigade, other soldiers often chided him for abandoning the tank and running away. "You should have just cleared the bricks," they had said, to which Gustav replied: "Yeah, we should have gotten out of the tank and asked the Americans to stop shooting at us while we fixed our gun!"

Clarence smiled a guilty grin—"Sorry about that."

"No, I'm glad you shot the building on us," Gustav said. "If I had stayed in that tank, I would have died in it."

•   •   •

Farther along the sidewalk, the men stopped short of the massive intersection. Cars bustled in all directions. Warm light shone down on the square.

A somber mood settled over the two tankers.

This was where their lives had collided all those years ago. A bicycle was locked to the lamppost where the bullet-ridden black car had come to a screeching halt. Clarence looked down at the sidewalk.

"This is where I see her in my dreams," he said softly.

Gustav frowned and nodded. His lenses hid his eyes, but the emotion was there, internalized in his stoic, Germanic manner.

Clarence gazed across the intersection. A line of cars sat parked where his Pershing had once idled.

Everything was much closer than he remembered. Back on that fateful day, the boulevard had been emptier, too.

Standing there, seeing the reality of the scene, Clarence dispelled any doubt about what had happened when the car darted into his field of fire. The boulevard was a shooting gallery. It would have been impossible for him to miss. His worst nightmare was a reality. But at least he finally knew the truth. Clarence turned to Gustav. With his lip quivering, he admitted that everything had happened so fast, he hadn't had time to study his target. He thought the car belonged to the German military—so he shot it.

What Gustav said in reply stunned Clarence. "Well, that's why I shot it too."

"You shot it too?" Clarence said, his voice shaking with disbelief.

"Oh, yes," Gustav said. "The car came to a stop right in front of me."

Gustav explained that he thought the car was the American tank coming for them, so he squeezed the trigger and didn't let go until it was too late.

Clarence looked where Gustav's tank had been, then where his had been. It was unmistakable. Their respective lines of fire converged on this very spot. His eyes teared at the revelation: *We both did it.*

Something was bothering Gustav, something he hadn't said. He couldn't hold back any longer. He said it was irresponsible of Delling, the grocer, to have been on the road in the first place. He and Kathi should have sheltered in a basement instead of driving into a battle—if they had just waited two more hours, none of this would have happened.

Clarence nodded. Gustav had a point.

"It's war," Gustav said, shaking his head. "It's in the nature of it. It can't be undone."

It's in the nature of it. The words gave Clarence pause. During the course of sixteen years of guilt and self-loathing, he had never considered that he might have been a victim of that day as well.

None of them should have been in that intersection.

Clarence should have been home in Lehighton on roller skates at Graver's skating rink. Gustav should have been watching the trains on the Hamburg–Bremen line. And Kathi should have been playing with a niece or nephew in a park, not driving through a raging battle.

Clarence felt a weight lift as this realization set in.

It's in the nature of it.

It wasn't their fault, or hers.

It was war's fault, and the fault of those who had orchestrated it.

The wrought-iron fence swung open with a groan. Clarence and Gustav stepped inside the grotto of St. Gereon's Basilica, the ancient church about two hundred yards from where they had once fought.

The shady grotto was enclosed by evergreens and walls covered with vines. It was cold, colder than the neighboring streets. And it was eerily quiet.

Gustav wore his black beret snugged tightly and Clarence kept his coat zipped high. Each carried a pair of yellow roses, brought along for a special purpose. Clarence's connections in the city had assured him: this was the place.

The men followed a path of stepping-stones through a sea of leafy shrubs. Gustav's lenses had become clear in the dim light, revealing eyes that were serious with remorse.

Stone crosses rose up out of the undergrowth around the men.

The grotto was a small cemetery.

Clarence and Gustav stopped at a particular stone cross and read the inscription:

MICHAEL JOHANNES DELLING

1905–1945

Clarence looked on with regret. Forty. Delling was only forty when he died behind the wheel that day—still a young man, in Clarence's eyes.

Gustav laid a rose at Delling's grave and Clarence did the same.

From there they moved across the cemetery to a knee-high wooden cross that held an iron crucifix.

A plaque on the cross read: THE UNKNOWN DEAD.

Clarence's and Gustav's heads sank lower. This was where Kathi's story had come to an end.

After the battle, her body had been separated from her briefcase for reasons yet unknown. Without identification papers on her, she was buried in this shared grave.

A small pail for flowers sat in front of the cross. Empty.

Clarence shook his head. It was painful enough to accept how Kathi's life had ended, but this made it even worse, seeing her forgotten, as if she had never even lived.

Gustav leaned forward and placed his rose in the pail before stepping back to make way for Clarence. Bent at the waist, Clarence leaned forward with his rose clenched in a shaking hand. He became unsteady and was on the verge of losing his balance. Before he could fall, Gustav grabbed him by the arm. Steadied by his former enemy, Clarence placed his rose in the pail and righted himself.

Clarence and Gustav stood side by side without speaking. Wind stirred the trees and the vines and the yellow roses. Where he was and what he was doing still seemed surreal to Clarence.

An innocent woman—once a stranger, now someone somehow familiar to him—lay buried at his feet, and his former enemy stood beside him.

Nowhere else in Cologne was the tragic truth more plainly on display.

War touches everyone.

Clarence shut the gate behind them after he and Gustav emerged from the grotto. But he wasn't finished here. He lingered outside, gazing into the dim environs as his fingers gripped the fence. Even if she lay in a nameless grave, he knew she was there.

In silence, Clarence made a vow to Kathi Esser.

He would never forget her.

As Gustav watched an unmoving Clarence fixate on the wooden cross, he became worried. Gustav urged the interpreter to check on his friend.

"You okay, Clarence?" the interpreter asked.

Clarence released his grip from the fence and stepped away. He shrugged and nodded. "I'm okay now."

Clarence and Gustav removed their hats when they entered the narthex of St. Gereon's Basilica. Faded medieval frescos lined the dark antechambers, but the dome overhead was full of light.

The men approached a row of candles still burning from the morning Mass. Clarence and Gustav dropped coins into the poor box before lighting a pair of votive candles. Each man added his own candle to the row of flickering flames.

In stillness they paid their respects, silent words the world would never hear.

After Clarence and Gustav left the basilica, they were met with a surprise. Clarence's German journalist friend had arranged an unexpected meeting for them with a slender young man. He was a history professor at the University of Cologne who had slipped out between classes to meet the veterans. His name was Marc Hieronimus. He was thirty-nine, with a long coat, glasses, and a closely cropped beard. More importantly, he was Kathi Esser's grandnephew.

Clarence froze.

This man was Kathi's family, after all. Gustav hovered behind in Clarence's shadow, leaving his larger friend to sort out the situation.

Marc defused any tension with a smile as he greeted the men in English. Clarence grinned and Gustav emerged from hiding.

Marc wasn't here to judge them. Instead, he had come to offer his help. Would they like a tour of his aunt Kathi's life? He would be their guide.

The silver van rumbled as the driver wound through Cologne.

Marc narrated from the passenger's seat while Clarence and Gustav sat behind him, listening with boyish awe as the sights passed outside their windows.

Kathi's home, a row house made of red brick.

Her favorite park, where the entrance to an air-raid shelter still stood.

The street that she had bicycled down each day to go to work at Delling's grocery store.

After a morning spent in somberness, Clarence and Gustav were back to smiling again. Marc's tour was uplifting, a fond remembrance of the life that Kathi had lived.

At the tour's conclusion, the van pulled over near a gate in the city's Roman wall.

Marc spun around in his seat. Before returning to the university, he wanted to extend an invitation to Clarence and Gustav: "Next time you come to Cologne, let's have dinner together?"

And it wouldn't just be dinner with him. His invitation was for dinner with Kathi's family—as friends.

The gesture wasn't lost on Clarence. Marc was offering them forgiveness.

Clarence couldn't stop smiling.

It was a good thing that Buck had stayed behind that morning. A call from the front desk summoned him from his hotel room. He had a visitor.

Buck discovered a woman waiting in the lobby to meet him. She wore a long black jacket, neatly accented by a tan scarf. Her shoulder-length blond hair framed a face with an unforgettable beauty that stirred Buck's memory.

She looked like Annemarie.

But how could that be? She wasn't even half the age she should be.

The woman introduced herself as the owner of the home that Buck had visited—the engineer had passed Buck's business card along to her. Her name was Marion Pütz. She was Annemarie's daughter.

Buck took Marion's hand and held it. He couldn't get over her likeness—"You look just like your mother!"

Marion said that meeting Buck was special for her. Her mother had died a decade before, and this was a chance to remember her by learning a bit more about the life she had lived.

The pair settled into seats at the side of the lobby.

Buck told Marion how he had met Annemarie and the story of their brief friendship. He expressed his lament that he had forgotten her so quickly after the war, but Marion urged him not to feel any guilt.

"You were there at the right time for her," Marion said. "When things were difficult, you gave her hope."

Buck leaned forward to ask the question that had been burning inside him ever since he came to Cologne: "Did she have a good life?"

Marion said that her mother had studied dental medicine and continued working in her father's practice. She became one of the first women in Cologne to get a driver's license and one of the first to buy a car—a Volkswagen Beetle.

Annemarie went on to marry a wealthy factory owner; she gave birth to Marion, and although her marriage didn't endure, she lived a happy life, splitting her time between Germany and a house on a Swiss lake that she loved to cruise in her motorboat.

Buck was pleased to hear all this—and thankful.

Marion gripped Buck's hand as she stood to leave. "I want to thank you for making my mother happy," she said.

Buck choked up at the sentiment. "Well, she made me happy too."

The next morning

While Gustav's son retrieved his car, the veterans approached Cologne Cathedral. In their short time together, they had become a team. A reunion of enemies had become a gathering of friends, and none of them wanted the visit to end.

But Gustav's son had work the following day and had to head back. And the Americans had families waiting at home. There was just one thing left to do.

The veterans stopped in the cathedral square and posed for photos together, passing their digital cameras back and forth.

Buck hopped into a photo with Gustav and joked about their matching heights.

Chuck took a turn alongside Gustav. Seeing Clarence aiming his camera and hearing him shout—"Say cheese!"—Chuck knew that the journey had been worth it. His friend was going to be all right.

Ultimately, Clarence and Gustav wound up smiling for the camera with their arms intertwined right in front of the cathedral. Cameras beeped and flashed. Buck, Chuck, and even their interpreter kept snapping pictures.

Then, Clarence did something unexpected. He reached down and hugged Gustav. He held the hug for the cameras and refused to let go. Gustav returned the hug with equal enthusiasm.

Passing teenagers might have laughed at the two old men—the towering American and the diminutive German—chuckling as they embraced in the bustling city square. But a passing group of teenagers would never have known just who these men were.

The veterans found Gustav's son waiting with the idling car at the hotel. He was ready to drive his father home.

Clarence knew what this meant. This would likely be the last time he would ever see Gustav.

The German veteran had confided that his health was poorer than he let anyone, including his family, know. But even so, he hoped to stay in touch with Clarence for as long as he possibly could.

They parted ways that morning with an understanding. Whatever guilt remained from the war—they would share it. Whatever nightmares surfaced—they would face them together.

Before Gustav stepped into the car, he gave the interpreter one last message for Clarence.

What he said made Clarence dab his eyes.

"Tell Clarence, in the next life, we will be comrades."

AFTERWORD

As America's largest fighting force in Europe during the Cold War, the **Spearhead Division** went on to hold the line against the Soviet Union, ready for the tank-on-tank clash that never came.

The division's next battlefield would instead be in the desert. Summoned from Germany, the 3rd Armored Division spearheaded the ground assault during the Persian Gulf War in 1990, waging the first major tank engagement since World War II. After battering the Iraqi Republican Guard, Spearhead helped bring the war to a cease-fire—in one hundred hours.

And that would be its final battle.

The Cold War had ended. Terrorism was the new threat to freedom. So the mighty armor division was retired and its units spread piecemeal among the U.S. Army. Now Spearhead remains a slumbering giant, at rest until the day when machines will again fight machines.

In September 2017, the WWII veterans of the 3rd Armored Association held their last reunion in Philadelphia. Just three tankers were able to attend. Two were Easy Company men: **Clarence Smoyer** and **Joe Caserta**.

Clarence's crew died long before they could gather again. At reunions, Clarence learned how their lives played out.

Homer "Smokey" Davis became an electrician and lived out his years in the woods of rural Kentucky.

William "Woody" McVey worked in an automotive repair shop near Detroit, where his skills were put to use test-driving cars.

John "Johnny Boy" DeRiggi's facial wounds healed during a year spent in army hospitals—from Greenland to Valley Forge—and he later became a steelworker in Levittown, Pennsylvania.

Bob Earley attained the farm of his dreams in Fountain, Minnesota, trading his perch in a tank turret for a seat on a tractor. He married, raised sons, and was known for riding his motorcycle cross-country to attend reunions.

Clarence never saw Earley after they'd parted in Germany but was at peace with how they sealed their friendship—with a long handshake and thankfulness that they'd made it through together. Earley died in 1979. After staring down the barrel of the Panther in Cologne, every additional day of life was a gift, and Bob Earley spent his well.

Seeking information about Paul Faircloth, Clarence called countless numbers in the Florida phone book before finding Paul's nephew.

The nephew informed Clarence that it would be difficult to visit Paul's grave because he was buried far away, at Épinal American Cemetery in France.

Determined to see his friend remembered on his native soil, Clarence donated money in Paul's name toward the construction of the 3rd Armored Division Memorial that now stands in a park at Fort Knox, watched over by a silent Sherman tank.

According to Chuck Miller, his trip to Cologne with Clarence was "the thrill of a lifetime."

Chuck died the following year. In his funeral procession, his grandson's motorcycle club escorted the hearse, filling the air with thunderous noise, reminiscent of an armored column on the move.

Everyone who knew him said the same thing: Chuck would have approved.

Frank "Cajun Boy" Audiffred married the company sweetheart, his girlfriend, Lil, a month after returning from the war. Despite being nearly deaf in both ears from that day at Blatzheim, Audiffred spent a career as a machinist with Standard Oil of Louisiana.

Before his death in 2019, Audiffred's body was still shedding German shrapnel. When dental hygienists found slivers of steel in his mouth during routine checkups, Audiffred would just chuckle.

In 1955, **Buck Marsh** and **Bob Janicki** attended their first division reunion together in St. Louis. Buck discovered that his battlefield mentor hadn't lost a step, despite wearing a false leg. Using his disability compensation, Janicki had opened a motorcycle dealership in Freeport, Illinois, a business that would later expand to three stores, allowing him to purchase—and fly—his own private plane.

In the 1960s, Buck found **Byron Mitchell** living in Atlanta and phoned him. Never one for words, Byron gave a brief report: "I'm driving a concrete truck and I really like it."

These days, Buck serves as the honorary sergeant major of his former unit, the army's **36th Infantry Regiment**, and he makes appearances at schools to teach children about World War II.

Without exception, some youngster will always ask: "How many Germans did you kill?"

Amused by the naïveté of youth, Buck gives the same answer every time: "I wish the number was zero."

On the other side of the Atlantic, **Gustav Schaefer** attended reunions of **Panzer Brigade 106** for decades, hoping to see **Rolf Millitzer**.

The gatherings were small enough to fit in any restaurant's back room—the brigade had been all but wiped out—yet Rolf never walked through the door.

After his POW sentence, Rolf was likely repatriated to his home in the Soviet-controlled zone of East Germany, and there he vanished behind the Iron Curtain.

It didn't take until "the next life" for Clarence and Gustav's friendship to take root.

The duo became pen pals, exchanging letters and Christmas cards. Clarence gave Gustav a gift: a small, die-cast Panther tank.

They even Skyped on their computers. With an interpreter joining in, the veterans would talk face to face, despite being thousands of miles apart. In the background behind Gustav was a clock with a pendulum, a bookshelf filled with atlases, and the little model of a Panther tank.

After hanging on four years longer than even he had thought possible, Gustav succumbed in April 2017 to cancer. At his funeral were flowers from family and friends, and one ribboned bouquet bearing these words:

> I WILL NEVER FORGET YOU!
> YOUR BROTHER IN ARMS,
> CLARENCE

When he stood at the grotto of St. Gereon's Basilica, Clarence had vowed that he would never forget **Kathi Esser**. Every year since his visit, yellow roses are placed on the unmarked grave where her body remains.

On March 6, they will appear once again.

After he met Gustav, Clarence's nightmares disappeared. Painful memories from the war remain—and always will—but he can live with them.

It took some time for him to revisit the VA hospital, but he did.

Clarence approached the conference room's open door. Familiar upbeat voices poured forth—another group therapy session was about to commence.

This time around, a different Clarence Smoyer paced those sterile hallways.

A survivor.

He had faced his PTSD and emerged victorious. Talking about it, with someone who listened and understood, had saved him.

And maybe that's what those younger veterans needed to hear. Maybe he could encourage them to keep talking—or maybe he could be that someone who would listen?

When Clarence reached the open doorway, he didn't slow his step or pause beyond sight. There was no turning back from what he'd come to do.

Someone has to help those guys.

Clarence stepped inside.

ACKNOWLEDGMENTS

I'd like to extend my deep thanks to the following people for their help with *Spearhead:*

To the World War II veterans at the heart of this story—Clarence Smoyer, Buck Marsh, Gustav Schaefer, Chuck Miller, and Frank Audiffred—you relived the most difficult years of your lives so that we might discover the human cost of war. Thank you for entrusting me with your stories.

To the armor and infantry veterans whose technical advice and supplemental interviews brought poignancy and depth to this book: Joe Caserta, Harry Chipp, Bill Gast, John Irwin, Robert Kauffmann, Marvin Mischnick, Ray Stewart, George Smilanich, Walter Stitt, Harley Swenson, Les Underwood, and to German tank commander Dieter Jähn, who taught us about the hopes and fears of men on the other side. You're each worthy of a book of your own.

To the Cologne journalist Hermann Rheindorf, it was your research that first identified Kathi Esser and brought Gustav, as well as Kathi's family, into Clarence's life. You are the unparalleled documentarian of your great city—Cologne.

To Clarence's daughter, Cindy Buervenich, you watched over your mother, Melba, so your father could travel overseas to meet Gustav. This book was born of that trip—thanks to your support.

To Frank Audiffred's daughter, Sherry Herringshaw, you unearthed priceless wartime letters and relayed our countless questions so that we might discover an amazing Cajun—your dad.

To Kathi Esser's grandnephew, historian Marc Hieronimus, you stepped away from your classroom to give Clarence and Gustav an unforgettable day and the greatest gift: the chance to heal.

To Marion Pütz, who opened the doors to her family's history to us—you're everything that one would expect from the daughter of Annemarie Berghoff.

To our "man on the ground" in Cologne, Dierk Lürbke, whose study of the cathedral tank duel is so forensic that even Clarence learned a thing or two. Thanks for always being on call to lend a helping hand.

To the family and friends of our "cast of characters," your memories, documents, and myriad contributions enriched these pages: Glenn Ahner, John DeRiggi, Craig Earley, John R. Faircloth, Patricia Fischer, Bernard Makos, Wanda Marsh, Jim Miller, Dr.-Ing Günter Prediger, Deborah Rose, Charles Rose, John Rose, Luke Salisbury, Charles Stillman, Deborah Stillman, Carol Westberg, Helene Winskowski.

To my dedicated agent, David Vigliano, who deftly guided this young adult edition of *Spearhead* into the hands of Delacorte Press, and to my editor, Beverly Horowitz, who gave life to this book and whose impeccable sense of "story" polished the manuscript to its final form. To the president and publisher of Random House, Gina Centrello, and to the publishing team who worked on this book for Delacorte Press: Cathy Bobak, Colleen Fellingham, Rebecca Gudelis, Nathan Kinney, Tamar Schwartz, and Ray Shappell, thank you all for bringing *Spearhead* to the world.

To our guides to Paderborn, who took me and my research team "back to the battle": Dr. Friedrich Hohmann, the region's grandfather-historian, and Colonel Wolfgang Mann, a tank commander of the modern-day German Bundeswehr. To our escorts in the Ardennes, the incomparable expert Reg Jans, and to Bob Konigs, who welcomed us to his Guesthouse BoTemps.

To our armor advisers: Bill Boller, the armor guru and trustee of the Collings Foundation, who could be found crawling over a World War II tank with a measuring tape in hand to answer our toughest of questions. Rob Collings, CEO of the Collings Foundation, who made his stable of tanks available to us and lent his historical input for this, our third book in a row. To Kevin Wheatcroft, the world's preeminent expert on German armor and the owner of the Wheatcroft Collection, a jaw-dropping tank collection in England, thanks for ensuring our accurate portrayal of the machines of the other side. And ultimately to "The Chieftain," Nicholas Moran, who gave the manuscript its final check ride, summoning his encyclopedic knowledge of all things armor and bringing to bear his real-world experience as a tank platoon leader in Iraq.

To the historians who made the Spearhead Division come alive for us: Vic Damon and Dan Fong, who run the 3rd Armored Division History Foundation at 3ad.com; Jan Ploeg, who remembers the doughs at 36air-ad.com; A-Company historian Dan Langhans; and Steven Ossad and Don Marsh, authors of *Major General Maurice Rose: World War II's Greatest Forgotten Commander General*.

To the dedicated authors, experts, and researchers who provided vital data, photos, and artwork for this book: Kevin Bailey, Justin Batt, David Boyd, Rita Cann, Lamont Ebbert, Tim Frank, Daniel Glauber, Timm Haasler, David Harper, Gareth Hector, Nick

Hopkins, Craig Mackey, Douglas McCabe, Jeannette McDonald, Russ Morgan, Darren Neely, Jaclyn Ostrowski, Debra Richardson, Gordon Ripkey, Matt Scales, Susan Strange, Bill Thomas, Bill Warnock, and Steven Zaloga; and to Nicolas Trudgian, whose primer on wartime train travel turned me into a rail fan for life.

To Thomas Flannery Jr., the veteran development editor who coached my writing from the first chapter to the last. Your eye for sharpening and polishing made this a better book.

To the early readers who lent a discerning eye to this manuscript: Matt Carlini, Joel Eng, Jaime Hanna, Lauren Heller, Matt Hoover, Tricia Hoover, Joe Gohrs, and Rachelle Mandik.

To my "early-warning system," my sister, Erica Makos, and mother, Karen Makos, who read every first draft—your feedback helped steer this book. To my grandparents, Francis and Jeanne Panfili, for your encouragement, to my youngest sister, Elizabeth Makos, for the entertainment; to my sister-in-law Agata Makos, whose delicious meals kept us going; and to my dear friends Helga Stigler and Georgea Hudner, who cheer me on from afar.

To my friend Pete Semanoff, who first discovered Clarence while interviewing veterans for his Eagle Scout project. You introduced me to his story and urged me to talk with him while we were in college, and after college, and even when we spoke in the desert of Iraq. Finally I met Clarence and came to know why he's your hero. This book is the result of your tireless efforts.

To our German researcher and comrade, Franz Englram. After interpreting for Clarence and Gustav in Cologne, you became one of our team, interviewing Gustav for us and poring through countless foreign documents to research his unit. During the war, your great-uncle, Gerard, died on the Eastern Front at age nineteen. By the sensitive way you treated the veterans of *Spearhead,* you honored his memory.

To my dad, Robert Makos, who "spearheaded" our interviews and countless cold calls for this book, your lifetime of experience in the psychology field made you more than a great researcher—you were irreplaceable.

To my brother, Bryan Makos, this book's research director and co-creator, you led us to Cologne three times, and to the Black Forest and back. Your task was lofty: to conduct history-gathering across two continents, five countries, and both sides of the Second World War. Clarence and Gustav, theirs is a one-in-a-million story. But your talent made this a one-in-a-million book.

Lastly, thanks to you, the reader, for riding along with us through the pages of *Spearhead.* I hope this story will remain with you long after you close this book. If you enjoyed your experience, please leave a review online, or tell others of these heroes that you've come to know. Nothing is more powerful than your endorsement.

If you're hungry to learn more, you'll find plenty of bonus content—including the wartime footage of Clarence's tank duel and film of his emotional reunion with Gustav—on my website: AdamMakos.com.

On behalf of Clarence, Buck, and the last living heroes of *Spearhead,* I pass the torch to you, dear reader. The legacy of great men and women lies in your hands.

SOURCES

This book is the product of a treasure trove of historical sources. We unearthed a paper trail of after action reports, wartime interviews, original orders, radio logs, morning reports, vintage newspapers, unit histories, and more, from archives such as:

Bundesarchiv-Militararchiv Freiburg, Germany
National Archives and Records Administration at St. Louis, Missouri, and College Park, Maryland
National Archives (UK)
U.S. Army Heritage and Education Center, Carlisle, Pennsylvania
Dwight D. Eisenhower Presidential Library, Abilene, Kansas
The 3rd Armored Division Association Archives at the University of Illinois
Maneuver Center of Excellence Museum Division, Fort Benning, Georgia.

But what was our greatest source of all? The veterans. Clarence. Buck. Gustav. Chuck. Audiffred. Caserta. Each was alive during the composition of this book and shared his memories in the best detail that he could remember.

We interviewed them anywhere and everywhere: Gustav on the street in Cologne. Chuck in a frigid field at Blatzheim. Buck visited us in Colorado and we visited him in Alabama. I interviewed Joe Caserta at his kitchen table in New Jersey and my team traveled to Louisiana to work with Frank Audiffred.

We dropped by Allentown, Pennsylvania, so many times to interview Clarence that we came to know the staff of the Holiday Inn by name. We talked with him by phone, too, almost weekly for five years. And when the manuscript was finished, Clarence, Buck, and our other core characters read this book cover to cover before giving their stamp of approval.

If I cited every fact from the stories that Clarence and his fellow veterans told us, our notes section would be longer than the book itself. So, for any facts not directly cited, you'll know where they came from: the men themselves.

But not every historical nugget was recited verbally. The veterans supplied us with written material. There were oral histories, like the one Clarence did in 1985—now thirty-three years ago. There was wartime correspondence—Audiffred's family saved every letter that he sent home. And some supplied accounts penned by their own hands, such as Buck Marsh's brilliant 200-page memoir, *Reflections of a World War II Infantryman*.

Armed with these desk-swallowing mounds of history, we married records, memories, writings, and information gleaned from the sources to follow to reconstruct this story as accurately as possible.

Gustav's interviews were translated from German into English, and I took the liberty of converting German military ranks into their American equivalents and metric measurement into imperial standards for the American editions.

But everything else is as we found it.

PHOTO CREDITS

JACKET ART

Easy Company commanders confer: Chuck Miller

Medics tend to Kathi Esser: National Archives

Background map: Bryan Makos, Valor Studios, Inc.

Panther as seen from cathedral spire: U.S. Army photo by William B. Allen, courtesy of Dave Allen and Darren Neely

Fury: Steven Zaloga

Photo of Clarence in cap: National Archives

A-Company doughs relax after securing Cologne: Buck Marsh

Sketch of Clarence: Clarence Smoyer

Spearhead dough in Cologne: National Archives

INSERT 1

Pg. 1: Spearhead M4: National Archives via Darren Neely

Pg. 1: Panther G: National Archives via Steven Zaloga

Pg. 2: *Fury:* Steven Zaloga

Pg. 3: Panzer IV H: Steven Zaloga

Pg. 3: Sherman crosses bridge: National Archives via Darren Neely

Pg. 4: Sherman in Stolberg: National Archives

Pg. 4: Sherman parked between houses: Frank Audiffred

Pg. 5: Tankers take a meal: Clarence Smoyer

Pg. 6: View through the periscope: Photograph by Jim Bates, courtesy of Special Collections, Pikes Peak Library District, 161–8919

Pg. 6: Audiffred and his M4A1: Frank Audiffred

Pg. 7: Spearhead crews in the Ardennes: National Archives

Pg. 7: Clarence and McVey with shell: Clarence Smoyer

Pg. 8: M4 in Baneux: National Archives via Darren Neely

Pg. 8: Sherman and vanquished Panther: National Archives via Steven Zaloga

INSERT 2

Pg. 1: Pershing approaches Cologne cathedral: Photograph by Jim Bates, courtesy of Special Collections, Pikes Peak Library District, 161–3326

Pg. 1: A second Sherman approaches cathedral: National Archives

Pg. 2: Sherman absorbs a hit: National Archives

Pg. 2: Pershing advances through Cologne: National Archives

Pg. 3: Pershing fires at Panther: National Archives

Pg. 4: Bartelborth and crew flee Panther (three photos): National Archives

Pg. 5: Burning Panther: National Archives via Darren Neely

Pg. 6: Bulldozer clears the street: U.S. Army photo by William B. Allen, courtesy of Dave Allen and Darren Neely

Pg. 7: Hohenzollern Bridge: U.S. Army photo by William B. Allen, courtesy of Dave Allen and Darren Neely

Pg. 7: Pershing stands guard: National Archives via Darren Neely

Pg. 8: McVey on the Pershing: Craig Earley

Pg. 8: Clarence and his fellow tankers: Clarence Smoyer

Photos on pages 320–321: Valor Studios

INDEX